Developing a Neo-Peircean
Approach to Signs

Bloomsbury Advances in Semiotics

Series Editor: Paul Bouissac
Formerly Continuum Advances in Semiotics.

Bloomsbury Advances in Semiotics publishes original works applying semiotic approaches to linguistics and non-verbal productions, social institutions and discourses, embodied cognition and communication, and the new virtual realities of the digital age. It covers topics such as socio-semiotics, evolutionary semiotics, game theory, cultural and literary studies, human-computer interactions, and the challenging new dimensions of human networking afforded by social websites.

Editorial Board

Zuanglin Hu, Peking University, Beijing
Marcel Kinsbourne, New School for Social Research, New York City, USA
Franson Manjali, Jawaharlal Nehru University, India
Mihai Nadin, University of Texas at Dallas, USA
Kay O'Halloran, National University of Singapore, Singapore
Jerzy Pelc, Warsaw University, Poland
Goran Sonesson, Lund University, Sweden
Jef Verschueren, University of Antwerp, Belgium
Anne Wagner, Universite du Littoral Cote d'Opale, France and China University of Political Science and Law, China
Ruth Wodak, Lancaster University, UK
Hiroshi Yoshioka, Kyoto University, Japan

Titles published in the series:

The Social Semiotics of Populism, Sebastián Moreno Barreneche
Systemic Semiotics, Piotr Sadowski
The Semiotics of Architecture in Video Games, Gabriele Aroni
Semiotics of the Christian Imagination, Domenico Pietropaolo
Computational Semiotics, Jean-Guy Meunier

Cognitive Semiotics, Per Aage Brandt
The Semiotics of Caesar Augustus, Elina Pyy
The Social Semiotics of Tattoos, Chris William Martin
The Semiotics of X, Jamin Pelkey
The Semiotics of Light and Shadows, Piotr Sadowski
Music as Multimodal Discourse, edited by Lyndon C. S. Way and Simon McKerrell
Peirce's Twenty-Eight Classes of Signs and the Philosophy of Representation, Tony Jappy
The Semiotics of Emoji, Marcel Danesi
Semiotics and Pragmatics of Stage Improvisation, Domenico Pietropaolo
Critical Semiotics, Gary Genosko
The Languages of Humor, edited by Arie Sover
Semiotics of Happiness, Ashley Frawley
Warning Signs, Marcel Danesi
Semiotics of Religion, Robert A. Yelle
Computable Bodies, Josh Berson
The Semiotics of Clowns and Clowning, Paul Bouissac
The Semiotics of Che Guevara, Maria-Carolina Cambre
The Visual Language of Comics, Neil Cohn
The Language of War Monuments, David Machin and Gill Abousnnouga
A Buddhist Theory of Semiotics, Fabio Rambelli
Introduction to Peircean Visual Semiotics, Tony Jappy

Developing a Neo-Peircean Approach to Signs

Tony Jappy

BLOOMSBURY ACADEMIC
LONDON • NEW YORK • OXFORD • NEW DELHI • SYDNEY

BLOOMSBURY ACADEMIC
Bloomsbury Publishing Plc, 50 Bedford Square, London, WC1B 3DP, UK
Bloomsbury Publishing Inc, 1385 Broadway, New York, NY 10018, USA
Bloomsbury Publishing Ireland, 29 Earlsfort Terrace, Dublin 2, D02 AY28, Ireland

BLOOMSBURY, BLOOMSBURY ACADEMIC and the Diana logo are
trademarks of Bloomsbury Publishing Plc

First published in Great Britain 2024
Paperback edition published 2025

Copyright © Tony Jappy, 2024, 2025

Tony Jappy has asserted his right under the Copyright,
Designs and Patents Act, 1988, to be identified as Author of this work.

For legal purposes the Acknowledgements on p. x constitute an
extension of this copyright page.

Cover design: Elena Durey
Cover image © Chain Circle – filo/istock

All rights reserved. No part of this publication may be: i) reproduced or transmitted in
any form, electronic or mechanical, including photocopying, recording or by means of
any information storage or retrieval system without prior permission in writing from
the publishers; or ii) used or reproduced in any way for the training, development or
operation of artificial intelligence (AI) technologies, including generative AI technologies.
The rights holders expressly reserve this publication from the text and data mining
exception as per Article 4(3) of the Digital Single Market Directive (EU) 2019/790.
Bloomsbury Publishing Plc does not have any control over, or responsibility for,

any third-party websites referred to or in this book. All internet addresses given
in this book were correct at the time of going to press. The author and publisher
regret any inconvenience caused if addresses have changed or sites have ceased
to exist, but can accept no responsibility for any such changes.

A catalogue record for this book is available from the British Library.

A catalog record for this book is available from the Library of Congress.

ISBN: HB: 978-1-3502-8881-2
PB: 978-1-3502-8885-0
ePDF: 978-1-3502-8882-9
eBook: 978-1-3502-8883-6

Series: Bloomsbury Advances in Semiotics

Typeset by Integra Software Services Pvt. Ltd.

For product safety related questions contact productsafety@bloomsbury.com.

To find out more about our authors and books visit www.bloomsbury.com
and sign up for our newsletters.

Contents

List of Figures		viii
List of Tables		ix
Acknowledgements		x
List of Abbreviations		xi
Introduction		1
1	The Problem of Relevance	7
2	The System of 1903	33
3	The Transition	61
4	The System of 1908	87
5	Approaches to Semiosis	113
6	Perspectives	141
Conclusion		171
Notes		173
References		188
Index		195

Figures

1.1	Abridged version of the 1902–3 classifications of the sciences	11
2.1	The determination sequence from object to interpretant	44
2.2	The alleged 'unlimited' action of the sign as suggested in 1902	45
2.3	Peirce's scheme for the association of the nine subdivisions of signs	52
2.4	Table of ten classes of signs	53
2.5	The action of the sign in 1903 represented as ellipses	56
2.6	Generic structure of a sign with image hypoiconicity	57
2.7	Generic structure of a sign with diagram hypoiconicity	57
2.8	Structure of a sign with metaphor hypoiconicity	58
4.1	Six correlates set out in 'determination' order	103
4.2	The three principal subjects of semiosis	103
5.1	The first page of post-scriptum scraps	116
5.2	Possible preparatory workings for the post-scriptum diagram	118
5.3	Three relata arranged in correlate order	119
5.4	Three relata arranged non-linearly	120
5.5	Three relata arranged in the order of semiosis	121
5.6	The class of collective gratific tokens as its corresponding class of semiosis	121
5.7	Basic semiosis in which the object mediately determines the interpretant	122
6.1	Sound spectrogram of spoken utterance (2)	149
6.2	Appeal for information concerning a lost kitten	154
6.3	Formal structure of a sign with image hypoiconicity	157
6.4	Formal structure of a sign with diagram hypoiconicity	158
6.5	Metaphor structure of *This man is a fox*	159
6.6	*Mona Lisa*	161
6.7	Portrait of Beatrice Cenci	163
6.8	Example of the diagram structures composing the Beatrice Cenci photograph	164
6.9	*Untitled (Your Body Is a Battleground)* by Barbara Kruger	165
6.10	Metaphor structure of the pictorial element of Kruger's poster	166
6.11	Metaphor structure of the verbal element of Kruger's poster	166
6.12	Diagram structure of a typical simile	167

Tables

2.1	The single-division of signs of 1867	46
2.2	The three-division typology of 1903 integrating the hypoicons	55
3.1	The 1904 six-division typology described to Lady Welby set out in tabular format	64
3.2	Four versions of the subclasses of the icon	71
3.3	Seven of Peirce's six- and ten-division typologies from the 1905–6 period	78
3.4	Signs distributed according to object and interpretant type in R318: 373–9	84
4.1	Fourteen six- and ten-division typologies established between 1904 and 1908	101
4.2	The 1908 six-division 28-class typology	105
4.3	The order of divisions yielding 28 classes of signs	106
5.1	The ten-class post-scriptum table	122
5.2	The ten post-scriptum classes	123
6.1	The table yielding twenty-eight classes of signs	152
6.2	The stages participating in the materialization of intentionality	169

Acknowledgements

In producing this study I have become indebted to a number of people and institutions.

For the visuals, to Barbara Kruger and the gallery Sprüth Magers for generous permission to reproduce her dramatic poster opposing the overruling of Roe v. Wade by the Supreme Court – it is, unfortunately, just as relevant now as it was in 1989; to the Picture Library of the Science Museum Group for permission to reproduce Margaret Cameron's 1866 photograph, *Beatrice*; and to the Agence photographique de la RMN-GP musée du Louvre, for its very generous permission to reproduce the Mona Lisa.

As this is essentially an argumentative approach to the defence and development of Peirce's logic, for permission to quote appropriately I am indebted to certain copyright holders of the printed versions of his voluminous output: especially to Professor Elize Bisantz, director of the Institute for Studies in Pragmaticism at Texas Tech University, for *Semiotics and Significs*, the Peirce-Welby correspondence; to publishers De Gruyter for the Bisantz edition of *The Logic of Interdisciplinarity: The Monist-Series*; and to the University of Indiana Press for *The Essential Peirce, Volume Two*. I am also indebted to the editors of two semiotics journals for allowing me to re-use copyright material: to the general and managing editors of the Chinese semiotics journal *Language and Semiotic Studies*, and to the editorial board of the *Revue Roumaine de Philosophie*. I am also indebted to Susan Petrilli for having retrieved for me Alberto Mioni's 1983 paper on diamesic variation; to Chiara Ambrosio and Rossella Fabbrichesi and to Zoe Hill of the Houghton library, Cambridge, MA, for their help with the manuscript version of the Peirce-Welby correspondence, RL463; to Stetson Robinson for allowing me to consult his DPhil dissertation 'Straws in the Wind: the correspondence of Charles S. Peirce and the Open Court Publishing Company'; to Pascal, for his suggestions for a logo that wasn't to be.

I am very much indebted, too, to the team at Bloomsbury, to Morwenna Scott and Sarah MacDonald, my commissioning editors, and to the thankfully vigilant Laura Gallon, my editorial assistant, for accepting the initial proposal, and for their constant support in sometimes difficult circumstances (and to the anonymous reviewer of the proposal whose adverse comments strengthened my resolve to actually produce the study!). None of the aforementioned can in any way be held accountable for the ideas that the study advances or for any errors and shortcomings it might contain: they are my sole responsibility.

Finally, heartfelt thanks yet again to F., for the proofing, for the food – for the Albert Hall! – and for the inestimable patience and moral support.

Abbreviations

References to standard primary Peirce sources are referenced in the text by abbreviations in parentheses.

Peirce, C. S., (1931–1935, 1958), *The Collected Papers of Charles Sanders Peirce*, 8 Volumes, C. Hartshorne, P. Weiss and A. W. Burks, eds, Cambridge, MA: Harvard University Press. (CP followed by volume, paragraph number and year).

Peirce, C. S., (1940), *The Philosophy of Peirce: Selected Writings*. J. Buchler, ed., London: Routledge and Kegan Paul.

Peirce, C. S., (1976), *The New Elements of Mathematics*, Vols 1–4. C. Eisele, ed., The Hague: Mouton (NEM followed by volume number, page number and year).

Peirce, C. S., (1982), *The Writings of Charles S. Peirce*, 8 Vols, M. Fisch, E. Moore and C. J. Kloesel, and the Peirce Edition Project, eds, Bloomington: Indiana University Press (W followed by volume number, page number and year).

Peirce, C. S., (1992), *The Essential Peirce: Selected Philosophical Writings, Volume 1: 1867–1893*, N. Houser and C. J. Kloesel, eds, Bloomington: Indiana University Press, Reprinted with permission of Indiana University Press. (EP1 followed by page number and year).

Peirce, C. S., (1998), *The Essential Peirce, Volume 2: 1893–1913*. Peirce Edition Project, eds, Bloomington: Indiana University Press, Reprinted with permission of Indiana University Press. (EP2 followed by page number and year).

Peirce, C. S., (2009), *The Logic of Interdisciplinarity: The Monist-Series*, E. Bisanz, ed, Berlin: Akademie Verlag GmbH., (LI followed by page number and year).

Peirce, C. S. and V. Welby-Gregory, (1977), *Semiotic & Significs: The Correspondence between C. S. Peirce and Victoria Lady Welby*, C.S. Hardwick, ed, Bloomington: Indiana University Press (SS followed by page number and year).

The text cites various generally unpublished Peirce manuscripts, numbered according to the standard Richard Robin catalogue. These are referenced by the letter R immediately followed by the sheet number and year, e.g. R478: 62, 1903 and R339: 339v, 1908. The Houghton Library in Cambridge, MA, which holds these manuscripts, is to be thanked for making them available in digital form for research purposes. The call number for the entire collection of Charles S. Peirce papers is MS Am 1632, consequently each citation is to be understood as, e.g. MS Am 1632, R339: 239v, 1904, this being a reference to the verso side of sheet 239 of the manuscript version of Peirce's Logic Notebook, R339. Note that in the particular case of manuscript R339, the recto/verso pagination established by Don Roberts, e.g. 339: 239v, is also accompanied for the convenience of the reader by the Houghton Library sequence number, thus: (R339: 239v, H450, 1904).

Introduction

Important purposes of any Introduction are to explain the title of the study, to say what it is about and why it was written. In the present case, it takes the form of answers to certain questions concerning title and content. Why should anybody be writing a book with a gerundive in the title, suggesting a possibly inchoate content? Why 'neo-Peircean' and not plain 'Peircean', and why not 'post-Peircean'? Why should anybody want or need to develop a semiotic system that is well-known and, for many if not most, has already proved its worth in numerous domains?

The simple answer to the first question is that the enterprise is worth attempting as there are valuable Peircean concepts in his legacy that Peirce himself never developed, and there is consequently potential for taking this legacy forward, as semioticians the world over have been doing for some time. Furthermore, as the gerundive in the title suggests, this is work in progress, not job done. Now, work in progress implies that the undertaking has already started, that the concept itself, therefore, is not new. And this is indeed the case, for the term 'neo-Peircean' itself is not in any way original, as an Internet search will show. Personally, I was introduced to the term, although the concept is implicit in his earlier study (Shapiro 1983), in a paper given by Michael Shapiro entitled 'Aspects of a Neo-Peircean Linguistics: Language History as Linguistic Theory' (Shapiro 2002b) at an international colloquium organized by the University of Perpignan in 2001[1] and published in the English language selection of papers to be found in Shapiro (2002a). In the paper, Shapiro's conception of neo-Peircean studies concerned the relation between semiotics and linguistic change, an entirely legitimate conception of what might be neo-Peircean but one that is quite unlike that of the present study. The concept also appears in Kalevi Kull's 'reinterpretation' of Peirce from within the field of biosemiotics (2012: 13), and elsewhere, too.[2] While not original, the concept has a respectable pedigree; and, returning to the gerundive nature of the enterprise, it has to be said that this study is a contribution to an existing field of enquiry, a possible version of the enterprise, not the entire story.

Second, an alternative title, 'Developing a Post-Peircean Approach to the Sign' suggested itself briefly, but was dropped since it would have implied some sort of Kuhnian paradigm shift in which the heuristic potential of Peirce's earlier definitions would have been rendered redundant or irrelevant by the later, 1908, conceptions of the sign and semiosis. This is not the case, as the study seeks to show how elements from what are posited as two very different approaches to signification are not necessarily incompatible and can be combined in a single hybrid approach. In short, the study seeks to offer an innovative developmental approach to signs from within what its author considers to be an authentic Peircean framework, but one which for obvious reasons cannot receive the great man's caution.

However, the recent history of the term is not the full story: there is also an epistemological justification for such a project. For it seems potentially deceitful to call contemporary Peirce-based semiotics 'Peircean', as Peirce never sought to develop a number of what are generally considered to be Peircean semiotic concepts himself: he was far more interested in identifying all possible signs in his broad conception of logic, and in classifying them. Therefore, 'neo-Peircean' is surely a more appropriate description of the sort of semiotic enquiry being conducted by myself and by others. While there is nothing dishonest in adopting the term 'Peircean', it seems to me to be misleading, hence the present attempt to present Peircean concepts from a different angle and under a more realistic denomination. What Peirce himself would make of present-day analyses and pronouncements in semiotics is impossible to determine, but in certain cases to be reviewed, not difficult to imagine. One thing is certain, he would only have had a passing interest in the sorts of problems that exercise contemporary Peircean semioticians; his theoretical preoccupations lay elsewhere. In view of his avowed scant, almost utilitarian interest in existent signs, how, and of what, is a neo-Peircean study to be composed? I wasn't the first to ask the question: 'Suppose that Peirce had succeeded in writing *A System of Logic, considered as Semeiotic*, or rather suppose that he were writing it today, in full knowledge of developments in logic and in semeiotic since his time. What would be its distinguishing features?' (Fisch 1986: 351).

The hard-pressed Peirce claimed on many occasions to be in the course of developing a complete, thoroughly 'Peircean' study of logic, but, owing no doubt to painful bouts of ill-health, unremitting impecuniousness and the sheer extent and evolving complexity of his all-encompassing conception of the subject, was never able to complete such a project. Any researcher or commentator attempting to follow his initiative is similarly hampered: the material evidence of this exhaustive conception of the sign that is available is vast, and is largely unpublished in any editorially sound form (the most up-to-date volume of the promised *Writings* presents documents from the nineteenth century, while the thematically organized *Collected Papers* are a potentially misleading resource). Thus, the most important of Peirce's statements on signs have to be sought piecemeal from scattered published and unpublished sources, with the unfortunate consequence that the recently coined sobriquet 'neo-Peircean' denominates a research enterprise fraught with difficulties.

***

What is the study about? One concern is to show that much of what passes for Peircean semiotics is a re-working of the concepts and principles expounded in lectures that Peirce gave on logic in 1903, and that there is significant material to exploit in the later pronouncements. Moreover, much of this re-working does not always seem to me to respect the original principles of the theory, which means that it might qualify as neo-Peircean but not exactly Peircean. This being the case, another purpose of the study is, in taking the semiotics forward, in developing hitherto unworked concepts, to emphasize the basic principles as I see them. Thus, while the study in no way seeks to project itself as a hectoring form of 'Peirce policing', respect for the original definitions and conceptions remains a constant preoccupation. What is advanced in the course of the six chapters is the thesis that Peirce's conception of signs and of how to classify them developed from the well-known 1903 period into a quite different approach. We therefore examine the appropriate aspects of what will frequently be referred to as the 'system of 1903', show how it began to develop into a more comprehensive conception of signs, objects and interpretants and their mutual cooperation, and then proceed to describe what, like other authors, I shall refer to as the 'later system' or as the 'system of 1908'. Such a division might be understood as a suggestion that the two suddenly became quite distinct, but, in fact, there is a gradual development from one to the other, without the first being dismissed by Peirce. Which is to say that the study doesn't in anyway reject the early 1903 conception of signs and their classes. It simply appeals for a greater effort to understand the later system in spite of the impoverished data at our disposal, namely the limited and, in places, cryptic information that Peirce has left us. This later system, I am convinced, can be shown to be just as relevant to our understanding of the relation between signs and the world as a number of recent developments in cognitive science and semiotics, a task for which the 1903 system is less well equipped.

***

To elaborate its purpose and further justify the title, the study first reviews an important aspect of Peirce's career-long interest in classification and assesses the largely hostile critical reception accorded to Peirce's late systems, one of the central concepts of which, semiosis, nevertheless merits a thorough investigation. Furthermore, subsequent developments in semiotics outside the Peircean sphere and in the cognitive sciences invite us to reaffirm the continuing relevance of a century-old approach to signs. These very different issues are all synthesized in an unavoidably 'patchwork' Chapter 1, but should provide the reader with an understanding of the problematic background to the approach to signs proposed in this – and in any – study seeking to exploit and develop Peirce's logic.

Thereafter, the book is divided into two distinct parts. In the first, Chapters 2 and 3 review material from one of the high points in Peirce's interest in signs until the introduction of the concept of semiosis. Chapter 2, entitled 'The System of 1903', thus concentrates on the lectures on logic that Peirce delivered in November and December 1903 at the Lowell Institute, and in particular, on the full manuscript version of the abridged Syllabus that accompanied the course of lectures. Chapter 3 deals with a transitional period between 1904 and the introduction of the concept of semiosis in 1907. The chapter examines an emergent conception of the sign which coincides with Peirce's renewed interest in pragmatism and the development of more complex sign taxonomies. Forming a sort of 'prolegomena', this two-part review of early material is warranted by the fact that it is easier to present and understand the lesser-known concepts to be introduced later, or those not known at all, by contrasting them with the better known, and also by virtue of the important principle whereby developing a 'neo-' approach to signs doesn't in any way preclude employment of more established concepts. In short, there are concepts with which the reader needs to be acquainted before the development of any new approach.

Chapters 4 and 5 compose the second part of the book, in which the elements of a neo-Peircean semiotics are brought to the fore. Chapter 4, entitled 'The System of 1908', presents the reader with a more sympathetic review of the later period of Peirce's thinking on signs than it has received from many renowned Peirce specialists. This period corresponds broadly to the years 1908 and 1909, and is based principally on correspondence between Peirce and his English correspondent, Lady Victoria Welby, between Peirce and William James, and on draft letters to both seemingly never sent. It was a period during which Peirce introduced a number of far-reaching modifications to his descriptions of signs, including a significant change in the theoretical framework on which he came to construct his later typologies. As these modifications form the basis of much of the hostile critical assessments of his late semiotics mentioned above, the chapter sets the scene, so to speak, for the theoretical arguments to follow.

The initial sections of Chapter 5, drawing on the conclusions from Chapter 4 examine a curious ten-class system left in a draft by Peirce apparently as an enigma for Lady Welby. The second part of the chapter then returns to the problem of relevance developed in Chapter 1, and compares certain features of what is presented here as Peircean semiosis with alternative models advanced by other specialists, mainly in biosemiotics. In particular, the study reviews at this point the nature of 'looking', observation, and investigates the ways in which Peirce's conception of the scopic relation holding between observer and the observed object, and more broadly between an organism and its environment, contrast with positions canvassed by contemporary biosemioticians, on the one hand, and by enactivist theory on the other. Chapter 4 thus deals almost exclusively with what I consider to be a faithful reconstruction of Peirce's concept of semiosis, while Chapter 5 reviews what is interpreted here as an abridged model of semiosis and returns to the problem of relevance by comparing and contrasting modern developments in semiotics and the cognitive sciences with Peirce's original statements.

Chapter 6, entitled 'Perspectives' and drawing on verbal, pictorial and socio-politically inspired issues, attempts to synthesize the later system with the better-known semiotics of 1903 by associating the potential for purely formal analysis provided by a class of signs from the system of 1903 with the dynamism of semiosis in verbal and pictorial case studies. Such an approach to signs illustrates the way a hybrid neo-Peircean semiotics can contribute to our understanding of the complex phenomena to be found in our semiosphere.

Chapters 2, 3 and 4 are given in chronological in order. There is good reason for such an organization, for while there is considerable development of Peirce's thinking on a range of philosophical problems, logic included, over a period of almost half a century of scientific enquiry, there are clear, persistent and constant features of his highly personal approach to these problems. For present purposes these require a chronological as opposed to a thematic approach such as the one adopted, for example, by Parker (1998), whose purpose was very different from the present one. Chronology, and concomitantly, as precise as possible dating of the quotations advanced as proof of such and such a point, determine the order of these chapters, and in this we leave the final word to Peirce on Plato from a list he drew up of 'ultimate ends':

> As to Plato, unless we are content to treat the only complete collection of the works of any Greek philosopher that we possess as a mere repertory of gems of thought, as most readers are content to do; but wish to view them as they are so superlatively worthy of being viewed as the record of the entire development of thought of a great thinker, then everything depends upon the chronology of the dialogues.
> (R434: 22–3, 1902)

It should be mentioned at this point that while there is in places an overlap in content with my earlier book (Jappy 2016), the purpose of the present study is entirely different. The topics of Chapter 4, namely a review of the letter to Peirce's English correspondent, Lady Victoria Welby, dated 23 December 1908, have already figured in that book and in a number of papers published since. While the contents of the letter are an important aspect of Peirce's development as a logician, I feel that they have not received the critical attention they deserve. They are also vital for the theory of semiosis and agency that I am advancing here, and I unashamedly examine the problem anew, this time in much greater detail. As mentioned in the Acknowledgements section, I also reutilize material extracted from various papers published relatively recently in semiotics journals. Chapter 5, for example, draws on my 'Peirce's other ten-class typology', *Language and Semiotic Studies*, 7(1): 1–33, (Jappy 2021), Chapter 6 reproduces material from my 'Hypoiconicity, semiosis and Peirce's immediate object', *Language and Semiotic Studies*, 5(2): 1–36, (Jappy 2019b), while Chapter 6 also draws on my 'Three problems for Peirce's metaphor', (Jappy 2022), *Revue Roumaine de Philosophie*, 66 (1): 11–28. Once again, I would like to thank the editorial boards of both journals for permission to re-use copyright material.

As the study seeks to advance Peircean ideas left undeveloped by their conceptor, more attention will be given to the textual sources than to secondary material provided by the work of other scholars. Consequently, with several notable exceptions, in discussions of such sources I have tried to avoid polemics: Peirce's very complex theories have engendered multiple interpretations, all of which, given the absence of the final arbiter, Peirce himself, ineluctably reduce to opinion, and the present study is no exception. I do, however, object to what I feel to be incorrect reformulations of Peirce's definitions, complaints of 'abstruseness' in his terminology and to self-styled specialists' disinclination to consult the manuscripts. There is no shortcut to enlightenment, and attempting to understand Peirce involves effort and debate: the study is thus both expositional and argumentative. It should nevertheless be noted that, while not intended as an introduction to a semiotics drawing on Peirce's logic, the study can obviously be used as such, as the first four chapters review a number of essential features of what we can legitimately refer to as his multifaceted theory of the sign. As the title clearly suggests, however, the purpose of the book is less concerned with popularization than with presenting and justifying an innovative position: the two central tasks of the study, then, are 'kite-flying', suggesting legitimate developments, and exposition of the principles of a hopefully just interpretation of Peircean sign theory. This latter task will require the drawing of an important distinction in the next chapter that further vindicates the 'neo-' element of the title.

1

The Problem of Relevance

The chapter launches the study by examining aspects of Peirce's semiotic legacy which, in the light of contemporary research, semiotic and otherwise, merits review and validation. What we consider as mainstream Peircean semiotics is now, like Saussure's *Cours*, over a hundred years old, and has been challenged by new semiotic practices and principles and, indeed, by branches of cognitive science. The Introduction advanced the idea, moreover, that there is misapprehension within and without the Peirce community of how semioticians work with Peircean concepts, and that this misapprehension is prejudicial to such research: it renders the theoretical background problematic by undermining the validity of even the most basic concepts.

One purpose of this chapter is, then, before beginning the review of the pertinent Peircean semiotic concepts to be developed in the later stages of the study, primarily to dispel once and for all this misapprehension. To this end, the sections immediately following this outline address the important issue concerning the way Peirce is esteemed as a semiotician, internally, so to speak, and also externally: they explore the relation between Peirce's steadfast interest in the classification of sciences and signs, and the way contemporary semioticians go about their business. Both pertain to the way his work is perceived and received within the Peirce community.

As was also mentioned in the Introduction, the study takes the notion of Peircean semiosis as its central theme. As the concept is in many ways problematic, not least because Peirce offers scant information that we can be certain of and work with, the chapter then reviews a number of disagreements internal to the Peirce community that threaten the relevance of any attempt to accord it its just theoretical importance. The most recently available reference to the concept occurs late in Peirce's career, and the later writings on signs in general have not met with the same understanding and critical analysis accorded to the better-known earlier descriptions of the sign, for which, significantly when one examines their critical analysis by the specialists, Peirce conveniently has supplied his own – oft-quoted – examples.

Finally, the chapter addresses further problems which are potentially harmful to any attempt to promote later conceptions of the sign. These take two forms. One is the fairly common complaint that Peirce is inconsistent with his terminology and the principles it refers to. To which, we can add the rider that the chronology of the various texts that researchers are able to deal with is not stable even a hundred years after Peirce's death. The second is more insidious, and is an issue that challenges any attempt to develop Peirce's ideas beyond the theoretical boundaries, which for reasons of extreme poverty, ill-health and old age he was constrained to set himself. This second issue is epitomized by the various attempts to apply his theory of the sign either in some form of hybridization with alternative – and potentially conflicting – theories of the sign, or by adopting the theory piecemeal and discarding 'bits' that might embarrass a given semiotician's project. As the reader will have realized, the study seeks to promote what its author hopes will be an impenitent form of Peircean orthodoxy.

***

But to return to the general theme of the study, consider the following statement: 'Peirce has gotten in with the wrong crowd, the semioticians.' T.L. Short, a philosopher and an extremely conservative Peirce scholar, had an agenda. This was the very first sentence in the Preface to his monograph, *Peirce's Theory of Signs* (2007). He was seeking to 'rescue' Peirce from the semioticians: from researchers like the author of this study, for example, and from the many practising academic semioticians seeking to further our understanding of cultural artefacts, social practices, the life sciences and our enveloping digital semiosphere, and from others out there in the wider world of industry and business working very legitimately, individually or with corporations on commercial ventures, on advertising projects or brand management, for example. Thus, while Short's irresponsible, deliberately divisive and utterly unPeircean remark can be interpreted as a less than oblique attempt to block the way of enquiry, it also provides me with a useful way of explaining the reasoning behind the title of my study. For, unfortunately, Short isn't alone in his criticism of contemporary Peircean semiotics, with the result that any semiotician attempting to take up and apply Peircean semiotic principles is confronted with a number of recurring difficulties, including almost theological reservations about the legitimacy of such an enterprise. Consider, for example, this remark by another renowned Peirce specialist: 'Contemporary semiotics is not Peirce's Semeiotic: that is not an expression of a personal idiosyncrasy, it is simply a historical fact. To identify Peirce's work as "semiotics" would be to invite the same kind of confusion that occurred with "pragmatism," an illness that Peirce cured by prescribing "pragmaticism"' (Ketner 2009: 44).

This is simply opinion, obviously, not any sort of historical fact. But Ketner is far closer to the truth than Short: contemporary semiotics is most often *not* Peirce's semeiotic. His assessment is, nevertheless in all probability, an expression of the sort of problems attending any attempt to employ Peircean theoretical constructs in, for example, contemporary cultural and biological research. Short and other Peirce philosophers, too, in all probability, with their 'wrong crowds', are afflicted by a kind of epistemological blindness, for they very clearly misapprehend the role and place of contemporary Peircean semiotics within the general field of Peircean research and within Peirce's own conception of the divisions of research. Another important purpose of this chapter, then, is to expose and rebut such blindness, and to show that there is a valid approach to signs from a seemingly novel but in fact long-established, authentic Peircean perspective. To understand the pointlessness of the hostile judgements on contemporary work in semiotics expressed by Short and others it is useful to place in perspective what seems to have been the research priorities of Peirce himself before expounding those of this study. This requires, among other things, that we review two fields extensively explored during Peirce's career-long interest in classification: sciences and signs.

Classification and semiotics

Two objects of Peirce's classifications: Sciences and signs

In this chapter we deal principally with the first interest, the classification of the sciences, as all the chapters to follow review Peirce's statements on the sign and, more rarely, his classifications of signs. Born in the first half of the nineteenth century, Peirce very much adhered to many of the research objectives of the age, one of which being to organize and classify the vast accumulation of knowledge acquired since the Enlightenment and before. Peirce studied the basic principles of classification under Jean Louis Agassiz, a Harvard professor of zoology (CP: 1.229, 1902; Fisch 1982: xxi), principles which he then applied himself in his own classificatory work (see below, for example, the extracts from CP: 1.229–1.231, 1902). Like John Locke (1964 [1690]), like Jeremy Bentham, like the Grimm brothers and their classifications of languages and folk tales, like Charles Darwin, and like Auguste Comte, whose classification model he partially adopted, as a systematic philosopher Peirce sought to organize not only his own research objectives but, as a preliminary, to classify knowledge gained by others in the form of a classification of the sciences involved in the acquisition of that knowledge: 'Every systematic philosopher must provide himself with a classification of the sciences. Comte first proposed to arrange the sciences in a series of steps, each leading on to another. This general idea may be adopted; and we may adapt our phraseology to the image of the well of truth with flights of stairs leading down into it' (R1345: 1, n.d.).

Typically, as we shall see over and over again, Peirce prefaces the introduction of important new concepts and principles by first presenting the theoretical background on which they are based. In this case, before introducing, for example, his principles of philosophy, he begins by showing his reader/audience just where philosophy stands in relation to other areas of enquiry. Not, perhaps, an undertaking that many modern philosophers or semioticians might embrace, but one that is characteristic of Peirce's whole approach to the acquisition of knowledge. Accordingly, in the following text, non-dated, Peirce explains how the various sciences he recognizes are organized by introducing a dependency principle, this being applied according to the nature of the observations the scientist undertakes, observation, as we see below, being the cornerstone of Peirce's conception of scientific enquiry:

> In the development of science, a point is soon reached at which men have to receive special training and be armed with special instructions in order to collect their facts. Thus, arise special classes of minds fitted for different kinds of inquiries. It now becomes necessary to distribute sciences in general into departments. It thus becomes necessary to classify the sciences according to the different sorts

of observations which they make ... Another reason [for the classification of the sciences], already pointed out by Auguste Comte, one of the first to employ this type of classification, further recommends it. It is, that the less general sciences have to employ the results of the more general, which because of their being less embarrassed by minutiae, are earlier developed.

(R1345: 37–9, n.d.)

Although he never again produced such detailed systematic arrangements of the sciences as those to be found in CP: 1.180–1.231 from 1902 and 1903, Peirce returns to the same broad divisions of the sciences of discovery in a late text, retaining the 'scopic' distinction between cenoscopy and idioscopy, two quite different sciences requiring distinct types of observation:

Let Heuretic Science be divided into, first, *Mathematics*, which assumes no responsibility for the truth of its premises, but only for its conclusions necessarily following from those premises; second, *Philosophy*, or, as Bentham calls it, Cenoscopy, which makes no new observations, but merely draws such conclusions as it can from universally undoubted truths and universally admitted phenomena; and thirdly, *Special Science*, Bentham's Idioscopy, which is chiefly occupied with bringing to light phenomena hitherto unnoticed. In idioscopy two wings must be observed; one *Psychical*, or Humanistic, the other *Physical* ... Under Philosophy, we shall find ourselves again forced ... to make a trichotomy; recognizing first, Phenomenology; second, the Critical, or Normative, Sciences, and third, Metaphysics, the science of Reality.

(EP2: 458–9, 1911)

Figure 1.1 is an abridged version in graphic form of the classification of the sciences that Peirce proposed in 1903 in the Syllabus distributed during a series of public lectures on logic given at the Lowell Institute in Boston.[1] Although it was by no means the earliest,[2] this particular version distinguished three major types of sciences: the theoretical sciences, that is, the sciences of discovery (heuretics), by which Peirce means the discovery of knowledge, followed (on the complete classification) by the sciences of review and the practical sciences. The latter two are simply indicated by dotted lines in Figure 1.1, for, in order to understand the error of Short's censure, we need only consider Peirce's organisation of the three sciences of discovery, mathematics, followed by the general science of philosophy (cenoscopy) and the idioscopic sciences.

Within Peirce's particular chosen path, then, namely the heuretic sciences, philosophy or cenoscopy, earlier spelled 'coenoscopy', a term constructed from one of Bentham's (CP: 1.241–1.242),[3] follows mathematics and precedes the 'sciences' of applied inquiry which Peirce, again drawing on Bentham, calls 'idioscopy', the difference being that cenoscopy doesn't observe actual events and data or use special instrumentation, but, based on common sense and careful reasoning, enables logically determined analyses with which to conduct applied research. Cenoscopy is, he writes, a 'Philosophy of Common Sense', 'the sort of science that is founded upon the common experience of all men' (CP: 8.199, 1905), of which, more below. Idioscopy, on the other hand, provides new knowledge.

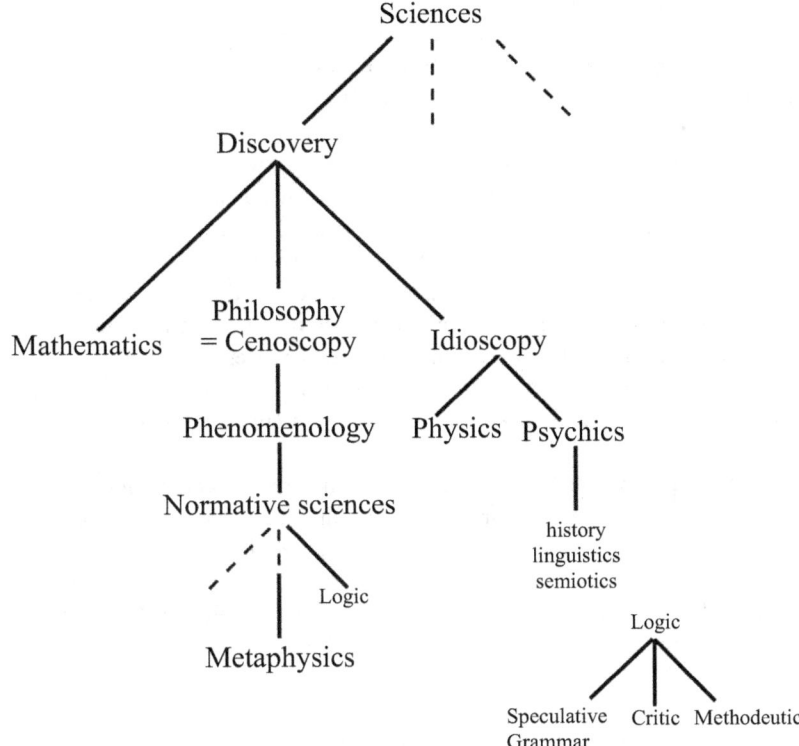

Figure 1.1 A much abridged version of the 1902–1903 classifications of the sciences, showing the respective positions in the classifications of Peirce's Speculative Grammar and contemporary semiotics.

Cenoscopy thus subdivides trichotomously into phenomenology, followed by normative science and, finally, metaphysics. The normative sciences, says Peirce, distinguish what ought to be from what ought not to be (CP: 1.186), and by doing so enable the scientist to distinguish between correct and incorrect reasoning. According to the dependency principle holding between sciences, the normative sciences, resting 'largely on phenomenology and on mathematics' (EP2: 259, 1903), form three distinct divisions: esthetics, ethics and logic, where 'each division', Peirce notes, following Comte's step-like arrangement, 'depends on that which precedes it' (EP2: 260, 1903; cf., too, EP2: 458, 1911). Logic considered as 'semeiotic', as Peirce on occasion named his logic (CP: 1.444, 1903), the 'cenoscopic' theory of the sign, in other words, enables the researcher to make accurate analyses based upon correct reasoning and to formulate valid hypotheses, based on what are in fact principles of common sense.

Characteristically, logic, too, is composed of three distinct but interrelated branches. The first is Speculative Grammar, that is, 'the general theory of the nature and meanings of signs, whether they be icons, indices, or symbols' (EP2: 260, 1903). This is followed by 'Critic', by which he meant the narrower, traditional conception of logic. This discipline classifies inferential processes and determines the validity of inferences within each of the major kinds of reasoning: abduction, which is a variety of inference governing the formation of hypotheses, together with the traditional types, deduction and induction. For Peirce, in combination they played an important role in the discovery and validation of knowledge.

Finally comes Methodeutic, to which he had also referred earlier as 'speculative rhetoric' and which he understood as that part of logic which determines the relations between logic and the methods that ought to be pursued in any scientific investigation. This is how he describes the science in a manuscript from 1906: 'The third division, *Methodeutic*, discusses the relations of signs to their interpretants, that is, their knowledge producing value' (R793: 20). In his unsuccessful 1902 Carnegie application, Peirce had earlier defined methodeutic, considered as the methodology of logic, as being characterized by the processes of definition of concepts and the establishment of divisions of their varieties. In other words, the diverse classification systems produced by Peirce are the product of his employing this particular methodology of definition followed by division.[4]

As we see in Chapter 2 and as all Peirce scholars and commentators know, this is how, in his Speculative Grammar, he established his ten classes of signs. Few contemporary semioticians would conduct their research into 'nudging' or the abuses of social media, or compose publicity campaigns with agencies, by strictly imposing Peirce's methodeutic, even if they could work it out completely, which is another reason for evoking a *neo*-Peircean approach to signs and semiotics.

The analyses of cenoscopy and the discoveries of idioscopy[5]

It is important that we understand how Peirce sought to organize his discussions of the sign by detailing the theoretical background underwriting them. This, as seen above, takes the form of a classification of the sciences leading, in the case of discussions of the sign, to logic. However, for the general theme of this and a later chapter, namely relevance, one of the most important distinctions he made in the 1902 and 1903 classifications concerns the two 'scopic' sciences, namely cenoscopy and idioscopy, the latter being the generic term for the special sciences 'out in the world', as it were, bringing to light new facts and research results. These are the facts ('truths') in what he saw as the purely physical world and the psychic world of animate and principally human activity indicated respectively as 'Physics' and 'Psychic' in Figure 1. This is how Peirce presented them in the second chapter of the Minute Logic of 1902:

> All knowledge whatever comes from observation; but different sciences are observational in such radically different ways that the kind of information derived from the observation of one department of science (say natural history) could not possibly afford the information required of observation by another branch (say mathematics) ... Among the theoretical sciences [of discovery], I distinguish three classes, all resting upon observation, but being observational in very different senses.
>
> (CP: 1.238–1.239, 1902)

We note that he presents these as 'observational' sciences; in other words, as examples of scientific pursuits that involve 'looking' in some form.[6] However, he claims, the nature of the observation in each case is different, even in the case of mathematics, a science which does not enter the explicitly named 'scopic' dichotomy, and which is not relevant to the present discussion, although it clearly underwrites Peirce's virtually career-long interest in, and promotion of, diagrammatic reasoning:

> The first is mathematics, which does not undertake to ascertain any matter of fact whatever, but merely posits hypotheses, and traces out their consequences. It is observational, in so far as it makes constructions in the imagination according to abstract precepts, and then observes these imaginary objects, finding in them relations of parts not specified in the precept of construction.
> (CP: 1.240, 1902)

The basic distinction between cenoscopy and idioscopy as sciences involved in the pursuit of knowledge is between what was referred to earlier as the discovery of knowledge using principles of sound reasoning – by the application of 'common sense', in other words – the discovery of knowledge unaided by exosomatic instruments such as stethoscopes and computers, etc., as opposed to the discovery of facts and new truths as a consequence of specialized training, travel or special instruments. As Figure 1.1 is intended to show, in Peirce's view the specialized sciences of physics and psychics derive, or should do, their investigative principles from philosophy. One wonders how many present-day scientists would admit that their research draws on general philosophical principles, and yet that is exactly what Peirce is saying: scientific research depends initially on sound reasoning, which is what his logical branch of methodeutic was intended to provide. Moreover, one wonders, too, how many contemporary philosophers would admit that their major systematic preoccupation is based upon observation.

There is at least one notable case: the late John Deely. To the best of this author's knowledge, John Deely is the only philosopher/semiotician to have adopted the cenoscopy/idioscopy distinction introduced by Bentham and developed by Peirce, and this in two stages. In a clearly Peircean conception of the two sciences in Deely 1990 he invokes the need to establish the basic principles of anthroposemiotics and biosemiotics cenoscopically: 'I will move in chapter 5 to the specific consideration of the action of signs within our experience, because it is best to establish the basic notions of a science cenoscopically considered, that is to say, in terms that are derived from what is accessible to everyone, namely, common experience' (1990: 19). To which we can add the following statement which clearly positions idioscopy in Deely's thought at the time: 'It is for this reason that I have resisted the temptation of tying the basic categorial concepts and terminology of biosemiotics to the latest biological theories which have for solid reasons ... replaced the traditional two kingdoms with five (not unlike the manner in which the traditional five external senses provide a cenoscopic framework of discussion for psychology in which idioscopic research is able to demonstrate that there are actually more refined discriminations which validate recognition of a greater number of sensory channels)' (1990: 25n8).

Now, by 2008–9 Deely had taken both 'sciences' a stage further, developing the nature of cenoscopy and renaming them both respectively as 'coenoscopy' and 'ideoscopy'. Consider this statement of the difference between the two types of knowledge, which he places understandably within his conception of biosemiotics, and a distinction which he draws between object and thing:

> So we need to distinguish between coenoscopic knowledge as critically accessible to any human animal as semiotic, and ideoscopic knowledge which presupposes coenoscopy but goes beyond it by mean of specialized researches and the testing of hypotheses often by mathematical means, and yet always returns to coenoscopy as the sole indispensable support of the difference between the closed unto itself objective world of pure animal perception (*Umwelt*) and the objective world which includes human understanding (*Lebenswelt*) as an opening to the infinite through the very action of signs which created the objective world in the first place as transcendent and superordinate to while inclusive partially also of the physical environment, the world of things in their own being independent of being known.
>
> (2009b: 5)

The distinction is important to Deely, though unlike the present author, he sees contemporary semiotics as cenoscopic like Peirce's logic (2009b: 129), rather than idioscopic, and his conception of signs and semiosis diverges significantly from that of Peirce and the one advanced in this book, as we see in Chapter 2. Nevertheless, as Deely affirmed, the distinction is important. Herewith cenoscopy and idioscopy as defined in the Minute Logic:

> Class II is philosophy, which deals with positive truth, indeed, yet contents itself with observations such as come within the range of every man's normal experience, and for the most part in every waking hour of his life. Hence Bentham calls this class, *coenoscopic*. These observations escape the untrained eye precisely because they permeate our whole lives, just as a man who never takes off his blue spectacles soon ceases to see the blue tinge. Evidently, therefore, no microscope or sensitive film would be of the least use in this class. The observation is observation in a peculiar, yet perfectly legitimate, sense. If philosophy glances now and then at the results of special sciences, it is only as a sort of condiment to excite its own proper observation.
>
> (CP: 1.241 1902)

> Class III is Bentham's *idioscopic*; that is, the special sciences, depending upon special observation, which travel or other exploration, or some assistance to the senses, either instrumental or given by training, together with unusual diligence, has put within the power of its students. This class manifestly divides itself into two subclasses, the physical and the psychical sciences.
>
> (CP: 1.242, 1902)

To complete this discussion of cenoscopy and idioscopy, there are two significant points to consider. First, it is important to note that 'cenoscopy' and 'idioscopy' are denominations in which, according to the *Oxford English Dictionary*, '-scope' is a suffix representing mod. L. – *scopium* from Greek σκοπεῖν, 'to look at', 'examine', which itself derives from the Indo-European root **spek-*, 'to observe'. Thus, for Peirce, and as the terms indicate, both cenoscopy as philosophy and the idioscopic sciences significantly involve 'looking', observation. This is an important point to which we return in Chapter 5, as conceptions of the relation holding between the observer and the observed have evolved considerably since 1903.

Second, it is inferable from the critical statements made by Short and others, no doubt, that such authors might have thought that for Peirce the idioscopic sciences were less important than their cenoscopic predecessor in the classification, and upon which they are shown to be dependent. To show the error of such a judgement, that an idioscopic discipline like contemporary semiotics was in no way for Peirce (or for the contemporary semiotician) a subaltern science or an epistemological 'illness', we need simply to turn to his review of Wundt's *Principles of physiological psychology*. Here we find: 'Wundt's great service to man ... has consisted in teaching the students of cenoscopy the beauty of those virtues upon which the students of idioscopy, especially those on the physical wing, have always insisted – virtues that will necessarily result from *any well-considered desire to know the truth*' (CP: 8.201, 1905, emphasis added). Naturally, as a scientist and fully trained chemist, Peirce was an advocate and indeed exponent of the 'physical wing', but was equally interested in the 'discoveries' of psychology and 'the vast and splendidly developed science of linguistics' (CP: 1.271, 1902). The following passage offers a clear indication of the difference between the two sciences of discovery and their relative values: for Peirce, cenoscopy advances by the analysis of everyday experience through observations which the uninitiated are unaware of, while idioscopy, encompassing contemporary semiotics and neo-Peircean semiotics, produces results – 'truths' – upon which further research may reliably be based:

> [L]ittle given is idioscopy to expressing itself in big books. It is not work of heuretic science of any kind. It is a product of that useful industry of collecting, arranging, and digesting the deductions of mathematics, the analyses of cenoscopy, and the discoveries of idioscopy – a service of which the Germans have assumed the burden, and which, as being the "systematization of knowledge," they as well as the general public are too apt to mistake for the business of science ... [Wundt] explicitly says that whatever is not based upon the *results of the special sciences* has no real basis at all.
>
> (CP: 8.202, emphasis added)

And, finally, we have a statement from a pragmaticism draft entitled 'Phaneroscopy: Or the natural history of concepts' which shows clearly that, while as a logician Peirce's primary theoretical interest was in the components of cenoscopy – phenomenology, the normative sciences and metaphysics – he prized the results provided by what he considered as idioscopic research no less than the analytical system of cenoscopy, affirming yet again the theoretical dependency of the former upon the latter:

> Now science, in the sense in which I have defined that word, – namely, as the cooperative business, or life-occupation, of finding out and making sure of the truth by the speediest methods known, – is an undertaking ... *We have to consider that the great body of truth can only be discovered and ascertained by specially devised observations made by specially trained senses with specially informed intelligences behind them.* I follow Jeremy Bentham in calling all that business by the name of Idioscopy. But in its entirety and in every part, Idioscopy presupposes a considerable body of other truth, which may be roughly described as instinctive, that is, traditionally hereditary, but familiarized by the everyday experience of everybody ... That study ... will constitute the department of science that Bentham called Cenoscopy for the reason that it rests on the experience of all men distributively taken, and must be acknowledged by all.
>
> (R299: 1, 1906; emphasis added)

We thus see that what Short, and others, too, probably, fail to see, a consequence of their epistemological blindness, is that Peirce was a *logician* working within his philosophy, his cenoscopy, whereas, present-day semioticians are 'idioscopists', certainly drawing on the logic, but adapting it in order to construct a semiotics enabling them to observe the world in a practical manner.

Some Peircean contributions to the idioscopic sciences

Now the fact that Peirce's principal preoccupation with the development of cenoscopy doesn't mean that he has not already had an influence in the applied sciences. Indeed, in the course of his long career as a logician, he had introduced a number of highly innovative semiotic concepts which he never developed himself but which were taken up by inspired semioticians, philosophers and linguists who recognized their heuristic value. Herewith, briefly, a number of these. His chemical theory of valency which anticipated dependency grammars (e.g. Tesnière 1988) is one example (cf. CP: 4.309); his complex theory of the diagram and diagrammatization which he never completed was taken up, by amongst others, Sowa (1984) and Stjernfelt (2011); applications of the dicisign (Stjernfelt 2014) and recent developments of the heuristic potential of abduction (Barrena and Nubiola 2019; Liszka and Babb 2019). Claudio Guerri and his co-workers, too, have developed a completely new analytical tool, the nonágon, that has taken the development of Peircean semiotic theory into an entirely new field (Guerri 2016, 2019). Finally, developments drawing on Peircean concepts are cybersemiotics (Brier 2010) and examples in biosemiotics too numerous to cite.

More broadly, Peirce's theory of the index was taken up in philosophy by, among others, Bertrand Russell and his concept of the egocentric particular (1950), while Bar-Hillel (1954) discusses indexicality (and the type-token distinction) and mentions his sources and fellow philosophers: 'It was C. S, Peirce who introduced the terms "indexical sign" and "index", Bertrand Russell used instead "ego-centric particular", Nelson Goodman coined "indicator", and Hans Reichenbach "token-reflexive word".

I decided to use Peirce's term since it provides an adjective easily combined with "sign", "word", "expression", "sentence", "language", "communication" alike' (Bar Hillel 1954: 369). The concept of the index had already been exploited by Collinson (1937), who introduced the ugly expression 'indicater', in his study of indication, and in linguistics most notably by Roman Jakobson in his work on shifters: as early as 1950 he had already employed the index in a paper presenting his theory of the shifter (1957).

Finally, Pierce's early statement on what is now known as the type/token ratio (TTR), a basic methodology in any statistical work, is offered as exemplary of how Peirce' influence has entered non-semiotic idioscopic research. The type/token distinction, which Peirce introduced explicitly in 1906 as the triad, type, token and tone, has entered the various disciplines of statistics in a binary state, and is commonly employed, particularly in corpus linguistics, as an easy-to-compute but rudimentary measure of lexical density: the higher the value of the ratio between the two, the more likely a text is to be composed of different words; the lower the value, the more likely the text is to be composed of many occurrences or instances of different words. Any serious introduction to the use of the TTR would hopefully quote a foundational passage from the 'Prolegomena',[7] as it makes the three distinctions on which TTR is predicated yet today: type, token and occurrence (instance). It is important to note, however, that Peirce's interest in general types and existent, individual tokens predates the paper from 1906, although formulated with different terms. See, for example, this definition of the legisign and its replicas in the terminology of the Syllabus of 1903:

> A *Legisign* is a law that is a Sign. This law is usually established by men. Every conventional sign is a legisign [but not conversely]. It is not a single object, but a general type which, it has been agreed, shall be significant. Every legisign signifies through an instance of its application, which may be termed a Replica of it. Thus, the word "the" will usually occur from fifteen to twenty-five times on a page. It is in all these occurrences one and the same word, the same legisign. Each single instance of it is a *Replica*. The Replica is a Sinsign. Thus, every Legisign requires Sinsigns. But these are not ordinary Sinsigns, such as are peculiar occurrences that are regarded as significant. Nor would the Replica be significant if it were not for the law which renders it so.
>
> (CP 2.246, 1903)

Now, with the possible exception of the later type-token-(tone/mark)[8] distinction and the graphs, the problem with these examples of Peirce's contributions to idioscopy is that the majority derive from the sign classes defined in the Syllabus of 1903, and for a long time, there was little to be found on semiosis or on developments of the late typologies. Thus, although type and token both appear in the typologies of 1908 and in what will be advanced later as the structure of semiosis, without the curiosity of Thomas Sebeok and the biosemioticians who followed him, the supremely important semiotic concept of semiosis might still be in a state of relative neglect.[9] We return to this problem in Chapters 4 and 5, for the examples given above suggest that Peirce's relevance is maintained almost exclusively by the classes of signs derived in the great system of 1903.

Logic as semeiotic

Peirce used the term 'logic' in two distinct ways, according it a narrow sense and a broad one. In the first case, logic was, he claimed, the standard or traditional study of the conditions of sound reasoning, this involving in his case three forms of inference: hypothesis-formation, deduction and induction. On the other hand, in his broader sense of the term, logic was also 'general semeiotic, treating not merely of truth, but also of the general conditions of signs being signs' (CP: 1.444, *c.* 1896).[10] In this broad sense, then, as can be seen in Figure 1.1, for Peirce, logic was the general science of signs, composed of three different branches – speculative grammar, critic and methodeutic – whereas in the narrow, standard or traditional sense, it was simply the second of those three branches, critic. Thus, the terms 'semeiotic', 'semiotic' or 'semiotics' were all terms which Peirce used as synonyms for 'logic' in the broad sense, for in his view, knowledge was representation (EP2: 271, 1903), and representation can only be realized by signs. In this study, semiotics, if placed in Peirce's 1902–3 scheme, would qualify as a psychic idioscopic science in Figure 1.1, and the term 'semiotic(s)' is the chosen usage, though many American scholars prefer the spelling 'semeiotic', sometimes used by Peirce himself with no noticeable difference of meaning. While the theory of signs discussed in this study (and in other contemporary studies) is semiotics, it is important to realize that Peirce's own theory of signs was an expanded version of *logic*.

The following extract from another course of lectures given earlier in 1903, in this case on pragmatism, offers a perfect idea of how Peirce conceived of his work in logic by classifying the organic relation uniting the three different branches of logic:[11]

> The ultimate purpose of the logician is to make out the theory of how knowledge is advanced. Just as there is a chemical theory of dyeing which is not exactly the art of dyeing, and there is a theory of thermodynamics which is quite different from the art of constructing heat engines; so *Methodeutic*, which is the last goal of logical study, is the theory of the advancement of knowledge of all kinds. But this theory is not possible until the logician has first examined all the different elementary modes of getting at truth and especially all the different classes of arguments, and has studied their properties so far as these properties concern / the/ power of the arguments leading to the truth. This part of logic is called *Critic*. But before it is possible to enter upon this business in any rational way, the first thing that is necessary is to examine thoroughly all the ways in which thought can be expressed. For since thought has no being except in so far as it will be embodied, and since the embodiment of thought is a sign, the business of logical critic cannot be undertaken until the whole structure of signs, especially of general signs, has been thoroughly investigated. This is substantially acknowledged by logicians of all schools. But the different schools conceive of the business quite differently. Many logicians conceive that the inquiry trenches largely upon psychology, depends upon what has been observed about the human mind, and would not necessarily be true for other minds … Other logicians endeavouring to steer clear of psychology, as far as possible, think that this first branch of logic

must relate to the possibility of knowledge of the real world and upon the sense in which it is true that the real world can be known. This branch of philosophy, called epistemology or *Erkenntnislehre*, is necessarily largely metaphysical ... I, therefore, take a position quite similar to that of the English logicians, beginning with Scotus himself, in regarding this introductory part of logic as nothing but an analysis of what kinds of signs are absolutely essential to the embodiment of thought. I call it, after Scotus, *Speculative Grammar*.

(EP2: 256-7, 1903)

This long extract calls for a number of remarks. First, like the relation holding between the three branches of logic, Peirce's whole classificatory edifice is constructed according to an 'architectonic' principle that Peirce adopted from Kant,[12] while, as seen earlier, from Comte he adopted the idea that there is an organic relation holding between the sciences such that the more complex feed principles to those following in the classification. Figure 1.1 is thus a partial representation of the architectonic structure displaying the internal dependencies Peirce established between the different scientific disciplines that philosophy was defined to engage with: the later draw on principles established by the former. In this way, for example, phenomenology draws on and exploits results and principles established within the field of mathematics. In the extract, he is indicating the dependencies holding between the three branches of logic in the broad sense.[13]

Second, it is important to note that speculative grammar, which is that part of logic which determines what sort of entity qualifies as a sign, is a philosophical, cenoscopic field of concepts, whereas the sort of contemporary semiotics practiced by followers of Peirce, Saussure, Greimas, Lotman and others, is an idioscopic science, a science which, if we follow Peirce's classification, discovers new facts: were he to classify present-day semiotics, Peirce would presumably say of it that, like linguistics, it is a variety of classificatory psychics as shown in Figure 1.1 (CP: 1.200, 1903), while biosemiotics, on the other hand, would belong to both the physic and psychic branches. For Peirce speculative grammar itself was a classificatory branch of the logic, as it enables the logician to specify what counts as a sign and then, as we see in Chapter 2, by means of three phenomenologically derived divisions of signs, to establish a table of ten different classes of signs. However, few working semioticians would see the classification of signs *per se* as either a practical or theoretical pursuit, and it is certainly not the primary research objective pursued by this book, although, obviously, without some basic form of classification it is not possible to name the entities the researcher is interested in. Nevertheless, we note that for Peirce classification was an essential instrument in the organisation of knowledge: 'All classification, whether artificial or natural, is the arrangement of objects according to ideas' (CP: 1.231, 1902).

Not all present-day philosophers would necessarily agree. Liszka (2018), for example, takes issue with the necessity of classification and even with attempts to understand Peirce's numerous attempts at the classification of signs, offering a quite different assessment of how contemporary Peircean semioticians appear to employ a theoretical framework more complex than the phenomenon to which the apply it:

> There's usually a problem when the theory is more complex than the phenomenon it hopes to explain, and that appears to be the case with the enterprise of sign classification as Peirce attempted it. He seems to violate his own dictum that the fundamental virtue of a classification scheme is its simplicity (MS 615: 29; Kent 1987: 54). There's a certain threshold of detail in analysis, below which, the analysis gets in the way of its mission.
>
> (2018: 157)

Liszka suggests that classification is a pointless form of reductionism, but disqualifies his position by the need to adopt a rudimentary form of classification himself, as he is obliged to name and distinguish hierarchically between the idiosyncratic types of informative semiotic levels he proposes in his version of semiosis: 'and so information is borne both quali-semiotically and sin-semiotically, if not legi-semiotically' (2018: 169). Without some form of classification these semiotic classes couldn't be referenced. And simply by naming the signifying units they are working with, all linguists and practising semioticians are necessarily indulging in some fundamental form of classification. One wonders, in this respect, how all those linguists like Sapir and anthropologists like Franz Boas would have fared in their attempts to rescue and record the declining Amerindian languages and culture without some basic form of classification. Peirce's numerous attempts to classify signs and the different classes thereof were surely part and parcel of a widespread contemporary scientific worldview.

Finally, in the system of logic as described in 1903, the principles defined within speculative grammar were free of what Peirce sees as the 'psychological or accidental human element' in reasoning (CP: 1.537, 1903): unlike the semiotics of modern schools, his system of logic does not 'trench largely upon psychology'. Yet in an earlier text, he seemed to relax this restriction within the branch of methodeutic (the earlier speculative rhetoric): 'In coming to Speculative Rhetoric, after the main conceptions of logic have been well settled, there can be no serious objection to relaxing the severity of our rule of excluding psychological matter, observations of how we think, and the like' (CP: 2.107, 1902). And psychology formed the basis of what in the idioscopic sciences as shown in Figure 1.1 he referred to as 'Psychics'.[14] And no present-day semiotic analysis of signs of human or cultural origin – anthroposemiosis – would hesitate to avail itself of psychological information, either: contemporary Peircean semiotic enquiry is determined by concepts and methods inherited from methodeutic *and* the relaxed constraint of appeal to psychological data. This fact, too, Short seems to have neglected or misunderstood.

***

It should now be obvious that scholars censuring semiotics as a betrayal of Peirce's original though are unaware of the way contemporary semioticians work, Peircean or otherwise. There is no reason to fear that 'the wrong crowd' of semioticians might damage Peirce's legacy. To suggest otherwise is to commit to a form of obscurantism. For one thing, the contents of the Syllabus and other statements by Peirce are as though writ in stone: nobody can change them, not even a Peirce philosopher like Short. At best, he can contribute to ever-increasing volumes of exegesis. For another, and more importantly, semioticians employing Peircean concepts are working in the field of idioscopy, not in cenoscopy, as Short and others appear to think: like Peirce himself, on occasions where he needed examples, the semioticians adopt and exploit powerful 'cenoscopic' concepts, certainly, not to prejudice or demolish the Peircean legacy, but for endorsement from the theoretical authority of such concepts in order to produce new facts.

Thus, in Figure 1.1 it is clear that cenoscopy/philosophy as Peirce engaged with it is a distinct science from the special sciences of idioscopy, and constituted Peirce's overriding epistemological concern, with the classification of signs central to that project. It can also be seen from Figure 1.1 that Short and others are unable to distinguish between the cenoscopic and the idioscopic analyses as practiced by contemporary Peircean semioticians, or else were unaware of the fact that, like linguists, semioticians produce new ideas and results, new 'truths' as Peirce might have put it. Interpreting the semiosphere, not epistemology, is the practising semiotician's overriding concern. Amongst other things, practising 'idioscopists' intercept and critique the excesses of the social media and artificial intelligence strategies that are engulfing us (e.g. see Guarda, Ohlson and Romanini 2018; Borges and Gambarata 2019), making use of concepts deriving from cenoscopy in the manner that Peirce's classifications prescribe; they don't – or shouldn't but see below – correct or rewrite Peirce's conception of signs as philosophers such as Murphey, Short and others have tried to do. As recent results amply demonstrate, the semioticians have borrowed principles and concepts from cenoscopy: ideas advanced all those years ago by Peirce which have contributed considerably not only to idioscopic Peircean semiotics but to theories of the sign developed within competing schools. In short, Peirce's logic as semeiotic was an augmented theory of logic, whereas contemporary semiotics is just that – semiotics, not logic.

Semiosis

'Semiosis' is a term deemed by the lexicographers to have been introduced into the English language by Peirce in 1907 in manuscript R318. This is the position of both the *Oxford English Dictionary* (henceforth *OED*) and *Merriam-Webster* online dictionaries and of the 1989 Second Edition of the *OED*, for example. As it happens, Francesco Bellucci, in an exhaustive study of classical inference referencing Peirce, his student Allan Marquand, Philodemus' *de Signis* and the term 'semiosis', considers the latter 'almost a *hapax*'. Bellucci doesn't mean that the word only occurs once in the manuscript, simply that it doesn't occur in any other, with the exception of a single earlier instance that Bellucci had found from 1894 in manuscript R411 (2016: 264): it is simply a very rare word in the available material. (The term must surely have appeared in Marquand's thesis under Peirce's direction, which, according to Bellucci, is now lost.) If that were indeed the case, it would put the earliest reference to the term in English at the beginning of the 1880s and not 1907.[15] Unfortunately for the Peirce researcher, as we see, for example in Chapter 2, there are other such 'almost' hapax legomena in the canon.

As for the denomination itself, obviously Peirce has no copyright on it, and once it has acquired general currency, a term like 'semiosis' is open to the use and interpretation of others, and there are, indeed, many different conceptions of what semiosis might be. More depressingly, there are many studies – monographs, manuals and papers – which cite the term mantra-like, without ever giving a definition: we learn of the contexts in which it is held to occur, the processes in which it is held to participate, even the 'results' it is held to yield, but rarely, very rarely, are we given an explanation as to how it functions and what its basic constituents, if any, might be. Moreover, there are Peirce scholars who barely afford the concept any theoretical importance at all. To return briefly to Short (2007), for example, we find that he mentions the concept five times: twice when he quotes Jacques Derrida quoting Umberto Eco discussing Peirce's alleged 'continuous semiosis'; twice when he quotes from Peirce's own 1907 definition; plus, the term 'semiosis' in the title of a work of reference by Johansen in the bibliography. Short has nothing to add to the concept himself. More surprisingly, Bellucci (2017), probably the most exhaustive and reliable contemporary presentation of Peirce's Speculative Grammar, only refers to the concept in two endnotes (2018: 125n3; 279n12).

The concept thus suffers from competing definitions, misinterpretation and a certain neglect from Peirce scholars who might have engaged with it further. This being the case, in order to comply with what I consider to be the spirit of Peirce's conception of signs and the action of signs, the approach to, and presentation of, semiosis adopted in this book is intended to be strictly Peircean. Although he defined the concept quite clearly in the manuscript from 1907, and also gave a number of examples of what can be considered as semioses in manuscripts and correspondence, he never developed the idea in a completely explicit manner. Hence another reason for introducing the prefix 'neo-' to this study: characterizing the concept, identifying its constituents and the way it functions as a process and illustrating it involves interpretation, and also benefits from the discussion of conflicting interpretations, a task undertaken in Chapter 4. Such an enterprise is, as we now see, not without problems, but vital as testimony of his continuing relevance …

Issues

The late systems and their critical reception

Since the central topic of the study is semiosis, the late period is crucial to the study, as this, I contend, was the only period in which Peirce gave us an account – albeit a brief, contested one – of how it might function. Unfortunately, critical reception of the material available from the period has been predominantly negative, although it should be borne in mind that scholars accepting the systems are more likely to get on with working with them rather than extolling their virtues, leaving it to those who dismiss them to voice their disapproval, often quite forcibly. Were it not for the fact that these critics are among the most highly respected authorities on

Peirce's philosophy, there would be no point in defending the concept here. This section introduces a selection of typical critical comments that Peirce's late systems have drawn, with most dismissive observations directed towards the post-1904 ten-division typologies and the order in which they are to be organized. There is thus no consensus as to how the ten divisions these projected typologies should be arranged, or even as to the viability of such an enterprise in spite of investigation into their theoretical potential being a necessity, as Nathan Houser here suggests: 'Perhaps in our present state of understanding of language and semiosis we have no need for such complexity [sixty-six classes of signs] – just as we once had no need for relativity physics – but where principal distinctions can be made, they should be made, and, in any case, they will probably someday be needed' (1992b: xxxviii). Houser further commends such a research project, insisting on the ordering problem associated with the ten-division typologies: 'A sound and detailed extension of Peirce's analysis signs to his full set of ten divisions and sixty-six classes is perhaps the most pressing problem for Peircean semioticians. What is needed first of all is a well motivated rationale for the ordering of Peirce's ten divisions of signs' (1992a: 502n). Although he dismisses as misguided attempts by the 'semioticians' to explicate Peirce's semiotics,[16] Ketner, too, sees this as a desideratum, and he echoes Houser in his introductory chapter to the Bisanz edition of the *Monist* series of Peirce's papers on pragmatism (Peirce 2009):

> Contrary to the claim that Peirce's semeiotical writings are fragmentary and scattered and unsystematic, they are voluminous, painfully detailed, and as systematic as any model one might care to mention from the history of the earth. Whether it is right or wrong, true or false, a boon or bane for mankind, must be left for the flow of science to reveal. But it is important to see *what* Peirce's hypotheses actually *were* – to give a truthful account of them. We will not be able to go beyond him until we have such an account (presently a desideratum), and lacking that, we can only go around him, which would be an unfortunate non-economy of research, not to mention also constituting an unnecessary delay.
>
> (2009: 45)

However, not all reputed Peirce commentators think that Peirce's late semiotics are worthy of such a project, a situation which, when examined carefully, casts doubt upon the validity even of the concept of semiosis itself. Consider, to begin with, this rather surprising summary of Peirce's semiotic achievements from Albert Atkin's internet introduction to Peirce:[17]

> Across the course of his intellectual life, Peirce continually returned to and developed his ideas about signs and semiotic and there are three broadly delineable accounts: a concise Early Account from the 1860s; a complete and relatively neat Interim Account developed through the 1880s and 1890s and presented in 1903; and his speculative, rambling, and incomplete Final Account developed between 1906 and 1910.
>
> (Atkin 2013, paragraph 2)

Peirce scholars do not all agree on the different periods in the development of Peirce's theory of signs, which is understandable when attempting to evaluate his multi-faceted career as a logician spanning almost half a century. Atkin's divisions correspond broadly to the chronology implicitly adopted in Chapter 2: the period 1866–7 when Peirce was developing his 'New List of Categories', the 'interim' period which Atkin here extends from the 1885 paper on logical notation to the Lowell Lectures and the Syllabus of 1903, a period which receives Atkin's measured approval, and, finally, the period discussed in Chapter 4. Peirce's thinking on signs in this period is, Atkin would have us believe, speculative, rambling and incomplete.

The following extract from Freadman (2004) is a more dramatic discussion of the late period and draws heavily on further opinions of the aforementioned philosopher, T. L. Short:

> The late classifications of signs are a very peculiar construct. T. L. Short calls them "darkest semeiotica," describing them as immense, obscure, crabbed with dense tangles, containing important suggestions, but tentative and difficult to clarify. Scholars from Lieb to Liszka have fought their way through its "thickets," elucidating the broad system, counting the classes, selecting those aspects of the classifications that seem most useful. I agree with Short that the first trichotomy is the richest and most fully developed of them all, and that the distinctions Peirce was drawing within the broad category of the object, and those, likewise, within the interpretant, are fraught with difficulties. I confess that as a descriptive semiotician, there is little from this period of Peirce's work that I am inclined to use. It should be clear from the foregoing what this is: the type/token relation seems to me to illuminate a very difficult issue in semiotic, as does the fallibility construal of the distinction between the "immediate" and the "dynamic" object. Some suggestions regarding the interpretant are also promising, but only to the extent that they show where, in a Peircean semiotic, we can accommodate insights into the effectivity of the sign that we know better from other sources.
>
> (2004: 167)

In a more circumspect and less deprecatory manner, Freadman, who describes herself as a descriptive semiotician, later draws an important distinction between what she sees as the 'classificatory protocol of genus and species', that is, the later post-1904 statements on signs, and the 'relational systems' of 1903. Her preference is, as is the wont of the philosophers, too, for the semiotics of the Syllabus, the 'relational systems' that yielded, for example, icon, index and symbol (this being the 'first trichotomy', the one that can be traced back to the 1860s), rather than for the numerous six – and ten-division classifications Peirce was experimenting with in the period from 1905 to 1908. What Freadman fails to mention, or hasn't bothered to perceive, is that all the ten-division classification systems were *combinations* of 'genus and species' and 'relational' trichotomies:

> To a certain degree, the problem of the late work can be glossed as a result of returning to a classificatory protocol of genus and species, instead of the relational

systems that Peirce had entertained at the turn of the century. He takes each relatum of the sign is a genus, then seeks its species, seeming to forget the relational analysis that has generated the terms in the first place.

(2004: 168)

Finally, consider Liszka (1996), whose general appreciation is seemingly far less damning:

> The final typology adds four new trichotomies, bringing the total to ten [note 29]. However, although the final typology is an interesting experiment, it is rather underdeveloped and tentative in Peirce. For this reason, and for the reason that the most detailed is associated with the interim typology [i.e., the system of the 1903 Syllabus], focus on the 1903 typology might be the most fruitful.
>
> (1996: 35)

In endnotes 27 and 29, however, Liszka discusses the final typology Peirce sent to Lady Welby in the letter of 23 December 1908. He sees it as posing a number of 'puzzles' (1996: 130) to the researcher, and provides a succinct summary of much scholarly reaction to the late semiotics (though the specification, when given by scholars, usually means the letters and drafts intended for Lady Welby), citing in particular David Savan (1988) and T. L. Short mentioned in the Introduction and elsewhere in this study, two eminent Peirce scholars whose contributions to the promotion of Peircean semiotics have produced varying results. These are discussed in Chapters One and Four in my study, which seeks precisely to justify Peirce's later statements on the sign. Liszka prefers, like Freadman and others, what he calls the 'interim typology', that is, the ten-class typology derived in the Syllabus of 1903. In a way, this is understandable as it is the first really exhaustive presentation of Peirce's theory of signs – 'the general semeiotic' – and was intended as a public introduction to the problem. Thus, in endnote 29 Liszka proffers a rather unhelpful appreciation of the late semiotics and, like others, declares it full of 'problems, contradictions and confusions': 'For all these reasons [ill-defined and ill-matched typologies], and despite Savan's interesting guesses at the characterization of signs involved in these typologies, I think that we have to agree with Short (1982: 306) that although there is promise here, there are many problems, contradictions and confusions in the very general and sketchy character of the final typology' (1996: 131).

In spite of such clearly negative views of the late semiotics, according to Houser and Ketner the 1908–9 sign-systems offer not simply a potential for further work in Peircean theory but represent a genuine need for such a task. Moreover, as we see in Chapter 4, any problems, contradictions and confusions associated with the late systems are those of the commentators, not of the semiotics. While Houser is presumably open to anyone undertaking such a task, especially in the case of the ten-division typologies, for Ketner though, this must be undertaken by genuine Peirce scholars. But perhaps the most significant comment on the problematic nature of the late systems and an assorted research programme of the sort urged by Houser and Ketner is that of T. L. Short:

For all the enthusiasm that Peirce's later taxonomy has elicited, with its promise of a vast system, an endlessly ramifying formal structure that applies everywhere and to everything, close examination of it disappoints. It is sketchy, tentative, and, as best I can make out, incoherent. Its importance lies not in what it contains but in the kind of project it defines. That project has not yet been adopted by any of Peirce's devotees. For it does not consist in formal elaboration of principles presumed to be apodeictic. Rather, it consists in a critical examination of proposed principles, in part by painstaking application of them to particular cases, and in their arduous reformulation, until a coherent and illuminating system is achieved. The initial three trichotomies that Peirce presented are deeply revealing, in fact essential: note, for example, the prevalence, in contemporary philosophy, of the type/token distinction and the idea of indexical reference. The need for further divisions is equally compelling. What is not compelling is the way Peirce attempted the latter within the formal framework he projected.

(2007: 261)

The problem with Short is that when any of 'Peirce's devotees' attempt to undertake the 'project' he mentions, he dismisses them as the wrong crowd. As for the formal framework in which Peirce tried to work out his final relatively explicit account of the way the sign functions in the letter to Lady Welby of 23 December 1908, Short either refuses to engage fairly with it or woefully misunderstands how it functions.

To their credit, some authorities, Savan (1988) and even Short himself, for instance, have taken the trouble to engage with and attempt to characterize the later typologies and identify some of their defining features. Others, Weiss and Burks (1945), Morand (2004), Diversey (2014), for example, have concentrated on reorderings of Peirce's original scheme. Yet others, like Sanders (1970) and Spinks (1992), have claimed that the task of identifying the sixty-six classes is, if not impossible, 'painstaking', potentially counterproductive, and likely to violate Peirce's own classificational principles. However, few working semioticians, descriptive or otherwise, are interested in a time-consuming attempt to organize a potential sixty-six concepts of Peirce's theory of logic: they are more interested in applying certain Peircean analytical instruments to cultural artefacts, social practices and the digital semiosphere enveloping the world around them from within a theory of semiotics.

In conclusion, we note that renowned Peirce scholars either choose not to discuss semiosis in detail or else reject the final semiotics, the typologies in particular but also the process which defines them, as being unfinished and sketchy. For many of them, Peirce's most interesting and finished period ends with the 'New Elements' of 1904 as the high note. They all, Houser included, seem to restrict the late semiotics to the complex ten-division typologies to be found in letters and drafts from July and December 1908, although Peirce had already constructed four such typologies between October 1905 and August 1906. Moreover, while criticizing the typologies, these same scholars neglect the process that Peirce describes to accompany them, namely semiosis. Clearly, in view of many Peirce scholars' suspicion or outright rejection of the later period of Peirce's theorizing on signs and representation any attempt, such as the present one, to develop the concept of semiosis is at the very least problematic.

Thus, Short's rather unpleasant jibe at the semioticians quoted earlier clearly illustrates the dubious theoretical status in which Peirce's final statements on signs find themselves within the Peirce community, even now, over a hundred years after he conceived them. And within this preoccupation with the taxonomies is the concomitant neglect of the nugget hidden away inside them, namely semiosis. At this point, we leave the last word to Peirce:

> The different varieties of signs and their modes of being have been a good deal studied by me. The same persons I have just been speaking of are apt to condemn all such inquiries as nonsensical. It is impossible to endeavour to aid them: the development of their intelligence will take its own course under the temporary handicap of their resolve not to listen to certain voices of reason.
>
> (R200: 89–90, 1907)

Misinterpretation

Critical condemnation of Peirce's later logical experiments is not the only problem encountered in any attempt to present Peirce's thinking on signs. His revisions of many of his important concepts are one source of potential misinterpretation, while another is the fact that in their enthusiasm (almost uniquely) for his 1903 Syllabus system, authors have diluted and even neutralized the power of the original statements, in this way offering to newcomers to the semiotics a potentially unscientific conception of Peirce's theory of the sign. As obstacles to a presentation of Peirce's statements on signs and their classes from the 1908 to 1909 period, to critical condemnation by the authorities we must also now add misinterpretation and misrepresentation.

In the first case, scholars have protested about putative inconsistencies in Peirce's terminology. A case in point is Murray Murphey. In the course of his study of Peirce's philosophical development, Murphey regrets the following situation: 'One sees here [CP: 1.556] a typically Peircean procedure: having set forth a doctrine with appropriate terminology, Peirce revises and refines the contents of the doctrine while retaining the form and terminology unchanged. Thus, extensive revisions of position pass unnoticed under a shell of changeless terminology, to the utter confusion of the reader' (1993: 88–9).

This comment draws attention to a particular consequence of the inevitable mutations which must surely occur within a theory which develops over a period of nearly half a century, and this was certainly the case with Peirce's evolving conception of logic. However, while Murphey's dismissal of the augmented informational depth of key terms associated with, in this case, Peirce's decision to give numerical values to his new categories (CP: 1.556, 1867), a decision which was in fact theoretically founded and maintained to 1909 and beyond; his reference to a 'shell of changeless terminology' was by contrast a misunderstanding, since the 'extensive revisions of position' similarly characterize another of Peirce's 'procedures', specifically, terminological hesitations – in other words, a constitutional reluctance to attribute once and for all a fixed denomination to certain key concepts if he deemed a change was necessary. One important example is the switch from the 1903 term 'phenomenology' to the choice, late in 1904, of 'phaneroscopy' to denominate the science of categories or 'appearances'. Changes of denomination for the same concept do occur. *Pace* Murray Murphey, it would be more charitable and more realistic theoretically to remember that while the terminology might change there will generally be a notional consistency in the concepts involved.

Another case of potential confusion due to terminological variation concerns the nature and function of his third branch of the grand logic, in particular the methodeutic versus speculative rhetoric distinction. Scholars reviewing this field of Peirce's logical enterprise have found considerable variation in the terms and definitions concerning it. Kent (1987: 206), for one, identifies nine different denominations for the speculative rhetoric/methodeutic branch of the logic, while Liszka (2000: 440) cites seven different names for it and nearly thirty different definitions.

One obvious explanation for the alleged spur-of-the-moment theoretical refinements decried by Murphey, for the terminological hesitations concerning speculative rhetoric, for the switch from phenomenology to phaneroscopy and for the late reference to a system of universes as opposed to categories in the classification of signs, for example, is that Peirce's appreciation of the scaffolding of the general theory required readjustment as his research into the subject progressed, not an unreasonable requirement in view of the complexity and architectonic organization of his approach to philosophy and the acquisition of knowledge which developed over nearly half a century: what Peirce referred to in 1903 as 'the ripening effect of time' (R467: 16).

Misrepresentation

As the topic will recur in the following chapters, offered as a paradoxical case of misrepresentation is Roman Jakobson's presentation of what in 1903 Peirce referred to as the 'hypoicons'. It is an interesting fact that it should have been in the field of linguistics, Saussure's preserve, so to speak, at a time when the principles of structuralism were the object of increasingly critical scrutiny, at a time, too, when in the United States Noam Chomsky's Cartesian linguistics had become hegemonic, that Peirce's theory of the sign came to prominence and became widely known beyond the strict confines of philosophy. For, after just over two decades spent in the United States, during which he had assimilated much American thought, and in what was subsequently acclaimed as a pioneering article, Roman Jakobson ([1965]1971) suggested that Saussure's model of the linguistic sign might be deficient in important respects, e.g. for the explanation of what Jakobson considered to be pervasive, quasi-universal and hitherto theoretically unexplained correlations between form and meaning,[18] and he invited linguists to acquaint themselves with a conception of linguistic motivation based upon Peirce's trichotomization of the icon.

Although not the first scholar outside the narrow and confidential confines of post First World War American philosophy to interest themselves in Peirce's logical theory, Jakobson was probably the one most responsible for bringing Peirce's semiotic theory to the notice of the wider world. As his disaffection for the European semiological tradition within which he had first conducted his research grew, he became increasingly aware of the linguistic implications of Peirce's logical concepts of the index and the icon. As early as 1950 he had employed the index in two papers dealing with his theory of the shifter; in 1959, in his reassessment of the Saussurean doctrine of the sign he had shown interest in the relation between symbolic signs and their indexical and iconic components:

> Finally, the issue of sound symbolism, on which I shall not further dwell here, remains, in spite of all the skepticism voiced in the past, an important and fascinating problem in the study of language. And so are all questions concerning the foundation of language symbols in image and indication (or, as Charles Sanders Peirce, the pioneer of the theory of signs, would have said: the problem of *iconic* or *indexical* symbols).
>
> ([1959] 1985: 29)

The icon, in particular, was becoming increasingly important in Jakobson's view of the relation between syntactic order and the order of experience in extralinguistic reality. In this way, by 1965 and drawing on the category-based implication principle expounded in CP: 2.247–2.249 from 1903, he was able to write: 'Thus Peirce's graphic and palpable idea that "a symbol may have an icon or … an index incorporated into it" opens new, urgent tasks and far-reaching vistas to the science of language. The precepts of this "backwoodsman in semiotic" are fraught with vital consequences for linguistic theory and praxis' ([1965] 1971: 357).

Less positively, it must be said that Jakobson initiated a certain interpretative tradition that was to have pernicious effects in subsequent discussions of iconicity, for he was ultimately unable to shake off entirely the binarism of the intellectual tradition which had nurtured him. This is particularly evident in features of his presentation of the theory of the hypoicons that he developed from Peirce. First, he seemed reluctant to abandon the binary and reifying conception of language as system of sound-meaning correspondences: as we see in Chapter 6, the putative dyadic sound-meaning relation is not a given, is not dyadic, is not a binary unit communicated whole from speaker to speaker, but the result of an inferential process in which Peirce's immediate object has a specific function. Second, the definitions Jakobson gives of icon, index and symbol are his own, not Peirce's, and they betoken a concern to dovetail these particular concepts into his own polar view of language as resemblance and contiguity (e.g. see ([1965] 1971: 346–7)). Third, he chose to discuss the major Peircean concepts in terms of the binary relation holding between a signans and a signatum, as though the Augustinian terminology was both a sufficient and necessary dignifying metalanguage. Finally, and most importantly, in his discussion of the hypoicons, to which we return in Chapters 2, 3 and 6, Jakobson found it necessary to reduce the original three to two, these being the *image* and the *diagram*, and neglected to describe the third hypoicon, *metaphor*, in Peircean terms, presumably because he felt that it competed with his own view of the metonymical and metaphorical axes of language. In conclusion, what we have here is a Jakobsonian, as opposed to a Peircean, or, better, as opposed to a neo-Peircean, approach to the icon and its subclasses.

In retrospect, Jakobson's beneficial contribution to the furthering of awareness of Peirce's importance to contemporary idioscopic research and the subsequent iconicity movement[19] that his article 'Quest for the essence of language'[20] inspired can be summarized in two facts. First, by 1965 he had categorically rejected Saussure's theory of linguistics as being incapable of accounting for the variety of data being brought to light by contemporary linguistic research, specifically of research into the relationship between language and the user's experience of the extralinguistic world. Second, he had become convinced that Peirce's semiotics, principally the, for him, highly novel concepts of the index and the icon, had a positive contribution to make in this field. And this canvassing of the value of Peirce's semiotics to linguistic research brought the rest of the theory to a far wider audience than hitherto, in spite of the efforts of Ogden and Richards (1923): linguistics was an example of idioscopic research for Peirce, and it was paradoxically through linguistics that his theory of the sign was brought to the notice of linguists and semioticians worldwide.

Nevertheless, the example of the highly personal manner in which Jakobson promoted Peirce's ideas and the contradictions to which it inevitably led should be a warning to anyone working in this field: any introduction and development of a Peircean concept in a field for which it was not originally and explicitly intended requires the careful respect of the general theory within which that concept was introduced. Developing a neo-Peircean, and therefore necessarily idioscopic approach to signs requires that we adhere to the general principles of cenoscopic logic. We can't change these; they are as they are – as writ in stone. But it is this author's contention we can, with respect, develop a number of them. One, for example, is the concept that Jakobson brought to the attention of scholars and researchers beyond the confines of classical logic and philosophy, namely Peirce's hypoiconicity; another is semiosis.

Summary and discussion

This first chapter has reviewed a broad variety of obstacles threatening the continuing relevance of a theory of the sign that is over a hundred years old. The first sections sought to show, through a summary of Peirce's classifications of signs and sciences, the specific nature of his philosophical objectives in order to highlight the differences between them and those of present-day semioticians. In doing so, it revealed contrasting attitudes of scholars to semioticians and to the 'late semiotics', that is, to developments in the logic after 1904, which present research into, and the development of, semiosis and other aspects of Peirce's various definitions of the sign with a situation fraught with problems. Reactions to the later pronouncements on the sign were seen to fall broadly into two groups: those who hold that our understanding of the period is incomplete and surely merits further investigation, and those who dismiss the period as bewildering and lacking in coherence, making any attempt to investigate the enterprise a waste of time. The response adopted in the chapter was to identify a neo-Peircean approach to signs as what Peirce in 1903 would surely have considered to be idioscopic research. Extant notable examples of such research were cited, but these, unfortunately, in spite of their undoubted heuristic value, were found to be almost entirely based upon Peirce's 1903 descriptions of signs and classes of signs. The present study seeks to sustain Peirce's relevance in one way by exploiting the material of the later period.

The chapter thus showed that Peirce identified his logic as 'cenoscopic', an approach to signs very different from the idioscopic practices of today. For example, with the notable exception mentioned in the chapter, semioticians would hardly bother to identify their research as idioscopy, as either 'physics' or 'psychics'. Nevertheless, the cenoscopic/idioscopic distinction reviewed in the chapter is still a useful way of separating the purely Peircean features of the material proposed in the chapters to come from the theoretical advances semioticians have suggested to principles and concepts that Peirce never had the time to develop. In this way, the chapter has introduced the following important distinction to be followed throughout the study. Peirce, working from within his cenoscopy, was a logician, and his semiotics was an extended and highly innovative logic. While attempting to show his continuing relevance, the study, placing itself explicitly within Peirce's idioscopy, approaches signs as a semiotics, not as a rewriting of Peirce's logic. It is this resolutely idioscopic approach to signs, the reader will have now noticed, that motivates the prefix 'neo-'.

Finally, the discussion of the cenoscopic/idioscopic distinction in the course of the chapter incidentally raised the problem of the nature of the scopic, that is, 'looking', process involved. Peirce's conception of observation, even if he posits three distinct versions of it in his classification of the sciences, is over a hundred years old. Since then, there have been other, completely different theories of the relation holding between observer and the object observed. Embodiment has entered the 'equation' with, for example, Lakoff and Johnson (1980) and Varela, Thompson and Rosch (1993), leading now to a strongly enactivist current in cognitive science (Noë 2009). More importantly, the research and influence of Thomas Sebeok has profoundly affected the way eminent semioticians conceive of the relation between observer and observed, between organism and environment. Thus, the sort of knowledge acquired using the instruments and principles of idioscopy now becomes problematic, and has been challenged, notably by the enactivists. An additional problem is that Sebeok has produced a semiotics that seems to lean heavily towards the enactivists' position. To show how Peircean semiotics deals with this important relation posing another threat to the continuing relevance of his conception of signs and observation, the problem of 'looking' as a test of continuing relevance will be taken up again later.

2

The System of 1903

There are at least three reasons for including an introductory chapter on the 1903 system in a book claiming to promote and exploit the later. First, it gives the newcomer to Peircean semiotics a fuller picture. Second, since one aim of the book is to show how in analyses of signs the later period complements, and can combine with, the earlier, it would be methodologically unsound to talk about the new without reference to the old. However, the purpose of this chapter is not simply to provide yet another description of the best-known period of Peirce's semiotics for the first-time reader – though it can serve this purpose – it is, as the third reason, to isolate the aspects of Peirce's logic that have contributed to the various 'schools' or versions of neo-Peircean semiotics generally, and, in particular, to introduce important concepts referenced in the development of the chapters to come.

At this point, in order to dispel any misunderstanding, there is an important distinction to be made. As seen in Chapter 1, the 'grand' logic, the last of the three normative sciences, followed phenomenology in the classifications. One of the principles guiding this study is the importance of understanding what is often referred to by semioticians as Peirce's semiotics. It is true that he designated his logic as 'semeiotic', that is, as a general theory of the signs to be employed in logic, since logic in 1903 was 'in short the Philosophy of Representation' (R465: 25, 1903). But it was a logic expanded to include the study of the signs of logic themselves, logic's very foundational units, not the sort of semiotics employed in his name today.[1] As mentioned in the Introduction, he explained to William James that he was only interested in actual signs to the extent that they reminded him that they existed (EP2: 500, 1909), for although he offers numerous examples of his various subdivisions of signs – icons, indices, types of argument, etc., he was interested principally in discovering all the possible signs that might be used in logic.[2] This, as was explained in the Introduction, is the reason for referring to the study as the development of a *neo-*Peircean approach to signs: it is not a presentation of semeiotic as Peirce understood the term, because he didn't understand the term 'semiotics' as we do today: he was, first and foremost, a logician.

As in the Introduction to Jappy (2019a), since it deals almost exclusively with the statements Peirce made on signs and signification in the Syllabus intended for his Lowell lectures on logic, and since these are to be found most conveniently in manuscripts R478 and R540, the chapter follows broadly Peirce's remarks as they occur in the two manuscripts. On a par with Saussure's *Cours de linguistique générale* as a monument of Western thought, the Syllabus had a similarly problematic emergence into the world of ideas. Whereas, though, the *Cours* was composed shortly after Saussure's death from students' notes, the first great Peircean system of signs is to be found essentially in the two manuscripts, which were only published piecemeal many years after his death. They form the basis of this chapter, but where there is disputed appreciation of how we understand what Peirce meant in the two manuscripts, these are dealt with in the appropriate sections.

However, to understand the nature of the novelty of the Syllabus it is useful to review briefly the general development of Peirce's thinking on signs as it evolved gradually between 1865 and 1909, that is, over a period of almost forty-five years. There is no real consensus among authorities on the stages in the evolution of his various systems of signs, but the following is offered as a guide. One approach to his evolving approaches to signs consists in associating the different periods with the number of divisions, or trichotomies, he established in his search for classes of signs: a single division in the long period from the mid-1860s to 1903, three late in 1903 itself. From 1904 he developed six divisions and ten from 1905 onwards. Such a characterization shows how Peirce's sign typologies grew in content and accelerated in their complexification in the first few years after the beginning of the last century.

It can also be shown that there are important developments in the theoretical background to the way Peirce conceived signs and the action of the sign beginning in 1905. Another way of reviewing his development is by distinguishing in it two distinct periods, again of vastly differing lengths and corresponding in this case to two distinct manners of classifying signs. The first runs from the mid-1860s to 1904, while the second, much shorter period runs roughly from 1905 to 1909. Here again we witness the acceleration in growth of content and a corresponding increase in complexity which can be explained by the fact that during the first, longer period, Peirce's phenomenological categories, once he had established their final form in 1902, formed the indispensable criteria to be used in the classification of signs, whereas in the second period the criteria he employed were three 'universes of existence'. It is to statements from the earlier period, the system of 1903, that this chapter is devoted.

Returning to R478, then, we begin this chapter by examining the principal aspects of the phenomenology, namely the three categories and an organizing principle which makes an important contribution to our understanding of the sign system that Peirce developed in 1903. This is followed by a section which examines the most relevant features of the logic that are of importance to the variety of neo-Peircean semiotics proposed in this study (and, obviously, in a number of other versions). Drawing on Speculative Grammar in the Syllabus, the section deals with definitions of the sign and with the sign-representamen distinction and the way it is interpreted; with the concept of continuous semiosis that authors have ascribed to the system of 1903; with the divisions of the sign, focusing principally on the icon-index-symbol division; and, finally, with the classification of signs and the nature and purpose thereof. Taking up material discussed in Chapter 1 that reviewed Jakobson's conception of iconicity, the final section offers a preliminary neo-Peircean presentation of hypoiconicity and the hypoicons as Peirce introduced them in the Syllabus.

Phenomenology

This presentation of the semiotics of 1903 reviews the outstanding aspects of a theory developed over the first, almost forty-year period in which Peirce came to use the categories forming the basis of his phenomenology in order to classify signs. In the earlier period, he first developed these categories from his logic and, then, after an exhaustive revision of what became his phenomenology in 1902, reversed the roles of each science, so to speak, and employed the categories to define and develop the principal concepts of his logic. The categories enabled him to establish the subdivisions which he retained throughout his subsequent statements on signs, and which, when combined in specific ways, eventually yielded ten different but organically ordered classes of signs.

As seen in the table of the classification of the sciences in the previous chapter, in 1903 Peirce founded the bases of logic on his conception of phenomenology, and in particular on three 'universal' categories and the relations holding between them. When we examine his categories it is easy to see the importance of having placed mathematics in initial position in the sciences of discovery. Consider this text from late in the nineteenth century, which clearly shows the mathematical origins of phenomenology, the science that followed mathematics in the classification:

> Having thus by observation satisfied ourselves that there are these three categories of elements of phenomena, let us endeavour to analyze the nature of each, and try to find out why there should be these three categories and no others. This reason, when we find it, ought to be interesting to mathematicians; for it will be found to coincide with the most fundamental characteristic of the most universal of the mathematical hypotheses, I mean that of number.
>
> (CP: 1.421, c. 1896)

This is the important description that he offered of the categories thus justified in 1902:

> I essay an analysis of what appears in the world. It is not metaphysics that we are dealing with: only logic. Therefore, we do not ask what really is, but only what appears to everyone of us in every minute of our lives. I analyze experience, which is the cognitive resultant of our past lives, and find in it three elements. I call them *Categories*. Would I could render them to the reader as vivid, as undeniable, as rational as they are to me. They will become so, if he will give thought enough to them. They appear in myriad shapes.
>
> (CP: 2.84, 1902)

Although Peirce had been working on the concept of categories since the mid-1860s, the important term in this current version is 'appears', as Peirce is at pains to dispel the idea that the categories might be construed as categories of material entities encountered in our everyday experience: they are not varieties of what *is*, but of the ways in which elements of our experience can *appear* to us, of which there are, as from 1867 on, three. These three ways he came to identify as Firstness, Secondness and

Thirdness. Originally, Peirce had conceived a system of five categories, of which two were subsequently discarded. The three remaining, identified at the time as *quality*, *relation* and *representation*, ultimately formed, when finally identified as the three mentioned above, the basis of his phenomenology, on which he continued to work for the rest of his life after having renamed it 'phaneroscopy' late in 1904.

The category of Firstness was, for Peirce, assimilated to freedom and independence and was characteristic of qualities, properties, qualities of feelings, for example. For Secondness, which he assimilated to effort and resistance – think of the resident of a house straining against a door that an intruder is attempting to push open – and is realized in individuality, fact, existence and brute action unrelated to thought. Finally, Thirdness, which he assimilated to generality, mediation and continuity, characterizes the complex phenomena of thought, habit and, within the phenomenology at the time, signs. Now, a fundamental operation involved in the phenomenology was a form of mental separation, or abstraction, which enabled him to identify relations between these three categories, a form of separation which he referred to variously as 'precision' or, preferably, 'prescission'. The principle involved had been established as early as 1867 in the article entitled 'On a New List of Categories' and figured prominently in Peirce's methodology in his later research in logic:

> I made use of three grades of separability of one idea from another. In the first place, two ideas may be so little allied that one of them may be present to the consciousness in an image which does not contain the other at all; in this way we can imagine *red* without imagining blue, and *vice versa*; we can also imagine sound without melody, but not melody without sound. I call this kind of separation *dissociation*. In the second place, even in cases where two conceptions cannot be separated in the imagination, we can often suppose one without the other, that is we can imagine data from which we should be led to believe in a state of things where one was separated from the other. Thus, we can suppose uncolored space, though we cannot dissociate space from color. I call this mode of separation *prescission*.
>
> (CP: 1.153, 1902)

Firstness, Secondness and Thirdness constitute discrete – Firstness is such as it is independently of anything else, for example – but related categories. This is how it is possible to prescind, that is, abstract mentally, Firstness from Thirdness as when *mentally* isolating the qualities of, say a cat, from the class of felines, since these qualities compose our knowledge of the entity in question from long acquaintance with it – from our experience of it, in other words. The phenomenological principle enabling abstraction of Firstness from both Secondness and Thirdness, and Secondness from Thirdness, but not the abstraction of Thirdness from either of the other two, thus constitutes a 'top-down' hierarchical organization of the phenomenology (cf. CP: 1.530–1.533, 1903).

It also follows from the operation of mental abstraction that the entire logic as it was presented in 1903 functioned on a presuppositional basis imposed by the phenomenology, in which elements characterized by Firstness are prescindable from, and, conversely, presupposed by, those characterized by Secondness, and in which the latter are themselves similarly prescindable from, and presupposed by, those characterized by Thirdness. This principle, which resembles the nesting of the well-known Russian dolls, had far-reaching implications for the establishment of the classes and subclasses of signs that followed. Looking at the principle from the opposite perspective, we see that the categories underwrite what amounts to an implication principle: if we can prescind Firstness from Thirdness, we can also say that Firstness is involved in, is implied by, Thirdness. With this in mind, we examine pertinent aspects of his logic as he presented it in the Syllabus of 1903.

The logic of the Syllabus

In November 1903, Peirce embarked upon a series of eight lectures at the Lowell Institute in Boston, entitled 'Some topics of logic bearing on questions now vexed', and it is on the two draft manuscripts (R478 and R540), prepared as a supplement for these lectures, that the following exposition of the semiotics of 1903 is based. The Syllabus, as he called the supplement, was indeed published, but owing to insufficient funds (SS: 12), this version omitted precisely that information which the audience would have needed most to follow a presentation of the vexed questions of the title of the lectures, namely the theoretical background to Peirce's very original and rapidly evolving conception of 'logic as semeiotic'. In view of this, then, there are good reasons why the discussion of this unique conception of logic should concentrate on the material to be found in this syllabus.

One important reason is that much of the material in the chapter will later be compared and contrasted with that to be expounded in Chapters 4 and 5, in which alternative conceptions of semiosis and approaches to looking and observation will be referenced. Another reason is that interpretations and applications of Peirce's logic proposed by various authorities often vary widely, making it important to refer to Peirce's original statements in this period. The reader might think that this is not important, but if the enterprise of developing a viable neo-Peircean approach to signs is to have any value, it is surely vital that the original statements and definitions be respected. Otherwise, anything goes, which perhaps is not the best way to conduct scientific research. For example, general presentations of Peirce's semiotics have on occasion been hybrid, in the sense that in genuinely seeking to be exhaustive authors have combined aspects of different stages without their context in the development of the theory, sometimes to the detriment of clarity and precision. Restricting the exposition to material written for the Syllabus is intended to avoid such a pitfall. It should be remembered, to begin with, that in this neo-Peircean study the concepts he developed and those that he introduced but never developed in the broader logic are addressed as semiotics, not as logic as he understood the term. The section of the Syllabus of interest in the following paragraphs dispenses with a description of the classification of the sciences, since that was dealt with in the previous chapter, while a discussion of his ethics of terminology as part of the theoretical background to the logic can be found in Jappy (2019a: 16–17).

The sign as defined and as understood

The statements concerning the sign in R478 are significantly prefaced by a description of phenomenology, the categories and the mental process of prescission. Not surprisingly, then, immediately before Peirce introduces his definitions of the sign he offers the following amplification, which makes the point that although Thirdness is the characteristic of thought and signs, there are nevertheless within the scope of Thirdness, signs of Firstness and signs of Secondness in addition to the signs of Thirdness itself, a phenomenologically derived organic structure that has to be borne in mind when considering all his pronouncements on signs, on their division and on their classification at the time:

> In the ideas of Firstness, Secondness, and Thirdness, the three elements, or *Universal Categories*, appear under their forms of Firstness. They appear under their forms of Secondness in the ideas of Facts of Firstness, or *Qualia*, Facts of Secondness, or Relations, and Facts of Thirdness, or Signs; and under their forms of Thirdness in the ideas of Signs of Firstness, or Feeling, i.e., things of beauty; Signs of Secondness, or Action, i.e., modes of conduct; and Signs of Thirdness, or Thought, i.e., forms of thought.
>
> (EP2: 272, 1903)

Having established the major principles obtained from his phenomenology, Peirce begins the process of exploiting the first branch of his grand logic, namely his Speculative Grammar, and defines the sign and the two associated correlates in terms of first, second and third, introducing as he does so, the concept of the triadic relation that he builds upon in the later manuscript (R540):

> A *Sign*, or *Representamen*, is a First which stands in such a genuine triadic relation to a Second, called its *Object*, as to be capable of determining a Third, called its *Interpretant*, to assume the same triadic relation to its Object in which it stands itself to the same Object. The triadic relation is *genuine*, that is its three members are bound together by it in a way that does not consist in any complexus of dyadic relations ... A *Sign* is a Representamen with a mental Interpretant. Possibly there may be Representamens that are not Signs.
>
> (EP2: 272–3, 1903)

This statement raises two points. First, although the object and the interpretant are indispensable participants in every act of representation, they are not in themselves the concern of Speculative Grammar, as they only occur or appear in the concrete act of representation and therefore cannot be classified in advance. This is especially understandable in the case of the interpretant, the effect that the sign has on an interpreter, as the reaction in an interpreter that a sign produces, even if deliberately 'targeted' in a manner described in Chapter 6, obviously cannot be determined with certainty before it has been produced. Thus, the scope of Speculative Grammar as Peirce understood the term is restricted to the conditions which determine whether some entity qualifies as a sign or not, together with its modes of representation and its informational value, and is therefore purely formal in nature. As for the sign's meaning, the Speculative Grammar of 1903, without 'access' to either object or interpretant, can only specify, as we see in what follows, *how* a sign means, not *what* it means.

Second, from the definition, in which the *or* is conjunctive (either term is valid for this definition), it follows that for all triadic relations the first correlate of the triadic relation is the representamen. However, in the special case where the interpretant of a representamen is mental in nature, is a 'cognition of a mind' – in other words when the sign produces an effect upon an animate, thinking being – then that representamen is a sign. A sign, thus, is defined to be a species of representamen, although as we now see, in this period Peirce employs both terms almost interchangeably for simplicity of exposition: either can be considered to be the unit of representation. The basic distinction is important nevertheless: representamens *without* mental interpretants are not signs but nevertheless theoretically extend the capacity for representation and interpretation to organisms such as plant life, etc., which *don't* possess mentality.

Such a definition of the sign has, unfortunately, given rise to a problematic alternative interpretation of the difference between sign and representamen, and this interpretation seems to have stemmed from Peirce's introduction to triadic relations in a later part of the Syllabus, namely the manuscript R540. This, together with the classification of the sciences, the ethics of terminology and the description of phenomenology and the operation of prescission in R478, constitutes the theoretical background to what Peirce is intending to introduce in his lecture. In order to understand fully the error of certain interpretations, notably of the difference between sign and representamen, it will be necessary first to review the theory of triadic relations with which the section in R540 begins. Being triadic, they are based on number, 'the most universal of the mathematical hypotheses' (CP: 1.421), and, as Peirce is careful to explain, organized by phenomenology: their scientific legitimacy is guaranteed by the two sciences that precede the normative in the classification of the sciences.

Triadic relations are composed, obviously, of three relates, and in Peirce's case, they are named in increasing complexity from First to Third, are divisible by trichotomy and can be grouped so as to form ten classes. Such an introductory system underwrites, as we see below, the theoretical framework for Peirce's later creation of ten classes of signs:

> Triadic relations are in three ways divisible by trichotomy, according as the First, the Second, or the Third Correlate, respectively, is a mere possibility, an actual existent, or a law. These three trichotomies, taken together, divide all triadic relations into ten classes. These ten classes will have certain subdivisions according as the existent correlates are individual subjects or individual facts, and according as the correlates that are laws are general subjects, general modes of fact, or general modes of law. … *In every genuine Triadic Relation, the First Correlate may be regarded as determining the Third Correlate in some respect; and triadic relations may be divided according as that determination of the Third Correlate is to having some quality, or to being in some existential relation to the Second Correlate, or to being in some relation of thought to the Second for something.*
>
> (EP2: 290, 1903; emphasis added)

In the italicized second part of the quotation, where genuine triadic relations are introduced, it is clear that Peirce is preparing a definition of the sign: in any usual, everyday case of the action of the sign some object will produce an effect or interpretant via, or through the mediation of the sign. If the triadic relation is genuine, says Peirce in the definition, the first correlate may be regarded as determining the third in some respect: the three specified respects correspond closely to the trichotomy specifying icon, index and symbol. We return to the importance of that remark below. In the meantime, we note that the correlates involved in triadic relations are identified by name as representamen, object and interpretant, these being the first, second and third correlate respectively: 'A *Representamen* is the First Correlate of a triadic relation, the Second Correlate being termed its *Object*, and the possible Third Correlate being termed its *Interpretant*, by which triadic relation the possible Interpretant is determined to be the First Correlate of the same triadic relation to the same Object, and for some possible Interpretant' (EP2: 290–1). Now, at this time, Peirce often introduces several statements describing signification with the formula 'A sign, or representamen, etc., etc. ... ' As a result, the relation between sign and representamen has become a theoretical issue of no little importance, some authorities having concluded from such statements that the sign is somehow either an entity 'containing' or comprising the triadic relation and its correlates, or in similar vein, constitutes the entire triadic relation.

Consider, for example, Benedict's exhaustive and well-researched paper on the importance in Peirce's logic of the representamen (Benedict 1985). In this, the earliest statement of this misleading principle that I have been able to find, he specifically bases part of his argument on the passages in R540 from which the quotations were extracted, and exploits them principally to 'reinstate' the term 'representamen', which, to Benedict's regret, Peirce was later to reject in a draft letter to Lady Welby in 1905: 'I formerly preferred the word representamen [to that of sign]. But there was no need of this horrid long word' (SS: 193, 1905). Benedict concludes thus:

> Concerning the matter of reinstating the term, there seems to be an *undeniable use* for the term in semeiotic. Of course, this assumes that the connotation of 'sign' includes its being a triadic relation. ... The foremost undeniable use for 'representamen' in semeiotic, particularly in Speculative Grammar, is to be the name of one of the three branches of the triadic sign relation. The other two branches have names, i.e. object and interpretant. The remaining branch frequently, nay almost universally, has been called a *sign*. However, that is really poor form! The word 'sign' should be reserved for the triadic relation. Refusal to do this has generated and perpetuated a source of ambiguity that has been unnecessarily deceptive.
>
> (1985: 265–6)

Surprisingly, this theoretical decision has been taken up by no few eminent Peirce specialists. For example, Winfried Nöth, in the section devoted to Peirce in his *Handbook of Semiotics*, writes: 'Theoretically, Peirce distinguished clearly between the sign, which is the complete triad, and the representamen, which is its first correlate'

(1990: 42). Jørgen Johansen, in his *Dialogic Semiosis* (1993), follows Benedict's lead with this statement: 'Peirce uses the word *sign* in both a broad and a narrow sense. In the broad sense, which is the most important, *sign* is used to designate the triadic relation between sign, object, and interpretant; in the narrow sense *sign* denotes one element, the *sign* or *representamen*' (1993: 62). Floyd Merrell, another noted Peirce scholar, offers this homely comment on the issue in a chapter on Peirce's concept of the sign: '*Peirce's* sign sports three components (Figure 2.1 [a propeller-type image with one of the three correlates located within each of three blades]). What usually goes for a sign in everyday talk Peirce called a *representamen* ... A fully-fledged sign must have a representamen, a semiotic object, and an interpretant, and each of these sign components must enjoy the company of the other two' (Merrell 2001: 28–9). More recently we have Barnham, examining Peirce through a Hegelian prism, informing the reader in an unreferenced claim that 'Peirce believes that the sign is more than just the representamen – it is the whole triadic relationship formed by the unity of the representamen, object and interpretant. But by reducing the sign to just one element of this relationship (e.g., the representamen) commentators thus impose Saussurean thinking on Peirce's sign structure' (2022: 136). Does it matter? John Deely offers the following reply:

> We are trying to understand what a sign is. We have no vested interest in protecting some particular 'model'. If a given model needs to be modified or changed or even abandoned, so be it. ... What's important about any given proposal is not whose model it is; what's important about it is whether it enables us to understand the phenomenon of signification. That is the whole and sole reason why Peirce always insisted that the sign was triadic; a brilliant insight, though by no means original with Peirce, who mainly gleaned it from the Latin teachers of Poinsot, the Conimbricenses.
>
> (2009b: 158–9)

This is surely the point: a theory of the sign must enable us better to understand signification, the process in which the sign functions. Problems arise, regrettably, when there is such a theoretical void between two conceptions of the signifying process's basic unit. Deely, too, adheres to the sign-as-triadic-relation position, as suggested in the quotation and in this extract from a text from 2015:[3]

> There is never just 'sign and signified', but always a 'hidden third' presupposed in semiosis. And it is the *relation* as irreducibly triadic and linking the three elements here and now that makes the foreground element *commonly called* 'sign', but *more technically better named perhaps* 'representamen', function formally to achieve semiosis (Deely 2014). On this view, it would be proper to say that it is *the triadic relation itself* (invisible to any direct perception) that is the *sign* formally speaking, whereas what is *commonly called 'sign'* is better identified technically as a *representamen*.
>
> (2015: 272)

Again, does it matter? It most certainly does, for whereas the texts by Nöth and Merrell had a general vulgarizing, popularizing purpose whose definitions the reader is at leisure to accept, reject or verify elsewhere, those of Johansen, Barnham and, above all, John Deely, summon the sign as the basic building-block to be integrated into a more complete theory of signification: respectively semiosis, the origin of conceptions, and, most importantly, the field of biosemiotics.[4] We find, in fact, that the sign-as-triadic-relation position has been adopted into mainstream biosemiotics, by Donald Favareau, for example, and others:[5]

> So, too, did the many of the now-forgotten scholars of Latinity discover at last that the unique property of the *sign* (a misleading term of reification for what is in every instance a *sign relation*) is that, as a subset of the genuine form of existential being that is 'relation' a sign relation simultaneously 'holds over' and exerts a uniquely organizing influence upon the *relata* involved in that sign relation (e.g., a word and its meaning, or a symptom and its cause).
>
> (Favareau 2009b: 18)

The question for any scientific enquiry, for a general semiotics and for a neo-Peircean semiotics in particular is this: just how valid can the rest of the theory be if the basic unit is misunderstood or incorrectly defined? It wouldn't matter in the least if the theoretical constructions such as those mentioned earlier had no claim to be Peircean (they, like the present study, too, are neo-Peircean). There is no reason whatsoever for a new field of enquiry such as biosemiotics not to redefine whatever concepts as are needed and validate them within the new discipline: in such a case a sign can very legitimately be redefined to be the relation of its constituents and not a constituent of the said relation. However, to claim that the definition is Peircean is another matter. Since I claim that the authors cited have made a very basic mistake which probably invalidates their whole conception of the sign, the onus is on me to prove their error. Consider the following long extract from the third draught of the third of the Lowell lectures on logic:

> I must begin the examination of representation by defining representation a *little* more accurately. In the first place, as to my terminology, I confine the word *representation* to the operation of a sign or its *relation* to the object *for* the interpreter of the representation. The concrete subject that represents I call a *sign* or a *representamen*. I use these two words, *sign* and *representamen*, differently. By a *sign* I mean anything which conveys any definite notion of an object in any way, as such conveyers of thought are familiarly known to us. Now I start with this familiar idea and make the best analysis I can of what is essential to a sign, and I define a *representamen* as being whatever that analysis applies to. If therefore I have committed an error in my analysis, part of what I say about signs will be false. For in that case a *sign* may not be a *representamen*. ... The analysis is certainly true of the representamen, since that is all that word means. Even if my analysis is correct, something may happen to be true of all *signs*, that is of everything that, antecedently to any analysis, we should be willing to regard

as conveying a notion of anything, while there might be something which my analysis describes of which the same thing is not true. In particular, all signs convey notions to *human minds*; but I know no reason why every representamen should do so.

(CP: 1.540, 1903)

To which we can add the following short extracts, all, of course, from 1903:

A *Sign* is a Representamen of which some Interpretant is a cognition of a mind. Signs are the only representamens that have been much studied.

(EP2: 290–1)

A *Sign* is a Representamen with a mental Interpretant. Possibly there may be Representamens that are not Signs.

(EP2: 272–3)

A *sign* is an object capable of determining in a mind a cognition of an object, called the *object* of the sign. A sign is a species under the genus *representamen*.

(R792: 2)

If, as Peirce remarks, the sign is a species of the genus representamen, if signs are the only representamens that have been much studied, and if there may possibly be representamens that are not signs, then the class of signs must be smaller than the class of representamens: in set-theoretic terms, the class of signs must be included in the class of representamens. An inclusion which is confirmed by this definition of the representamen from the same third lecture draft: 'My definition of a representamen is as follows: *A REPRESENTAMEN is a subject of a triadic relation TO a second, called its OBJECT, FOR a third, called its INTERPRETANT, this triadic relation being such that the REPRESENTAMEN determines its interpretant to stand in the same triadic relation to the same object for some interpretant*' (CP: 1.541, 1903). Nothing could be simpler than this definition: the representamen is one of the three subjects of a triadic relation, and is defined functionally as determining the third subject to enter into the same triadic relation to the object that it does itself. There are many such triadic relations, but in semiotics the sign occupies the representamen position when it determines a mental interpretant or conveys notions to human minds. It therefore simply is not possible for the sign to be defined as the triadic relation itself, comprises representamen, object and interpretant: we might call this the 'sign=triadic relation fallacy'. Now, there is no reason at all why commentators and system-builders shouldn't have their own theory of the sign, but in the conception of neo-Peircean semiotics being canvassed in the present study, it is essential from a theoretical standpoint to adhere as strictly as possible to what Peirce actually meant, as far as this can be ascertained.

Finally, consider anew the first sentence of a definition of the sign, which, in view of the dynamism inherent in the meaning of the verb 'determine', can be viewed as the description of a process: 'A *Sign*, or *Representamen*, is a First which stands in such a genuine triadic relation to a Second, called its *Object*, as to be capable of determining

Figure 2.1 The determination sequence whereby the interpretant is mediately determined by the object via the sign.

a Third, called its *Interpretant*, to assume the same triadic relation to its Object in which it stands itself to the same Object' (EP2: 272, 1903). To complete this discussion, then, the sequence of determinations described in the definition (where the sign is stated to be in such a relation to its object that it determines an effect or reaction – the interpretant, by definition – in some interpreting agency)[6] can usefully be represented by Figure 2.1, although Peirce never represented any such sequence involving the sign and its two correlates in this way.[7] The letters O, S and I are, respectively, the object, the sign and the interpretant *in that order*, though some commentators have queried this order and have proposed another. Merrell (2001), for example, places the interpretant – the correlate that Peirce describes as the effect produced by a sign on some interpreting agency – as the central mediating element of the sequence,[8] while Barnham, admitting that his general position might invite criticism (2022: 142) and viewing Peirce through his Hegelian prism, seems to be misled by his erroneous conception of the 'triadic' sign: 'Critically, with Peircean semiotics, this mediating entity is the "object" within his triadic sign' (2022: 133). This is to misunderstand the meaning of the verb 'mediate', and it therefore blinds Barnham as to how a sign has to mediate between object and interpretant; he is thus led to place the object in the centre of the determination sequence (2022: 112, 139–41). Any attempt to follow the conventional order (e.g. as shown in Figure 2.1) Barnham dismisses self-importantly as a reversion to some sort of 'secondary dualism', that is, to a dyadic Saussurean, as opposed to his triadic, Hegelo-Peircean, conception of the sign.[9] We return to this discussion and to the relation of the schema in Figure 2.1 to semiosis in Chapter 4 and review the above triadic conception of the action of the sign in Chapter 6.

'Continuous' semiosis

Before discussing the divisions of signs, there remains one aspect of the sign theory of the Syllabus period that requires comment. Interpretations of some definitions of the sign have led commentators to refer to the processual nature of the sign as conceived in the period 1902–3 as 'unlimited' (Eco 1996) or 'infinite' (Atkin 2013) semiosis. Neither is an expression ever used by Peirce but the general idea is neatly encapsulated in these two influential definitions from 1902, the first from the Minute Logic, the second from Baldwin's *Dictionary*:

> Genuine mediation is the character of a *Sign*. A *Sign* is anything which is related to a Second thing, its *Object*, in respect to a Quality, in such a way as to bring a Third

thing, its *Interpretant*, into relation to the same Object, and that in such a way as to bring a Fourth into relation to that Object in the same form, *ad infinitum*.

(CP: 2.92, 1902)

Anything which determines something else (its *interpretant*) to refer to an object to which itself refers (its *object*) in the same way, the interpretant becoming in turn a sign, and so on *ad infinitum*. No doubt, intelligent consciousness must enter into the series. If the series of successive interpretants comes to an end, the sign is thereby rendered imperfect, at least.

(CP: 2.303, 1902)[10]

The dynamic continuity of the action of the sign as ascribed to Peirce can be represented by Figure 2.2,[11] where O, S and I indicate, respectively, object, sign and interpretant, and where the arrow '→' stands for the process 'determine'. In this system, each subsequent interpretant would become a sign that determines a new interpretant, ($I_1=S_2$) for example, and so on in an endless series, as the two definitions state.

Although it might apply to the creation of habits, such a conception of how signs function is nevertheless counterintuitive, for if an 'eyes-right!' order is given to a squad of soldiers marching, and the soldiers obey, the order 'eyes-front!' might conceivably be considered a further sign; however, it is difficult to conceive of the second command as the interpretant of the original one, and while we might consider the two commands as a sequence regulated by some military code, in practice the second order wasn't directly determined by the first, it simply followed it chronologically. In some cases, then, the action of the sign ceases completely once the sign has been interpreted, and would have been termed 'imperfect' by Peirce in 1902. But at the time he used no notion of semiosis, being more interested in continuity and continuous series. As we see in Chapter 4, by 1908 he had redefined the signifying process in such a way that it covered all varieties of semiosis, continuous and non-continuous and also provided for interpretants that were qualities of feeling and discontinuous actions in addition to habits.

Divisions of signs

Having established the nature of the sign, it is now time to examine the ways in which Peirce 'divides' it, that is, how he established the trichotomies enabling him to derive the table of ten classes of signs. The manner in which this was achieved is important for future reference and requires returning briefly to the period before 1903 during which there are two stages in the development of his logic that deserve to be singled out, namely the presentation of an initial typology in 1867 and a general extension of the scope of logic in 1885.

$$O > S > (I_1 = S_2) > (I_2 = S_3) > (I_3 = S_4) \ldots (I_n = S_{n+1})$$

Figure 2.2 The alleged 'unlimited' action of the sign as suggested in 1902.

Table 2.1 The single-division of signs of 1867

Sign-Correlate
Symbol
argument
proposition
term
Index/sign
Likeness

Within the chronology of Peirce's thinking the first really important stage is the paper entitled 'On a new list of categories' from 1867 (EP1: 1–10). In this, he developed his three categories by defining them in terms taken from logic: representamen, ground, correlate (his term then for what would later become the object) and interpretant,[12] are all logical concepts, that of interpretant being Peirce's own contribution to logic that has proved to be an inestimable and universally adopted theoretical advance. Table 2.1 displays the single division of representamens from the period 1866–7, 'representamen' being at the time the term designating the unit of representation. The term 'sign', which was later to replace 'representamen', was at the time an early denomination of the index. The division was established on the relation holding between the sign and the 'correlate'. What was later to become the icon was identified as a 'likeness' in the paper. As a technical term for one of the three subdivisions of the relation holding between the sign and the object, the term 'icon' would only appear nearly twenty years later. In 1867, too, the symbol, which Peirce considered then the most important object of study of the logician – symbolistic – subdivided into the traditional tripartite distinction between term, proposition and argument as indicated in the table. The table for this early trichotomy illustrates the prototype for the well-known icon-index-symbol division, of which Peirce was later to write to Lady Welby that it was the one he most used.[13]

In a paper of 1885 contributing to the philosophy of notation Peirce then established that all three types of signs – symbols (referred to in the text as 'tokens'), indices and icons – were necessarily involved in any perfect system of logical notation: 'I have taken pains to make my distinction of icons, indices, and tokens clear, in order to enunciate this proposition: in a perfect system of logical notation signs of these several kinds must all be employed' (EP1: 226, 1885). The paper is important, too, for having introduced into this system the genuine-degenerate distinction which subtends the organization of the three divisions of 1903. This broader scope of signification can be measured in the following early definition of the sign, in which the expression 'in some respect or capacity', in other words, what Peirce sometimes refers to as the ground, that is, the theoretical justification of the relation, shows that icons and indices have acquired equal status with the symbol as the sign's modes of representation of its object:

There are three kinds of signs. Firstly, there are *likenesses*, or icons; which serve to convey ideas of the things they represent simply by imitating them. Secondly, there are *indications*, or indices; which show something about things, on account of their being physically connected with them. ... Thirdly, there are *symbols*, or general signs, which have become associated with their meanings by usage. Such are most words, and phrases, and speeches, and books, and libraries.

(EP2: 5, 1894)

This single division stood for almost forty years until the Lowell lectures on logic given late in 1903. Peirce had still maintained the single division in his Carnegie submission,[14] and even during the Harvard lectures on pragmatism that he had given in the spring of 1903.[15] Later, he went on to classify the three subdivisions as either degenerate or genuine: 'Of these three genera of representamens the *Icon* is the Qualitatively Degenerate, the *Index* the Reactionally degenerate, while the *Symbol* is the relatively genuine genus' (EP2: 163, 1903), which is both the practical application of the mental operation of prescission and an indication of how he was beginning to present the relations between the three. More interestingly, he then proceeded to intimate trichotomization of the icon itself: 'Now the *Icon* may undoubtedly be divided according to the categories but the mere completeness of the notion of the *icon* does not imperatively call for any such division' (EP2: 163, 1903).

Only a few months later in the manuscript version of the syllabus (R478) he divided the original single division into two distinct trichotomies. The first established what might be considered as the sign's three modes of representation – its three ways of representing its object – namely the types of relation, governed by the three categories in ascending order of complexity, holding between the sign and its object: 'Representamens are divided by two trichotomies. The most fundamental is into *Icons*, *Indices*, and *Symbols*' (EP2: 273). This, until the championing of the Peircean concept of semiosis by Thomas Sebeok in the 1970s and 1980s was probably the best known – and most contested – trichotomy in the Peirce canon. This is how Peirce describes the three subdivisions of the second trichotomy in the later manuscript section of the Syllabus, R540, and the implication relation holding between them, that is, the way the less complex subdivision is involved in the more:

An *Icon* is a sign which refers to the Object that it denotes merely by virtue of characters of its own, and which it possesses, just the same, whether any such Object actually exists or not. It is true that unless there really is such an Object, the Icon does not act /as/ a sign.

... An *Index* is a sign which refers to the Object that it denotes by virtue of being really affected by that Object. It cannot, therefore, be a qualisign; because qualities are whatever they are independently of anything else. In so far as the index is affected by the Object, it necessarily has some quality in common with the Object, and it is in respect to these that it refers to the Object. It does, therefore, involve a sort of icon, although an icon of a peculiar kind. ... A *Symbol* is a sign which refers to the Object that it denotes by virtue of a law, usually an association of general ideas, which operates to cause the Symbol to be interpreted as referring to that Object. It is thus itself a general type or law, that is, is a legisign. ... Now that which is general has its being in the instances which it will determine. There must, therefore, be existent instances of what the symbol denotes, although we must here understand by 'existent', existent in the possibly imaginary universe to which the symbol refers. The symbol will indirectly, through the association or other law, be affected by those instances; and thus the symbol will involve a sort of index, although an index of a peculiar kind.

(EP2: 291–2)

The three modes of representation of the object by the sign are thus, respectively, a basic form of similarity or resemblance, physical, spatio-temporal contiguity of some kind, and general convention. Moreover, since the index involves an icon 'of a peculiar kind' and the symbol involves a 'sort of index of a peculiar kind', it follows that by transitivity, a symbol will also involve an icon, albeit of a peculiar kind. Furthermore, as we see in the section 'Hypoiconicity' below, since the icon can be trichotomized as image, diagram and metaphor (EP2: 274), it also follows that symbols such as natural language signs can also involve the subdivisions of the icon, the subdivision the basis of whose mode of representation, earlier referred to as the *ground* of the relation, was its resemblance to its object, that is, the properties it had in common with the object, real or otherwise. It was Jakobson's genius to see how this would, at some level of analysis, sustain a view of language as motivated, thereby challenging the Saussurean doctrine of arbitrariness. Unfortunately, as seen in the previous chapter, unable to shed the binarism of his intellectual origins, he elected to disregard the icon's most complex subclass, metaphor.

The index provides an excellent example of what Peirce meant by genuine and degenerate entities. Being a form of Secondness of Thirdness, the index divides into two further subdivisions: 'An *Index*, or *Seme* (σημα), is a Representamen whose Representative character consists in its being an individual Second. If the Secondness is an existential relation, the Index is *genuine*. If the Secondness is a reference, the Index is *degenerate*' (EP2: 217, 1903). Examples of a genuine index are the veering of a weathervane or a photographic portrait, cases where there is an existential relation between the sign and what determined ('caused') it – the wind or the presence of a model – whereas an anaphoric item such as a relative pronoun or a definite article which refers back to some item already mentioned in the discourse is a degenerate index of its antecedent. The anaphor and antecedent are not related by a real, existential relation, as in the cases of the weathervane and the photograph, but simply by a reference relation that points back to another word inside a closed piece of discourse.

As mentioned in the previous chapter, the icon, in particular, received much critical attention after being introduced into mainstream linguistics in the mid – to late-1960s by Roman Jakobson and other researchers in the linguistic iconicity movement (Jappy 1999). There were nevertheless those who rejected the concept because of its theoretical association with the property of resemblance. For example, Bierman (1962) had already maintained that there could be no such thing as an iconic sign: 'I maintain that there are no iconic signs at all. There are no signs whose denotation and signification depend solely on their resemblance to that which they denote' (1962: 245). Amongst other things, suggests Bierman, dispensing with the icon allows us to appreciate the *Cratylus* all the better ... (1962: 249). He was followed in this by Umberto Eco, who in 1976 initially dismissed the icon as a culturally coded, conventional sign (1976: 327), while Nelson Goodman contested the idea that figurative paintings might resemble their subjects, claiming instead that they represented any other paintings: 'A Constable painting of Marlborough Castle is more like any other picture than it is like the Castle, yet it represents the Castle and not another picture – not even the closest copy' (1976: 5), his thesis being, in short, that since pictures are hung on walls and are (or were when Goodman made his silly claim) of a necessary shape surrounded by a frame, they all share the same 'structure'. Which is wilfully to misinterpret the function of pictorial representation.

What the champions of this conventionalist thesis concerning the icon don't realize is that any conventional content they find in what, within Peirce's logic, is the basic quality of a particular logical relation, comes from their own experience as they discuss a work of art or other pictorial sign – it can't be in the icon, a subdivision of the sign's mode of representation that is simply composed of intangible qualities, unperceivable on their own. In his introduction of the concept of the hypoicon, to be discussed below, Peirce makes this observation: 'Any material image, as a painting, is largely conventional in its mode of representation' (CP: 2.276, 1903), and it is this conventionality *in a concrete image* that the conventionalists see, not the abstract qualities of the icon, a *logical* concept which, manifestly, they don't understand.

The icon-index-symbol division has been reworked more recently by Barnham (2022), who idiosyncratically actuates semiosis within the trichotomy: his figure 11 (2022: 242) illustrates an upward-moving cyclical movement from icon to symbol that gathers conceptual and representational density as it travels to increasing complexity through the subdivisions. This resembles Thellefsen's 'sign displacement' process travelling upwards through the trichotomies (Thellefsen 2001), and contributes to a demonstration of how a Hegelian approach to Peirce's logic might lead to concept formation. There may well be a case for a Hegelian interpretation of Peirce, but there are three objections to be made to such 'displacements' from a strictly Peircean perspective. First, semiosis, which Barnham summons to operate such a displacement, is initiated not by a subdivision such as the abstract qualisign or the icon but by the dynamic object, which was not accessible to the logic of Speculative Grammar in 1903; second, although the content of the manuscript doesn't deal specifically with the subject, being more concerned with cenoscopy, the title of manuscript R299 (1906), 'Phaneroscopy: Or, the natural history of concepts' tells all: the concepts of logic (and, presumably, those of natural languages) are given by phaneroscopy, a remark Peirce makes on several occasions, and a situation derived from his placing phenomenology before the normative sciences in his classifications. Finally, within all Peirce's classification any 'movement' between the subdivisions is always from more complex to less: for example, as we see in Figure 2.3, a sinsign can be associated with an icon but not with the phenomenologically more complex symbol.

***

Peirce obtained the second trichotomy by subdividing the symbol. With the resultant subdivisions he then established the relation holding between the sign and its interpretant. Since this new relation set out the ways in which the sign represented the object to the interpretant, it is convenient to claim that it classified signs according to their 'informational value', and identified them in order of increasing phenomenological complexity as rhemes, dicisigns and arguments in place of the traditional trio of term, proposition and argument.

The dicisign was a remarkable innovation as it replaced the traditional subject-predicate proposition by an information-communicating unit that allowed for non-propositional signification, and hence for the communication of knowledge in non-propositional form. The new basic form was an index associated with an icon: the index being the subject, or in more recent terminology, the theme or topic of the communication, while the icon replaced the predicate, corresponding again in more recent terminology, to the rheme or comment of the communication. The transmission of knowledge as we understand it, had, since Aristotle at least, been assumed to be restricted to the structure of the proposition – 'propositional knowledge' – like the sentences on this page. Peirce's introduction of the dicisign had the effect of broadening the information-bearing channel, so to speak. In addition to the symbol status of natural language signs, these being the traditional 'vehicles' of information, within anthroposemiotics this now included complex, multimodal iconic and indexical signs such as the portrait of a woman with her name beneath, a photograph (EP: 2:282), or complex multimodal linguistic combinations of verbal and nonverbal communication; within biosemiotics it allowed for different forms of informational units within non-human species of animate and, perhaps, non-animate organisms. Finally in the second trichotomy he identified, as the name suggests and according to a long tradition in logic, the argument as a sign of reasoning, of which he distinguished three types: abduction, or the formation of hypotheses, deduction and induction.

In the later Syllabus manuscript, R540, Peirce was led to introduce a division of the sign itself, which he identified in order of increasing complexity as the qualisign, to account for any quality which functions as a sign, a quality of feeling, for example; the sinsign or singular, existent perceivable sign, such as the sudden change of direction of a weathervane; finally, the legisign, the sign by law or an element of some general system such as a human language. In the latter case, in order to be perceivable, and therefore interpretable, he posited a subclass of 'replicas', sinsign-type legisigns which occur in actual cases of representation. This set up a typological system in which a single non-relational division was associated, in a particular order, with two relational divisions. This is the order forming a typical triadic relation: the representamen followed by the object and, finally, the interpretant, an order (ROI) henceforth referred to as 'correlate order', the order of the correlates in any triadic relation.

There are several reasons why Peirce should have introduced the non-relational sign division. First, since the 'values' of the subdivisions were determined by their respective phenomenological complexities, the status of the two relational trichotomies holding between the sign and its correlates would have been difficult to validate logically without first having established that of the sign. For example, the symbol is defined as representing a general object, such as 'boot', that is, the class of durable items of footwear covering foot and ankle. Peirce no doubt realized that logically such a representation requires a sign which is equally general, one now identified in the first trichotomy as a legisign, e.g., *boot*. Second, it was in this later manuscript that he introduced the ten classes, and it would have been equally illogical to propose an exhaustive classification of signs without including some sort of specification of the sign itself. Finally, and most importantly, these divisions were defined within his Speculative Grammar, which, as mentioned before, identified the conditions under which a given entity qualified as a sign. This explains the lengthy descriptions of signs and representamens examined above, for one thing. Now, Peirce was necessarily aware of the traditional distinction between two objects in logic from his borrowing of the term representamen from the eighteenth-century Scottish philosopher Thomas Reid through his knowledge of Sir William Hamilton's edition of his work.[16] Moreover, although he never developed them, he also alluded to three interpretants in R478 as the immediate, the indirect and the imperfect.[17] Nevertheless, it is the conditions of signhood alone that prevail in Speculative Grammar.

As for the two relational divisions, these obviously had a historical origin since Peirce from the start had been preoccupied as a logician with the relation holding between sign and object (i.e. the correlate in 1867). The reason for this is obvious as was mentioned in a different context: logic as Peirce understood it dealt with representation, which he described in a text which still retains the single division of 1867:

> I must begin the examination of representation by defining representation a *little* more accurately. In the first place, as to my terminology, I confine the word representation to the operation of a sign or its *relation* to the object *for* the interpreter of the representation. The concrete subject that represents I call a *sign* or a *representamen*. I use these two words, *sign* and *representamen*, differently. By a *sign* I mean anything which conveys any definite notion of an object in any way, as such conveyers of thought are familiarly known to us.
> (CP: 1.540, 1903)

As the object is not necessarily known, is 'outside' the sign, and as the interpretant is inevitably a future event or effect and is impossible to access before the sign has functioned, the sign, the unit of representation defined in Speculative Grammar, is thus the only element that the logician can be sure of. Nevertheless, by basing the analysis on the phenomenology, it is possible to hypothesize the nature of the relation that might hold between the sign and the object and the nature of the way the sign represents that object to the interpretant, since the 'organic' structure of the categories provide the means to do so. Through the operation of prescission it is also possible to state the nature of the relations holding between the subdivisions in each trichotomy.

Classification

Having introduced a sign division and named the three divisions of signs Peirce then established his ten classes of signs. Figure 2.3, from a page in the Logic Notebook, diagrams Peirce's method for the establishment of the ten classes of signs. The

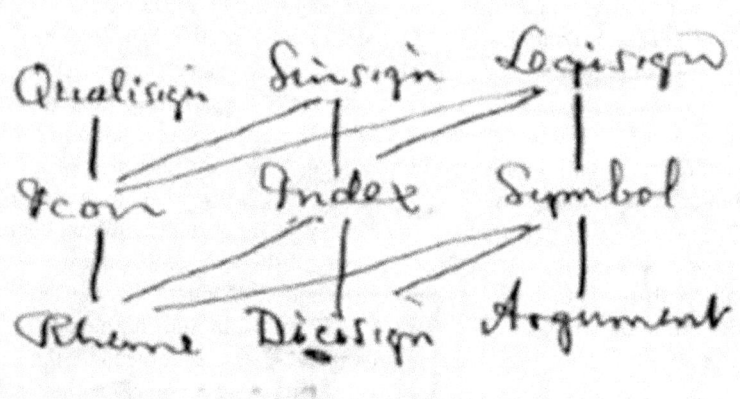

Figure 2.3 Peirce's scheme for the association of the nine subdivisions of signs. (R339: 239v, H450); MS Am 1632 (339), Houghton Library, Harvard University.

scheme in Figure 2.3 indicates the possible categorial affinities holding between the subdivisions of the three trichotomies. The vertical lines associating three subdivisions of the same phenomenological complexity form a class, a qualisign combines with an icon and a rheme, for example. The downward diagonals run from right to left, leading from the phenomenologically more complex subdivisions to the less. For example, it is possible to trace a class from sinsign to icon, which necessarily leads to rheme. Figure 2.3 shows that it is not possible for the Firstness of one division to 'move up', or 'displace itself' up the phenomenological scale to combine with a Secondness of the following division, or for a Secondness of one division to associate with the Thirdness of a following division. The system is thus 'top down': it is impossible within a Peircean conception of classification to 'climb' the three-stage phenomenological scale. By combining subdivisions in this way Peirce obtained ten classes of signs, which he established in order of increasing phenomenological complexity (see EP2: 294–6).

Although the elements of Figure 2.3 are displayed spatially, the classes yielded by such a system are simply composed of *three facets of the same semiotic entity*: a dicent indexical legisign is belongs to a class of signs whose semiotic value is assessed, or 'computed', from three different points of view. When one division's various subdivisions are correctly combined with subdivisions from the following divisions according to the admissible 'paths' in Figure 2.3, we obtain the ten classes which Peirce schematized in Figure 2.4, although he never explained how he obtained them, stating simply:

> The affinities of the ten classes are exhibited by arranging their designations in the triangular table here shown, which has heavy boundaries between adjacent squares that are appropriated to classes alike in only one respect. All other adjacent squares pertain to classes alike in two respects. Squares not adjacent pertain to classes alike in one respect only, except that each of the three squares of the vertices of the triangle pertains to a class differing in all three respects from the classes to

which the squares along the opposite side of the triangle are appropriated. The lightly printed designations are superfluous.

(EP2: 296, 1903)

The important point to note about these ten classes, however, is their artificial, 'laboratory-derived' theoretical status: they are the classes defined for the purposes of logic and, in Peirce's case at least, employed in the cause of logical analysis. They are not classes of natural objects such as fish, although Peirce exhorts us to define the sign as a zoologist might a fish. It is important to remember this, in particular in any discussion of semiosis, as semiosis is a dynamic process that is 'in the world', so to speak, not within the static three-division classification of signs. Figure 2.4 shows the characteristic V-shaped table on which Peirce presented them in MS R540. The classes obtained in each case are based upon a system of 'appearances' and are therefore of completely different natures.

Hypoiconicity

As seen above, the trichotomization of the icon had initially been mooted in one of the Harvard Lectures on Pragmatism delivered in April 1903. This distinctly Peircean

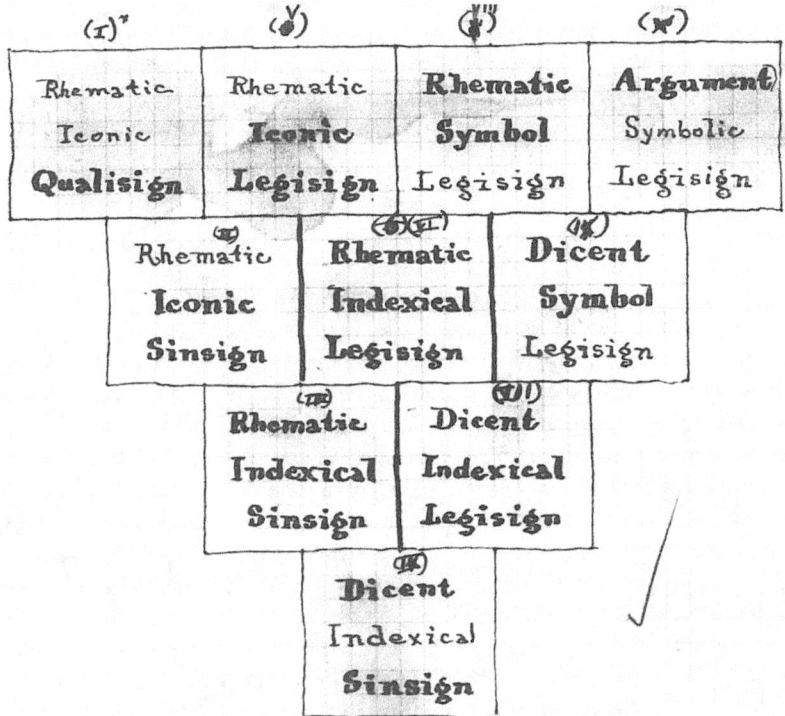

Figure 2.4 The table of ten classes of signs from manuscript R540: 16, 1903.

and highly innovative semiotic approach to the property of resemblance in signs – characteristically, Peirce identifies *three* ways in which a sign can represent its object qualitatively – reappeared in the Syllabus, where Peirce introduced the concept of the hypoicon:

> But a sign may be iconic, that is, may represent its object mainly by its similarity, no matter what its mode of being. If a substantive be wanted, an iconic [sign] may be termed a hypoicon. Any material image, as a painting, is largely conventional in its mode of representation; but in itself, without legend or label it may be called a *hypoicon*.
>
> (EP2: 273–4)

Thus, after having derived the icon subdivision through the process of categorial analysis, Peirce then proceeded to derive the three subdivisions of hypoicons by recursively applying these same categorial distinctions to the icon itself, a process recorded in the precisely formulated but initially forbidding statement establishing the three degrees of structural complexity, which are, in effect, the three forms of resemblance presented by the hypoicons. The trichotomy resulting from this category-based process is the definition – isolated and dignified as the single paragraph 2.277 in the *Collected Papers* – describing image, diagram and metaphor in order of increasing complexity:

> Hypoicons may roughly [be] divided according to the mode of Firstness which they partake. Those which partake the simple qualities, or First Firstnesses, are *images*; those which represent the relations, mainly dyadic, or so regarded, of the parts of one thing by analogous relations in their own parts, are *diagrams*; those which represent the representative character of a representamen by representing a parallelism in something else, are *metaphors*.
>
> (EP2: 274, 1903)

Since this analysis of the icon yields image, diagram and metaphor,[18] and since Peirce later maintained that an index involved a sort of icon, and a symbol a sort of index (EP2: 291–2), it follows, here too, by transitivity that indices and symbols can involve any or all of the three hypoicons, a heuristic potential that Jakobson understood before anyone else and exploited very successfully, if incompletely. Finally, it should be noted that as with the structural complexity of icon, index and symbol (CP: 2.304, 1902), the increase in hypoiconic complexity in the definition follows what Peirce had earlier referred to as the logical categories of the monad, the dyad and the polyad or higher set, which are 'categories of the forms of experience' (CP: 1.452, 1896). Table 2.2 sets out the relations between the nine subdivisions and corresponds to Figure 2.3 with the hypoicons added.

At this point, the 'neo-' interpretation of the 1903 system enters the picture, so to speak, with this introduction to Peirce's description of the hypoicons. The relation of these to neo-Peircean sign analysis stems from the fact that once Peirce had introduced them in manuscript R478, the earlier of the two discussed in this chapter, he never refers to them again as such. And yet, they hold considerable promise for idioscopic

Table 2.2 The three-division typology of 1903 integrating the hypoicons

	Category		
	Firstness	Secondness	Thirdness
Respect:			
Sign	qualisign	sinsign	legisign
Sign-Object	icon	index	symbol
	image		
	diagram		
	metaphor		
Sign-Interpretant	rheme	dicisign	argument

semiotics and they have already been exploited in many ways. However, the precise form of the graphic representations of the hypoicons to be developed in Chapter 6 merits a preparatory explanation. They are, of course, a necessarily personal conception of the hypoicons.

Interpreting the definition of the hypoicons

It has to be admitted that paragraph CP: 2.277 has been problematic for Peirce scholars, sometimes causing frustration or incomprehension. Short, for example, simply quotes the paragraph and leaves the reader to work out the meaning of the passage for her or himself (2007: 218). David Pharies, on the other hand, in a remarkably illustrated study of image and diagram, makes the following observation on the definition of the hypoicons from CP: 2.277: 'This is one of the more obscure passages I have had occasion to quote, and I do not profess to understand it completely. The central message, however, seems to be that hypoicons have three degrees of complexity' (1985: 36). Perhaps the most notorious example of misunderstanding or misrepresentation is that of Roman Jakobson, mentioned in the previous chapter.

Such misunderstanding, misrepresentation or misinterpretation is understandable as the passage is terse to the point of obscurity without careful examination. What most commentators seem to forget is that the hypoicons are three different types or subclasses of icon, and are thus necessarily three increasingly complex degrees of *form*. They are immaterial, can only inhere in a sinsign, for example, and above all they cannot trigger a process: they can't 'do' anything. The description of image, diagram and metaphor to be given later is my own reading of CP 2.277, but of course it is not the only one: there are other accounts of Peircean metaphor. Shapiro (1998), as I have mentioned elsewhere, is a notable microscopic study of a certain type of iconicity exhibited by Shakespeare's sonnets, and, by the same token, is the perfect illustration of the sort of analysis for which the hexad of 1908 described in Chapter 4 is totally ill-fitted.

Diagramming the action of the sign

The schemata to be developed fully in Chapter 6 derive from the definition of the sign in the Syllabus. Anticipating the description of semiosis of 1908, the sign thus presented in 1903 operates in a three-correlate potentially dynamic process, whereas the analysis in section 'The logic of the Syllabus' concluded that the ten classes of signs derived in 1903 are a-temporal and static, having only an indirect relation to the three correlates participating in the definition of the sign. The object and interpretant contribute to that definition but they do not provide independent trichotomies to the 1903 ten-class typology as they do in 1908. Summarizing the definition, we can state that a sign is determined by its object to produce an effect upon an interpreter, and when the sign of 1903 actually functions as a sign, no less than that of 1908, it mediates in a 'determination flow' from object to interpretant. That is, the object exerts an influence upon the sign such that it produces an effect upon an interpreter: this is a dynamic process but, as we see later, an over-simplified version of an actual action of the sign.

We recall how the all-important relation holding between sign and object – the sign's mode of representation – is defined in the Syllabus: 'The first and most fundamental [division of signs] is that any Representamen is either an *Icon*, an *Index*, or a *Symbol*' (EP2: 273). This was followed later by this further definition of the icon: 'An *Icon* is a sign which refers to the Object that it denotes merely by virtue of characters of its own, and which it possesses, just the same, whether any such Object actually exists or not. It is true that unless there really is such an Object, the Icon does not act /as/ a sign' (EP2: 291). While the 'ground' of the icon's mode of representation of its object is whatever properties or qualities it presents independently of anything else, in order to function at all the icon must nevertheless involve all three correlates, hence the specification also of both object and interpretant in Figure 2.5 and in figures in Chapter 6.

As a First,[19] the icon – identified as an iconic sinsign in all the following schemata – is, with respect to the definition, the *first* correlate in a triadic relation, which, according to the definitions of triadic relations, can be so determined by the second correlate, the object, as to determine the third correlate, the interpretant. In Figure 2.5, the three correlates display the determination process by which the sign is informed by its object and then communicates that form to an interpretant. Figure 2.5 is thus intended to represent the determination sequence, or determination 'flow', from dynamic object to final interpretant, and, as we see in Chapter 5, represents an earlier version of semiosis that is implicit in the 1903 definition of the sign. However, in order to illustrate the structural differences distinguishing the three hypoicons, the schema in Figure 2.1 will be replaced in Chapter 6 by the 'ellipses' in Figure 2.5.[20]

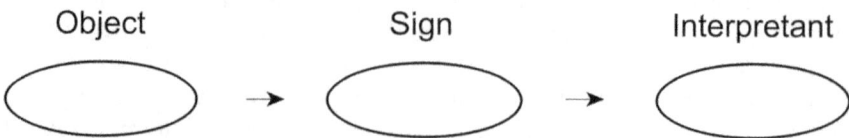

Figure 2.5 The action of the sign in 1903 represented as ellipses.

The hypoiconic structures characterizing image, diagram and metaphor

The three fundamental ways in which the icon can resemble its object by virtue of Peirce's categorial distinctions are represented as Figures 2.6, 2.7 and 2.8, rudimentary graphic representations of the structure of, respectively, Peirce's image, diagram and metaphor, in which the 'arrows' represent both the process of determination and the communication of the process by an inescapably 'sensible' – in other words, existential and perceivable – medium such as air, a piece of painted canvas, oils on a wood panel, the inked page of a book, the old-fashioned school chalk and blackboard or the pixelated glass on a smartphone.[21] Note that in all such cases the sign is necessarily a sinsign or the replica of a legisign, as it has to be perceivable – were it a legisign, it would be of the nature of law, thought or habit and would therefore be physically unperceivable. Note, too, that by definition it is the sign alone which has hypoiconic structure since it is the 'representing', mediating, correlate in the process.

Figure 2.6 is a very basic representation of some of the qualities (specific qualities of lines, shapes, colours; qualities of feeling; sounds) presumed to be inhering in features of the represented object which determine corresponding qualities, namely the First Firstnesses of the definition, in a portrait painting, for example, which is an iconic sinsign but also, minus any caption, an image at its hypoiconic level.

Since the qualities – First Firstnesses – thus represented are phenomenologically less complex than the Secondness of the existential medium – the canvas and oils of a painting, for example – the intended representation of the qualities in the object is in no way inhibited or quantitatively restricted by potential differences in complexity between the structure of the sign and the respective structures of its two correlates. In other words, since the qualities represented in this phenomenological conception of the process are less complex than the medium conveying them, the intended representation of the qualities in the object is in no way inhibited.

Figure 2.7 represents the structure of a very basic diagram (most signs with diagrammatic structure would, of course, be far more complex than this), an icon

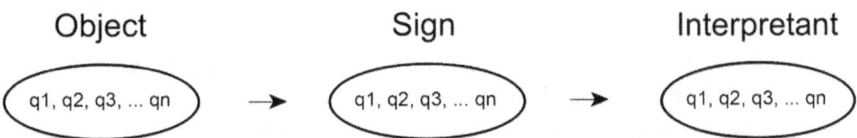

Figure 2.6 The generic structure of a sign with image hypoiconicity.

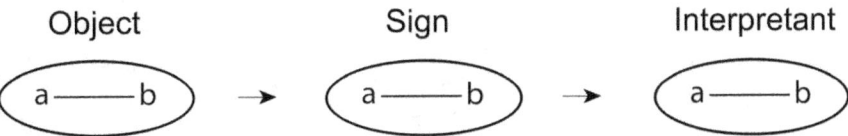

Figure 2.7 The generic structure of a sign with diagram hypoiconicity.

composed essentially of the Second Firstnesses implied in the definition, namely the dyadic relations mentioned there and represented as the relation **a—b** between the two partial objects **a** and **b** in the entity, fact or event represented by the sign, such relations being a step up the phenomenological scale from the necessarily vague, unstructured Firstnesses composing the image. These are interpreted to conform to an object, the portrait-painter's model, for example, but there is no necessary correspondence between the painting as hypoiconic image and the model. The diagram, by contrast, is an icon composed of lines, shapes, colours, rhythmic sounds organized by at least one dyadic relation inherited from the object that it represents (CP: 4.418, 1903), and, in more complex combinations of relations and partial objects, informs not only spoken and written sentences, the illustrations from geometry manuals and the graphic instructions on how to assemble furniture, all manner of informative exosomatic organs such as thermometers, speedometers, the complex form of sound spectrograms, but also the highly detailed blueprints for the construction of buildings and supersonic aircraft. In all such cases, nevertheless, the diagrammatic complexity of the sinsign partakes of the Secondness of the medium and Peirce's conception of phenomenology explains how the representation of the structure of the object is similarly in no way inhibited by the medium through which it is communicated.

Finally, as indicated in Figure 2.8, metaphor is the hypoiconic structure presenting the Third Firstness implicit in the definition, a phenomenological complexity compatible with convention, synthesis and representation. Like the symbol, metaphoric form in the Peircean sense requires the experience of the interpreter in the interpreting process in order to construe the nature of the unfamiliar association or comparison that is being communicated concerning two (or more) generally disparate domains of experience, and it is in this that metaphor is necessarily triadic. The monadic image has the capacity to signify whether it has an object and interpretant or not, the dyadic diagram requires the existence of an object in order to attain its signifying status since it is relations in the object which determine the diagram's structure, while metaphor could not function without an interpretant to confirm its meaning. Figure 2.8 is an attempt to represent this composite structure by the difference in sizes between the complexity in object and interpretant and the simpler structure of the unavoidable Secondness of the medium.

Hypoiconic resemblance is established in this complex case by associating in the simpler sign appropriate elements inherited from the parallelism in the object. As represented in the schema, the object ellipse involves an assimilation and thus has two parallel lines indicated by //. In this way, the **a' - b'** relation on the top line

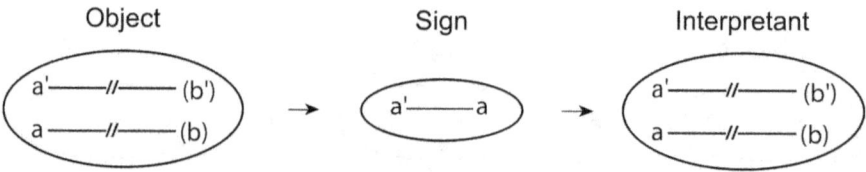

Figure 2.8 The structure of a sign with metaphor hypoiconicity.

represents the controversial, contentious or sometimes yet to be defined relation between individuals, events or states of affairs in another domain of experience which is being 'targeted' by the metaphor. On the other hand, the relation **a - b** on the lower line in the object constitutes the basis of the assimilation, namely a relation between individuals, events or states of affairs in some different domain of experience. It was to Peirce's immense credit that he was able to theorize the structure of signs more complex than the common diagrammatic type, metaphorical signs which synthesize in the guise of a judgemental comparison elements from two quite distinct relations. In the hypoiconicity of 1903 we thus see metaphor as a conflict between the complexity of the object, whatever that may be, and the constraints of an existential medium. We take up the illustration and exploitation of the formal structures of the hypoicons in Chapter 6.

Summary and discussion

The chapter has reviewed much of the logic material presented in the Syllabus and has sought to show what is required of a genuine neo-Peircean *semiotic* approach to signs, that is, an approach to signs using Peircean concepts but also developing concepts that he introduced but never gave substance to himself. There are pitfalls to avoid in such an enterprise, but also theoretical advances, and this final section discusses four of them.

First, the categories as described in 1903 had evolved over a period of nearly forty years before reaching the stage at which they became central to Peirce's conception of how the world appears to us. It is these categories that Peirce used as discriminating criteria when he established the various subdivisions of signs introduced later in the Syllabus and we return to the subject in the discussion of these divisions, noting that in the final Pragmatism lecture of 1903 Peirce remarks that all three categories, including the generality of Thirdness, appear to us in perception (EP2: 207, 1903), an important aspect of Peirce's logic to which we return and exploit in Chapter 5.

Second, the way the categories figure in contemporary research can be problematic. Would we expect, for example, the grammatical label 'action verb' to act on someone and make them run a marathon or chop logs? Would we expect a label such as 'count noun' to 'produce' logs, boots or a flock of sheep? Of course not. These are labels defined and used by linguists to classify features of certain human languages, they aren't used to activate what they label. However, authors have been tempted to make Peirce's categories 'do' things: initiate new types of semiosis, for one thing. The categories are labels for types of phenomena, they can't 'do' anything; they can't be recruited to activate some semiotic (or other) process.

Third, there is no reason in the world why semioticians of various non-Peircean stripes should not define the sign as a relation, as Benedict, John Deely and many others have done. There is no semiotics police to safeguard definitions, nor should there be. No more than with the concept of semiosis, Peirce has no copyright on the definition of a sign: once 'out there' it can be, and is, adopted and redefined according to theoretical requirements, and the concept most certainly appeared before he did. However, as papers and books by John Deely and other, more recent, biosemioticians claim very forcefully, the basic *semiotic* concepts of biosemiotics, the definition of the sign included, are Peircean in origin. This being the case, to claim, for example, that according to Peirce the sign constitutes the relation of its relates is incorrect, and invites judgement as the sign=triadic relation fallacy. It is simply wrong to claim that such a complex triadic relation was adopted by Peirce from some earlier tradition, and moreover, it is potentially invalidating for any research based on such a claim. For Peirce, as the chapter has sought to demonstrate, the sign is but just one of three correlates or constituents combining to establish an irreducibly triadic relation. To define the sign as the entire relation, one that regulates the trio representamen, object and interpretant, is to go against all Peirce's definitions. As we see in Chapter 4, in 1908 Peirce describes a more complex, hexadic, sequence in which the sign occupies a position between the immediate object before it in the sequence and the immediate interpretant following it. It is difficult to imagine how Peirce would have inserted at that sign position some sort of underlying triadic relation composed of representamen, object and interpretant as claimed by the proponents of the 'sign as relation' position, as there are two objects and three interpretants in the higher hexadic relation already, and to insert a triadic relation in place of the sign in such a hexad would be ludicrous.

Finally, the reader will have noticed that, although they were alluded to, little space has been given to the ten classes that Peirce established in the Syllabus. These will reappear briefly later in the study in relation to another typology involving ten classes, but they are not immediately important to the general thesis developed here. Moreover, few if any contemporary semioticians would actually spend precious time completely classifying in three, six or ten ways the signs they are dealing with. This, of course, was not the case with Peirce. As we see later in the study, he was anxious to identify as many classes of signs as possible. This was because Peirce the logician was interested in expanding the logic of his cenoscopy, whereas the semiotician, the 'idioscopist', is generally more interested in finding new facts and establishing new relations than in seeking, organizing and employing new classes of logical signs: the icon, index and symbol have apparently proved sufficient. In any case, to attempt to modify or add to the cenoscopy as Peirce left it would be the logical equivalent of re-writing *Hamlet* or adding to the Ten Commandments. Peirce alone was master of his philosophy. We can only try to understand it and apply it if we think it useful. We have no brief to modify it. What should be retained from the material of the chapter is that these are classes of representations; they are complex representations, as in addition to classifying the sign and its relation to its object – referred to in the text as the sign's mode of representation – they also include information concerning the informational scope of the sign. With hindsight from the chapters to come, what can be said, finally, concerning the ten classes of signs from the Syllabus is that they perfectly illustrate Peirce's conception of logic as a veritable philosophy of representation. What we see in the years to come is a movement away from this.

3

The Transition

In spite of what numerous commentators suggest from samples of the analyses of signs that they propose, Peirce's development as a logician didn't cease in December 1903. Their reluctance to engage fully with the later statements on logic is understandable in a way as the examples he gives in 1903 of divisions and classes of signs are obviously easier to work with, consequently authors referring to them cannot err in their pronouncements. Moreover, there are those who do use material and concepts from the later stages of Peirce's thinking, but can on occasion be content to exploit the two objects and various trios of interpretants, paying only lip service to the complexities of semiosis. The period deserves more, as what I have been referring to as the system of 1908 didn't appear out of the blue; it was the consequence of a slow but steady evolution in Peirce's logical theory, an evolution in which we find subtle, often perplexing and sometimes seemingly inconsistent changes of viewpoint and approaches to the problem of the sign. What I deem the most important stages in this evolution form the backbone to this chapter. It is presented in three chronologically organized stages, and they take us to a point where the correlates of the original triadic relation come to acquire the sort of active, creative influence within Peirce's 1908 concept of semiosis that was inconceivable in 1903.

The three stages might not be every commentator's choice, but they are not the result of contagion from triadomany;[1] moreover, the progression from one stage to another obviously didn't kick-start to a new level on the first of January of each year. They are intended to rationalize the continuity of the developments that led to a complete change of outlook in the theoretical foundations to the way in which Peirce approached the sign and the process in which it functioned barely five years after the remarkable construction to be found in the Syllabus. The first is the year 1904, during which Peirce expanded his typology of signs; the second deals with the very fertile two-year period 1905–6, while the final period sees Peirce's explicit (re)introduction[2] of the concept of semiosis, and naturally leads to the essential topics of Chapter 4.

1904

Features of Peirce's first hexad

At the time of the Lowell lectures on logic, Peirce had begun his correspondence with Lady Welby: in December 1903 he introduced parts of his logic and triadic relations, but there was nothing really technical in his contribution to the exchanges. Within a year of giving the Lowell Lectures, however, Peirce wrote to Lady Welby describing a more complex sign-system in which he had expanded the original triad of correlates to six: two objects, the sign and three interpretants, for which he devised a number of names in the four-year period that followed until they became 'standardized' as, in order of appearance in semiosis, immediate, dynamic and final in a later letter to Lady Welby (SS: 108–9, 1909).

Characteristically, Peirce prefaces his new typology with a review of the theoretical foundations of the material that was to follow. This, one of the most complete descriptions of the categories and genuine and degenerate cases that we have, occupied more than two thirds of the letter, and must have demanded much attention of Lady Welby as Peirce makes no concessions to technical detail, although he does give examples of the concepts he introduces. Before the paragraphs that deal in detail with the sign and classification the phenomenological statements in the letter conclude with this description of the relation he established at the time between the categories and signification:

> In its genuine form, Thirdness is the triadic relation existing between a sign, its object, and the interpreting thought, itself a sign, considered as constituting the mode of being a sign. A sign mediates between the *interpretant* sign and its object. Taking sign in its broadest sense, its interpretant is not necessarily a sign. Any concept is a sign, of course. Ockham, Hobbes, and Leibniz have sufficiently said that. But we may take a sign in so broad a sense that the interpretant of it is not a thought, but an action or experience, or we may even so enlarge the meaning of sign that its interpretant is a mere quality of feeling. A *Third* is something which brings a First into relation to a Second. A sign is a sort of Third. How shall we characterize it? Shall we say that a Sign brings a Second, its Object, into *cognitive* relation to a Third?
>
> (SS: 31, 1904)

There are two important remarks to be made of this prophetic passage. First, we have Peirce writing of the sign's mediating function, an innovative theoretical principle he develops in the following two years. Second, what will appear as the classes of signs defined by the three types of final interpretant (necessitant, existent, possible) in the typology discussed in the following chapter, that is, in the typology described to Lady Welby in December 1908, are anticipated quite clearly here in order of decreasing complexity: thought, action and quality of feeling. It is quite singular that the remarks concerning what Peirce identifies later as the three subclasses of signs defined according to the 'universe status' of the final interpretant don't appear in the descriptions of signs and divisions in the typology that he develops in the final paragraphs of the October 1904 letter. What Lady Welby made of the introduction of the relates of triadic relations in the passage was probably consigned to her diary, but she wrote back that she was interested in Peirce's description of the categories, and even shared parts of his letter with another correspondent (SS: 36, 1904).

***

I am now prepared to give my division of signs, as soon as I have pointed out that a sign has two objects, its object as it is represented and its object in itself. It has also three interpretants, its interpretant as represented or meant to be understood, its interpretant as it is produced, and its interpretant in itself. Now signs may be divided as to their own material nature, as to their relations to their objects, and as to their relation to their interpretants.

(SS: 32, 1904)

At this point Peirce begins his description of his new typology, but again characteristically, prefaces it with a definition of the sign. In this case, the number of relates in the signifying relation has been augmented by a second object and two further interpretants. As with his use of the term 'representamen', as he initially called the sign, the adoption of the two objects was probably due to his acquaintance with the philosophy of the eighteenth-century Scottish philosopher Thomas Reid. The following is a suggestive sample of Reid's discussion of cognition quoted by Deledalle (2000: 133):

The Leibnitio-Wolfians [...] distinguished three acts in the process of representative cognition: 1° the act of representing a (mediate) object to the mind; 2° the representation, or more properly speaking, *representamen*, itself as an (immediate or vicarious) object exhibited to the mind; 3° the act by which the mind is conscious immediately of the representative object, and, through it, immediately of the remote object represented.

The terminology and concepts in this short quotation are echoed in similar fashion by Peirce in his discussions of the sign and its two objects: 'representative object' and 'remote object' correspond, respectively, to what Peirce refers to in the letter to Lady Welby as the 'object as it is represented' and the 'object in itself', and thus, respectively, to what he refers to in the passage quoted, and retained subsequently, as the sign's 'immediate' and 'dynamic' (also 'dynamical', or 'dynamoid') objects. In view of this, we conclude that Peirce came to adopt the two objects according to a philosophical tradition in which, he notes on several occasions, past logicians had generally recognized two objects.[3]

Now, although earlier in the letter he had introduced three different types of final interpretant (thought, action, quality of feeling), which was a relate of the new hexadic relation in which the sign functions, the typology resulting from this increased system of correlates was, like the triadic system of 1903, essentially relational. It was composed, first, of a correlate division for the sign, followed by divisions holding between the sign and its five correlates (Table 3.1 in which the symbol S means 'sign'). Since it is the sign that occupied initial position as in Table 2.2 and not the object as in Figure 2.1 from the previous chapter, Peirce was clearly interested in establishing a new typology and not a hypothetical model of the action of the sign. Moreover, although such a typology was capable of yielding twenty-eight classes of signs, Peirce seems not to have envisaged the possibility; nor did he establish a viable dynamic process involving this new set of correlates that might furnish a means of triggering semiosis.

Table 3.1 The 1904 six-division typology described to Lady Welby set out in tabular format

	Category		
	Firstness	**Secondness**	**Thirdness**
Respect			
S	qualisign	sinsign	legisign
S-Od	icon	index	symbol
S-Oi	S of quality	S of experience	S of law
S-If	rheme	dicent	argument
S-Id	contemplated S	urged S	submitted S
S-Ii	S interpreted by feeling	S interpreted by experience	S interpreted by thought

Of note in the table, which, unlike Peirce's verbal description, sets the classes out in tabular fashion, is the order in which the relational divisions are proposed: the sign occupies initial position in the table, then we have the sign in relation, respectively, to dynamic object, immediate object, final interpretant, dynamic interpretant and, finally, immediate interpretant. The order reflects the application of the genuine-degenerate distinction both within the divisions and between them: within the sign-to-dynamic object relation the icon is doubly degenerate, while the index is simply degenerate with respect to the symbol; and this order continues through the interpretant divisions in the typology. Similarly, the dynamic object, for example, is genuine with respect to the degenerate immediate object. Hence the genuine-degenerate order in the organization of the interpretant divisions, and, no doubt the temporary inclusion of sign-to-immediate object and sign-to-immediate interpretant divisions. These he subsequently abandoned as, by definition, they were already 'present in' the sign, as we see below. There seems to be only one other six-division typology based upon this genuine-degenerate order, one from August of 1904 in the Logic Notebook, where Peirce is trying to work out values for the icon-index-symbol and rheme-dicent-argument divisions (R339: 239v, H450, 1904).[4] Peirce seems in the Logic Notebook to be experimenting with the division organization expounded more rationally in the October letter. As we see in the next section, Peirce modifies definitively the order of divisions within his subsequent typologies.

The August 1904 page from the Logic Notebook and the October letter were the continuation of work that Peirce had begun earlier in the year in the text 'New Elements'. This dealt quite exhaustively with the icon-index-symbol division in terms of the genuine-degenerate hierarchy that we find in these two texts. This was clearly an important distinction within the phenomenology as he conceived it at the time. The following passage is typical of 'New Elements' and clearly anticipates the two later descriptions of typology divisions:

A pure icon is independent of any purpose. It serves as a sign solely and simply by exhibiting the quality it serves to signify. The relation to its object is a degenerate relation. It asserts nothing. If it conveys information, it is only in the sense in which the object that it is used to represent may be said to convey information. An *icon* can only be a fragment of a completer sign. The other form of degenerate sign is to be termed an *index*.

(EP2: 306, 1904)

Further remarks concern the values that Peirce attributes to the subclasses of signs yielded by the final division, *S-Ii* in Table 3.1, and the denominations of the three interpretants.[5] In the first case, the subclasses of signs yielded by this relational division are the sign interpreted in order of increasing complexity as quality of feeling, action and thought. As seen earlier, the values of the three subtypes of immediate interpretant are in similar order, quality of feeling, action and thought: 'But we may take a sign in so broad a sense that the interpretant of it is not a thought, but an action or experience, or we may even so enlarge the meaning of sign that its interpretant is a mere quality of feeling', where by meaning in this passage Peirce means interpretant. As we see in the next chapter, these are the values that Peirce attributes not to the relation between sign and immediate interpretant, but to the final interpretant functioning as correlate. In the second case, the label 'dynamic interpretant' is stable throughout, whereas the immediate interpretant received several different denominations. The final interpretant, designated by a perplexing variety of terms in the numerous typologies that Peirce established in the years to follow, was to be the object of much critical debate.

The letter of 12 October 1904 appeared to be work in progress, as after having detailed the six divisions of his new typology, instead of offering examples of the classes of signs that it might yield, Peirce simply added as a post-scriptum the ten classes from 1903 (SS: 35–6, 1904). Towards the end of the year he renamed his phenomenology 'phaneroscopy' (CP: 1.286, 1904), and this might have heralded greater precision in, and an extension to, the construction of the typology of 1903. In the circumstances, however, it signalled the end of the classification of the sign simply as a 'representation' of its object, as simply 'standing for' its object. What we see in the following three years is the development of a different conception of the sign.

1905–6

Symbolistic, pragmaticism and the symbol

The two years following the October 1904 letter to Lady Welby are marked by a number of innovative decisions and revisions, with Peirce's own peculiar brand of meaning-seeking pragmatism forming a continuous theoretical background. Indeed, the years 1905–6 constituted a period during which Peirce also undertook a thorough revision of his logic: for example, he worked feverishly on his conception of pragmaticism, composing a large body of drafts and published papers, and also produced an impressive number of six- and ten-division typologies in his Logic Notebook between 10 October 1905 and 31 August 1906. In view of the importance of pragmaticism as a background theory to the evolution of ideas that resulted in the description of semiosis in 1908, what follows is an attempt to put into perspective the influence of pragmaticism and the importance within it of the symbol.

Peirce is now known as a logician and one of the founders of contemporary semiotic theory, but was, in his lifetime and for a long time afterwards, best known as a major protagonist of pragmatism. The term itself was described by Peirce in 1907 as 'merely a method of ascertaining the meanings of hard words and of abstract concepts' (EP2: 400, 1907), but the concept was initially enshrined (although not explicitly identified by Peirce at the time as 'pragmatism') in the following maxim from the 1878 paper, 'How to Make our Ideas Clear': 'Consider what effects, which might conceivably have practical bearings, we conceive the object of our conception to have. Then, our conception of these effects is the whole of our conception of the object' (EP1: 132, 1878). In the paper, Peirce was rejecting what he considered to be traditional conventions for establishing the clearness with which we conceive ideas, namely by a form of familiarity with them and by means of definitions – for example, the generally two-sided, 'recto-verso' entries associating word with sense to be found in our dictionaries. To counter these twin errors afflicting philosophical tradition Peirce, drawing on his experimentalist experience in the laboratory, later framed more completely his own theory of the clearness of conceptions and their meaning as follows:

> a *conception*, that is, the rational purport of a word or other expression, lies exclusively in its conceivable bearing upon the conduct of life; so that, since obviously nothing that might not result from experiment can have any direct bearing upon conduct, if one can define accurately all the conceivable experimental phenomena which the affirmation or denial of a concept could imply, one will have therein a complete definition of the concept, and *there is absolutely nothing more in it.*
>
> (CP: 5.412, 1905)

This was his pragmatist grade of clearness or understanding of meaning.[6] However, Peirce was not interested in the meaning of all words, but principally with the meaning of those connected with the communication of the ideas of science, in effect a relatively restricted scope of meaning. And this impacted his logic as it developed during the two-year period in question. He had already developed the concept of pragmatism in the course of the Harvard lectures on the subject in 1903, which, in retrospect were, in certain ways, a propaedeutic for the lectures on logic delivered later that year, especially the third which dealt with the categories and signs.

As a further stage in Peirce's undiminished interest in pragmatism we find him returning in the first of three articles for *The Monist* in 1905 to a problem raised in the Lowell lectures on logic, namely the ethics of scientific terminology – a sort of editorial counterpart to the more interpretive nature of pragmatism – and, of particular interest to the study, to the question of the symbol. As he states in the ethics of terminology, for Peirce the symbol, the most complex type of sign, was the essential vehicle of scientific thought: 'the woof and warp of all thought and all research is symbols, and the life of thought and science is the life inherent in symbols' (EP2: 219, 1903). Holding that new scientific ideas required a new concept-specific terminology, he furthermore required the inventor of a new conception, as he was doing in logic, to provide a new, concept-specific term (EP2: 266, 1903).[7]

Now, in order to bring out the defining characteristics of his version of pragmatism he introduces a dialogue between himself and an imaginary questioner, in the course of which he recognizes pragmaticism's restricted conception of meaning when asked what the expression 'George Washington' meant. To this he replied that: 'it must be admitted that pragmaticism fails to furnish any translation or meaning of a proper name, or other designation of an individual object', that 'the pragmaticistic meaning is undoubtedly general; and it is equally indisputable that the general is of the nature of a word or sign' and that the 'word "soldier," whether spoken or written, is general in the same way; while the name, "George Washington", is not so' (EP2: 341–2, 1905). In short, pragmatism, or pragmaticism, is a theory of meaning that is unavoidably restricted to the interpretation of the sorts of symbols mentioned in the earlier Ethics of Terminology, which set out 'rules' framing the technical language to be employed in the composition of scientific reports, for example (EP2: 266, 1903).[8] Consequently a theory of this sort is inapplicable to the determination of the meaning of indices such as proper names, and, logically, to the determination of the meaning of icons, too.

It is the concept, a symbolic entity, that is the subject of his famous formula 'The elements of every concept enter into logical thought at the gate of perception and make their exit at the gate of purposive action; and whatever cannot show its passports at both those two gates is to be arrested as unauthorized by reason' (CP 5.212, 1903): the rule doesn't apply explicitly to icons and indices. This is a particularly problematic statement considering that according to the classificatory system he established in 1903 all signs were either icons, indices or symbols, and that he had earlier claimed that meaning was communicated by signs.[9] Nevertheless, the theoretical priority thus accorded the symbol rationalizes the pervasive influence of the genuine-degenerate distinction that informs the typology of 1904 examined in the previous section, the relations holding in particular between the subdivisions in the icon-index-symbol trichotomy, and the reason why an icon 'can only be a fragment of a completer sign'.

Pragmaticism is, in short, then, a theory of meaning, and its relation to logic is obvious: only symbols have meaning, but symbols cannot function in logic alone, for as Peirce had determined as early as 1885, an exhaustive logical theory additionally requires indices and icons. What seems to run through much of his work in the 1905–6 period is a return to the symbolistic of his earliest years, and the idea that the symbol is the prime, albeit not the sole, subclass of signs that founds his conception of logic. This was how he initially conceived 'semiotic' as the science of representations:

Logic is objective symbolistic.
Symbolistic is the semiotic of symbols.
Objective symbolistic is that branch of symbolistic which considers relations to objects.
Semiotic is the science of representations.

(W1: 303, 1865)

Within this group, his own work consisted predominantly in objective symbolistic, the field which studies the relation between signs and their objects, this being, in fact, the basis of his first division of signs, the one to which he returned many times over the years, and the one which surely founded his theory of the diagrammatic representation of thought. It certainly evolves to become the division of signs in which we find the hypoicons presented abstractly in Chapter 2. With the importance of symbolism in pragmaticism in mind, it is to this division and the hypoicons that we now turn.

Mutations of the subdivisions of the icon

Peirce's descriptions of the icon and its three subdivisions in the Syllabus were introduced in the previous chapter, so the reader is referred back to the section 'Hypoiconicity' in Chapter 2 for more information. Since this wasn't relevant at the time to the discussion of the hypoicons, there was no mention of the fact that the terse formulation in which metaphor was defined as the most complex type of icon was not, in fact, Peirce's earliest attempt to trichotomize the icon, that is, to identify the three ways in which entities might, at a necessarily abstract level of analysis, resemble other entities through the application of the analytical principle which had earlier yielded icon, index and symbol to the Firstness of the icon itself. Although it appears on a later sheet in the same Syllabus manuscript (R478), together with a number of 'false starts' in Peirce's attempts to introduce his Speculative Grammar, this is the first of at least four formulations of the icon's subclasses:

> Icons may be distinguished, though only roughly, into those which are icons in respect to the qualities of sense, being *images*, those which are icons in respect to the dyadic relations of their parts to one another, being *diagrams* or dyadic analogues, and those which are icons in respect to their intellectual characters, being *examples*.
>
> (R478: 209, 1903)

By the expression 'intellectual character' Peirce no doubt had in mind the ideas of thought, Thirdness and the symbol, for the *example*, the most complex subclass in this initial definition requires, as we see later, a mental interpretant for the signification to succeed. No doubt the generality of the concept of an example as being representative of a group, collection or class influenced Peirce's choice of the term.[10] However, this relatively straightforward description was followed by what is now considered the standard definition of the explicitly termed 'hypoicons' with its concise phenomenological wording, repeated here for convenience from the previous chapter:

> Hypoicons may roughly [be] divided according to the mode of Firstness which they partake. Those which partake of simple qualities, or First Firstnesses, are *images*; those which represent the relations, mainly dyadic, or so regarded, of the parts of one thing by analogous relations in their own parts, are *diagrams*; those

which represent the representative character of a representamen by representing a parallelism in something else, are *metaphors*.

(R478: 62; EP2: 274, 1903)

This particular formulation emphasizes the specifically formal aspects of the hypoicons as opposed to the more general description given in the earlier passage, the striking definition of metaphor being noteworthy in this respect. The trichotomization of the icon and its resultant classifications turned out to be a relatively unstable logical concept, nevertheless. The following extract is from the Logic Notebook, dated 12 October 1905, written exactly a year after the letter to Lady Welby which introduced the hexadic typology involving the sign and five relational divisions (SS: 32–5, 1904):

A sign may represent its dynamical object simply by virtue of its own abstract quality. It thus represents whatever else has that quality. Such a sign is termed an Icon. Icons either represent unanalyzed qualities, when they are simple *likenesses* or they have structures like the structure of the object, when, […] they are *analogues*, or if made for the purpose are *diagrams*.

(R339: 257r, H487, 1905)

The *examples* and *metaphors* constituting the most complex types of icon in the two 1903 definitions from the Syllabus have now been reformulated as *diagrams*, with the phenomenologically less complex earlier *diagrams* now redefined as *analogues*, Peirce here reverting to two terms – 'likeness', 'analogue' – introduced in the 1860s (W1: 308, 1865). The 'intellectual' character attributed to the *example* and the complex parallel form of the object in the case of *metaphor* in the phenomenological phrasing of the entire second definition have now been replaced by what had earlier been defined as a phenomenologically less complex type of icon, the *diagram*. Moreover, the diagram is now defined by its coming into being for a 'purpose', which testifies to a growing consciousness of the dynamic nature of the action of the sign and of the importance of intentionality in signification. Note, however, that Peirce never used the term 'intentionality'. He referred instead to 'purpose' or 'intention' (the latter generally in the restricted, technical sense of 'first intention' and 'second intention'). The more symbolic flavour of the most complex icon is also symptomatic of the way Peirce was working towards the published version of his pragmaticism and the Graphs, namely the Prolegomena text of 1906.

But there is more. In the following extract from manuscript R284, one of a number of draft attempts at a 'Basis of Pragmaticism' from 1905, the earlier *diagram* in the Syllabus definitions is now simply described in the new phaneroscopy terminology as bearing 'brute Secundan relations of parts', whereas the *diagram*, here again in 1905 the most complex of the three subclasses but the only one to be named, presents 'intellectual relations' with respect to the icon's object, and partakes of a 'symbolic flavor', echoing the way in which the *examples* of the earliest definition were referred to in 1903 as 'those which are icons in respect to their intellectual characters':

> Icons are subdivided according to the nature of their significant likeness to their Objects which may be 1st in Priman characters or qualities of feeling; these alone have the iconic character in its purity; or 2nd in brute Secundan relations of parts; or 3rd in intellectual relations of parts. The last which are the most important may be called *Diagrams*. These partake of a symbolic flavor.
>
> (R284: 61v-63, 1905)

Such modifications indicate both the relinquishing of the strict phenomenological terminology framing the earlier hypoicons and a shift towards an attempt to reformulate the definition in the terminology of his newly named phaneroscopy: 'priman' and 'secundan' appear frequently in the texts of 1905. The reference to a 'symbolic flavor' is significant: it shows how the symbolistic influence in Peirce's pragmaticism is coming to the fore in the period under examination: this corresponds to the more 'symbolcentric' conception of the diagrammatic system founding the Existential Graphs, which we see quite clearly in manuscript R298 of 1906, where Peirce writes:

> But you have seen (or should you not be satisfied of it, the next following sections of this article shall make it clear to you), that Existential Graphs furnish a moving picture of the action of the mind in thought, – that is, to so much of that as is common to thoughts on all subjects. The study of that system, then, must reveal whatever common nature is necessarily shared by the significations of all thoughts. You 'catch on', I hope. I mean, you apprehend in what way the system of Existential Graphs is to furnish a test of the truth or falsity of Pragmaticism. Namely, *a sufficient study of the Graphs should show what nature is truly common to all significations of concepts.*
>
> (LI: 352, 1906, emphasis added)

Thus, the symbol-flavoured diagram has now to be a graphic aid to the revealing the commonality of the meanings of concepts – 'symbolhood' – hence its elevation to the most complex of the subclasses of the icon, no longer referred to as the 'hypoicons'. Moreover, the iconic purity of the image is now a quality of feeling: it is pure quality and cannot logically trigger semiosis (neither can the other two), which means that any reference to icon-based semiosis is nonsense. The four definitions of the subclasses of the icon proposed between the years 1903 and 1905 are displayed in Table 3.2, the latter of which also includes the newer terminology of phaneroscopy.

Now, the problem for a neo-Peircean semiotics, and for semioticians working with Peircean terms generally, is what do we make of this profound modification of the icon system? Obviously, any future investigation of, or research conducted on the basis of the hypoicons should mention the fact that Peirce reformulated them to suit ongoing theoretical concerns in 1905. In the Prolegomena text of 1906, for example, he devotes much effort to a new presentation of his Existential Graphs. Although the latter are diagrammatic in structure, they represent propositions – they are graphic representations of dicent symbols, in more Peircean terms. They are a perfect illustration of Peirce's synthetic, symbolcentric approach to logic: they are diagrams, that is, complex 'annotated' types of icons, that display indices, and without these the

Table 3.2 Four versions of the subclasses of the icon

	Manuscript and date			
	R478a 1903	R478b 1903	R339 1905	R284 1905
Discriminant:				
First Firstness	image	image	likeness	**Priman** — quality of feeling
Second Firstness	diagram	diagram	analogue	**Secundan** — relation of parts
Third Firstness	example	metaphor	diagram	**(Tertian)** — diagram

important informational content of their symbolic material could not be represented either verbally, or, as in the Graphs, graphically.

What of Peirce's definition of metaphor? It was a conspicuous example of the derivation of a complex representational *form* from the categories, and surely deserves not to be condemned to oblivion as yet another hapax. But it is important to remember that Peirce was a logician, and that any modifications that he makes to his concepts, as in the case of the hypoicons, serve that discipline; semiotics, on the other hand, as an idioscopic science, is under no obligation to follow him in these modifications as long as the basic principles are followed (otherwise the theory cannot claim to be Peircean). What is clear is that the precisely defined disparity between the structure of metaphor defined as a hypoicon and the medium conveying it has apparently been neutralized.

Finally, one important consequence of this is that although metaphor as Peirce describes it in 1903 is one of three types of icon, that is, three purely qualitative representations of their object, owing to the phenomenological bottleneck imposed by any existential medium, we are constrained to diagram metaphor, that is, represent it in a form compatible with the existential medium: Figure 2.8 from the previous chapter is a diagram in the Peircean sense representing metaphorical iconicity. The diagram shows how certain participants (in parentheses on the schema) in the original parallelism are as though 'filtered out', bracketed, by this unavoidable funnel or bottleneck effect caused by the sign's being a perceivable medium: were this not the case, we should be unable to hear or observe it. As a hypoicon, metaphor as defined in 1903 cannot function as an autonomous form of representation in which all the elements of the parallelism are represented on a two-dimensional page or pictorial sign: it is simply not possible to 'metaphorize' metaphor as defined in 1903 in a two-dimensional medium. What is perhaps less evident but also a theoretical consequence of Peirce's having constructed his classes on a phenomenological foundation is that not only can we not *metaphor* or 'metaphorize' image, diagram and metaphor itself, but we cannot *image* any of them or anything else in the strictly theoretical sense: like the parallel-structured metaphor, the image hypoicon cannot autonomously represent the others, or anything else, within its strict monadic framework. The diagram/analogue alone has the capacity to 'comply', to be 'compatible', with the constraints of two-dimensional existential media. Such compatibilities and incompatibilities were treated by Peirce in 1903 from a phenomenological perspective. Sections of Chapter 6 nevertheless return to this topic and illustrate the potential for qualitative analysis offered by the three types of icon, that of metaphor in particular, in conjunction with aspects of the later semiotics.

The sign as medium

In the final section of Chapter 2 much was made of the relation between a potentially obstructive medium and the form to be communicated to the interpretant by the sign. At this point it is now possible to return to the problem of the medium, as this concept figures prominently in Peirce's thinking in the 1905–6 period. However, there is an intermediate stage that merits examination.

As noted in Chapter 2, Peirce had defined the sign in the following manner, in which the continuing influence of his conception of phenomenology is clearly visible: 'A *Sign*, or *Representamen*, is a First which stands in such a genuine triadic relation to a Second, called its *Object*, as to be capable of determining a Third, called its *Interpretant*, to assume the same triadic relation to its Object in which it stands itself to the same Object' (CP: 2.274, 1903). Without rejecting the phenomenological basis of this definition, in the 1905–6 period Peirce nonetheless reformulated the definition in significant ways.

In a draft letter intended for Lady Welby from July 1905 (SS: 189–94), Peirce initially redefined the sign within the terminological framework of phaneroscopy, echoing the wording of the last of the four descriptions of the three types of icon examined in the previous section:[11]

> A 'Sign' is anything, A, which,
> (1) in addition to characters of its own,
> (2) stands in a dyadic relation r, to a purely active correlate, B,
> (3) and is also in a triadic relation *to* B *for* a purely passive correlate, C, this triadic relation being such as to determine C to be in a dyadic relation, S, to B, the relation S corresponding in a recognized way to the relation r.
>
> (SS: 192, 1905)

As ever, this definition was preceded by an introduction to this new conceptualization of the phaneron – 'whatever is before the mind in any way whatever & regardless of whether it be fact or fiction' (SS: 189) – in which Peirce went on to describe its three 'grades of structure', namely, Primans, Secundans and Tertians, which corresponded to the earlier Firstness, Secondness and Thirdness, terminological distinctions which he hadn't relinquished at that time (R339: 242r, H455, 1905). What is interesting in this new definition is the attribution of activity, or agency, to the correlate B, the dynamic object, and passivity to the correlate C, the interpretant. The relation is triadic and the active-passive relation implies dynamism. This definition is purely formal, but Peirce goes on a few lines later to describe the sign in more familiar terms, and at that point, repudiates the former term 'representamen' (SS: 193), this being the passage which troubled Benedict, as was seen in Chapter 2, and spurred him to attempt to 'reinstate' the term in definitions of the sign. The letter was apparently never sent, Peirce thinking, perhaps, that the combination of graphs and phaneroscopy was a little too taxing for his correspondent. The draft was followed the subsequent year by another, this time containing a more complex definition of the sign, together with its correlates.

This was a period in which he began to describe more clearly the manner in which the sign, which had always been implied or stated explicitly to mediate between object and interpretant in the definitions, could now be shown to function as a medium, and, by virtue of integrating the two objects and the three interpretants in his conception of the action of the sign, explicitly attributed to the sign itself this more precisely defined mediating role, as we see in the following extract from manuscript RL463, a draft letter to Lady Welby dated 9 March 1906:

> I use the word "*Sign*" in the widest sense for any medium for the communication or extension of a Form (or feature). Being medium, it is determined by something, called its Object, and determines something, called its Interpretant or Interpretand.[12] But some distinctions have to be borne in mind in order rightly to understand what is meant by the Object and by the Interpretant. In order that a Form may be extended or communicated, it is necessary that it should have been really embodied in a Subject independently of the communication; and it is necessary that there should be another subject in which the same form is embodied only as a consequence of the communication. The Form, (and the Form is the Object of the Sign), as it really determines the former Subject, is quite independent of the sign; yet we may and indeed must say that the object of a sign can be nothing but what the sign represents it to be. Therefore, in order to reconcile these apparently conflicting Truths, it is indispensible to distinguish the *immediate* object from the *dynamical* object.
>
> (SS: 196, 1906)

This important text calls for a number of remarks. First, this was not an isolated case of Peirce defining the sign as a medium: 'All my notions are too narrow. Instead of "Sign" ought I not to say *Medium*?' (R339 283r, H530, 1906) and this entry, too, in the Logic Notebook for 30 January 1906: 'A sign is a species of medium for communication' (R339: 271r, H515, 1906).[13] As noted by the editors of EP2, this was a prominent feature of Peirce's research into and on the sign in 1906.[14] This raises the problem of what we are now to understand by the term 'medium'. There are many possible interpretations. The one adopted in this study runs as follows. Conventionally, if we see a traffic light at a road junction, we take the whole instrument to be a sign – it signals the exact point at which the driver of a car must, by law, come to halt and take stock of the traffic situation before proceeding. If we see the photographic portrait of a relative from the pre-smartphone/selfie era, we take the complete photograph to be the sign. Similarly, we see the several occurrences of the English definite article on a printed page as instances of a general type of sign. However, with this new definition of the sign as being the medium for the communication of a form, the notion of sign takes on a more restricted sense. For example, the medium of the traffic lights is an assemblage of metal and glass in a specific shape and colour, the medium for the photograph is photographic paper coated with an emulsion, while the medium for the definite article is (or was ...) printers ink and paper. To give a more concrete example, the medium for a painting in the Louvre such as the *Mona Lisa* is a wood panel, oil and pigments; yet, the finished portrait is determined by the way the form communicated from the dynamic object is 'communicated' to this material medium via the immediate.

Now, a second point concerning the definition is that Peirce includes the two objects. This means that whatever form the signifying elements mentioned may have is a consequence of the influence of the immediate object which communicates form from the dynamic. And in the rest of this study, as in the *Mona Lisa* example, it is the combination of this form and the medium to which it has been communicated which constitutes the signifying element of the action of the sign.

What, in such a context, are we to understand by 'form'? Both the quotation from the 1906 draft and the extracts from R793 insist upon the fact that the sign is a medium for the communication of a 'Form'. Peirce offers an explanation for this in manuscript R793:

[That] which is communicated from the Object through the Sign to the Interpretant is a Form. It is not a singular thing; for if a Singular thing were first in the Object and afterward in the Interpretant outside the Object, it must thereby cease to be in the Object. The Form that is communicated does not necessarily cease to be in one thing when it comes to be in a different thing because its being is the being of a predicate. The Being of a Form consists in the truth of a conditional proposition. Under given circumstances something would be true. The Form is in the Object, entitavely as we may say, meaning that that conditional relation, or following of consequent upon reason, which constitutes the Form is literally true of the Object. In the Sign the Form may or may not be embodied entitavely, but it must be embodied representatively, that is, that is, in respect to the Form communicated, the Sign produces upon the interpretant an effect similar to that which the Object itself would under favorable circumstances.

(R793 4–5, 1906)

Now, if what is communicated from the object to the sign were an existent, 'singular', entity it would cease to be in the object once it found its way into the sign, and would cease to be in the sign as soon as it inhered in the interpretant. This is the basis of Peirce's (not entirely consistent) rejection of the term 'vehicle' as a correlate in a triadic relation.[15] In the 1905 text 'Issues of Pragmatism' (R283), for example, Peirce also introduces the definition of the sign as a medium of communication and justifies his reasons for not conceiving the sign as a vehicle at this time by suggesting that the transmission of a fever by a mosquito functioning as a vehicle is not a valid triadic relation since the 'entity of a zymotic disease' can't be in two places at the same time (EP2: 391, 1905).[16]

Continuing the discussion of form we see that it is necessarily a quality: that 'monadic element of the world' (CP: 1.426, *c*. 1896) and consequently the only category of being that can be simultaneously embodied in sign, object and interpretant: hence the importance of form in the analysis of the three types of icon discussed earlier.

In the abstract, the only forms that can be thus communicated are monads, dyads and triads, or combinations thereof. This is Peirce's earlier description of them 'the logical categories of the monad, the dyad, and the polyad or higher set ... are categories of the forms of experience', discussed in Chapter 1 (CP: 1.452, 1896). These are the basic forms structuring, for example, the predicates of Firstness, Secondness and Thirdness, the various subdivisions defined in all of his classificatory divisions and are, indeed, to be found throughout the logic. Media defined by the 1906 statement simply need to be perceivable and to accommodate such forms emanating, of course, from the dynamic – or what Peirce sometimes called the 'real' – object (e.g. CP: 2.310, 1903). Potential media, then, according to this view, are the artist's canvas and pigments, cinema-, computer – or TV-screens, glass neon hoardings outside department stores, metal panels and paints on roadsides, old-fashioned school blackboards and chalk, and even human skin. From now on, and in particular in the case of the analyses to be conducted in Chapter 6, the sign is considered as a medium to be informed by the immediate object.[17]

From this it follows that by defining the sign as a medium Peirce was beginning to attribute a far more explicit role in the action of the sign, too, to the object. The determining influence of the object now overtly involves the communication of 'form' via the immediate object to the sign conceived as a medium, which then communicates this form to the series of interpretants, and this independently of any utterer and interpreter as participants in the action of the sign.[18] Such a position, of course, raises the questions of what sort of entity the dynamic object is and what its semiotic scope may be, and how such a form may relate to the meaning of the sign. Consider another extract from manuscript R793, in which Peirce avoids human psychology in the logical nature of sign-action by identifying utterer and interpreter as quasi-minds, abstract theoretical constructs which suggest that the logic as conceived by Peirce at this time cannot yet accommodate intentionality, the intentionality of creation, for example:

> For the purposes of this inquiry a *Sign* may be defined as a Medium for the communication of a Form. It is not logically necessary that anything possessing consciousness, that is, feeling of the peculiar common quality of all our feeling should be concerned. But it is necessary that there should be two, if not three, *quasi-minds*, meaning things capable of varied determination as to forms of the kind communicated.
>
> (R793: 1–2, 1906)

He thus also introduced the concept of the quasi-mind in conjunction with the definition of the sign as a medium, enabling him to describe the general context of the communication of meaning from one mind to another in manuscript R283, a version of the 'Basis of Pragmaticism':

> At this point, some such question as the following may suggest itself: Is this new scientific concept of a Sign not to recognize the connection of every sign with two minds? The proper reply would first point out that two separate minds are not requisite for the operation of a sign. Thus the premisses of an argument are a sign

of the truth of the conclusion; yet it is essential to argument that the same mind that thinks the conclusion as such should also think the premises. Indeed, two minds in communication are, in so far, 'as one,' that is, are properly one mind in that part of them. That being understood, the answer to the question will go on to recognize that every sign, – or, at any rate, nearly every one, – is a determination of something of the general nature of a mind, which we may call the 'quasi-mind.'

(LI: 280, 1905–6)

Clearly, signs are the determination of the dynamic object, but for a logician like Peirce, just how that dynamic object initiates a process of determination requires explanation. Although in this same draft he cites ordinary conversation as a perfect example of communication, he eschews any form of appeal to any fallible psychological element in his theorizing, and adopts the far more abstract concept of two quasi-minds, between which, he says, the sign is the medium of communication (LI: 278–80). This introduction of a theoretical context for the exchange of representations by signs anticipates the later concept of semiosis.

The March 1906 draft letter is also remarkable for having presented a novel description of the three interpretants. After having introduced the dynamic (Peirce's term is 'dynamical', but for convenience the terminology has been standardized here, too) and immediate objects and the sign itself, Peirce goes on to complete the description of the process by describing the three interpretants as follows:

There is the *Intentional* Interpretant, which is a determination of the mind of the utterer; the *Effectual* Interpretant, which is a determination of the mind of the interpreter; and the *Communicational* Interpretant, or say the *Cominterpretant*, which is a determination of that mind into which the minds of utterer and interpreter have to be fused in order that any communication should take place. This mind may be called the commens. It consists of all that is, and must be, well understood between utterer and interpreter, at the outset, in order that the sign in question should fulfill its function.

(SS: 196–7, 1906)

The distinctions Peirce draws between the three interpretants are important in two ways. To begin with, actually identifying the interpretants is an important step. The intentional, effectual and communicational interpretants are surely identifiable as the three standardized later as, respectively, the immediate, dynamic and final interpretants. Peirce gives no indication that this is the case, although, as we see in a later section, the interpretant divisions in his hexadic or decadic typologies all follow the immediate, dynamic and final order. Moreover, there are other cases where he gives descriptions which either repeat the standard order or correspond to it, for example: 'A *Sign* has three Interpretants … The *Immediate Interpretant* … The *Dynamical Interpretant* … The *Final Interpretant*' (R339: 287r, H538, 1906) or 'We might call the three Interpretants The Impressional Interpretant the Factual Interpretant The Habitual Interpretant' (R339: 283r, H530, 1906), where 'Factual' obviously corresponds to 'Effectual', and 'Impressional' suggests 'Intentional'. This order is justified, too, from a strictly theoretical perspective, first by the definition Peirce gives of the term 'immediate' in the Logic Notebook: 'to say that A is immediate to B means that it is present in B' (R339: 243Av, H460, 1905). It would be difficult to place the interpretant defined as being 'present in' the sign in any other than first position in the interpretant order; second, referring back to Peirce's conception of mental separation, it is clearly possible to prescind the immediate from the dynamic, for example, but not the dynamic from the immediate, and so on; this suggests that the intentional interpretant, like the immediate, is in initial position in interpretant order. The question of the ordering of the interpretants is taken up again in Chapter 4.

Furthermore, the logical characterization of the intentional (i.e. immediate) interpretant as a determination of the mind of the utterer and the effectual (i.e. dynamic) interpretant as a determination of the mind of the interpreter is highly significant as it introduces, as I have argued elsewhere,[19] a semiotic 'differential'. Given the two distinct loci of this sort of determination, the 1906 draft explains how signs can produce an effect or reaction which diverges from the one intended: if the two agencies or theatres of consciousness involved in the communication have widely differing experiences of the world, then the non-deterministic basis of Peirce's semiotic theory explains those cases where the effectual interpretant is not congruent with the intentional, in other words, where the reaction to a sign is different from the one intended, where the interpreter reacts differently from the utterer's expectation.

The draft letter of March 1906 merits one further remark in that the definition of the sign it contains suggests a six-correlate 'system', by which is meant not only a definition of the sign but also that the order in which correlates are introduced (this applies in particular to the interpretants as described above) corresponds to an order of occurrence of the correlates in an actual case of sign action.

The ten-division typologies 1905–6: Combining facets and correlates

Although there is no explicitly stated link between the typologies that Peirce devised in the 1905–6 period and his work on pragmaticism, they are typical of the intense activity which characterized his thinking on signs in the period, and are an important stage in the development of his logic.[20] Consider Table 3.3, which shows seven of the complete typologies that he constructed in the Logic Notebook in the two years following the letter discussed in section '1904' above. It also contains a reconstruction of the typology implicit in the definition of the sign as medium from the March 1906 draft letter to Lady Welby (in italics in the table).[21]

The work on the classification of signs from this period is notable for a number of reasons. First, although there are only six complete divisions plus the italicized reconstructed one from Peirce's description in the draft letter, the Logic Notebook contains several other partial attempts at typologies that attest to his almost frenetic interest in new classifications. As these are incomplete, they haven't been added to the table.

Second, as is evident in Table 3.3, all seven typologies begin with the sign division followed, in 'correlate' order, by the object divisions and, finally, the divisions involving the interpretants. More precisely, they are always presented in the order: immediate, dynamic object, and in the case of the interpretants, immediate, dynamic and final (according to the terminology employed). This is the standard ordering of divisions

Table 3.3 Seven of Peirce's six- and ten-division typologies from the 1905–6 period

	Typology order	
	Divisions	
Date:		
07-07-1905	S, S-Oi, S-Od, A-Ii, A-Id, A-**Irational**, where A = sign's appeal to,	247r
08-10-1905	S, Oi, Od (equiv. S-Od), Ii, Id, **Isignificiant** (equiv. S-If)	252r
08-10-1905b	S, Oi, Od, S-Od, Ii, Id, S-Id, **Irepresentative** (=If), S-Irep, S-O-Irep	253r
13-10-1905	S, Oi, Odα, Odβ, Ii, Idα, Idβ, Ifα, Ifβ, Ify (If=**representative**)	262r
06-03-1906	S, Oi, Od, **Iintentional,** Ieffective, **Icommunicational**	EP2 278
31-03-1906	S, Oi, Od, S-Od, I**intended**, Id, S-Id, If, Pass(If), **normal**(If)	275r
31-08-1906	S, Oi, Od, S-Od, Iinit, Imid, S-Imid, purpose(**Ieventual**), infl(S on Iev), Ass(S to Iev)	285r

in all of Peirce's typologies. As we see in Chapters 4 and 5, any deviation from that order – that is, when the initial division is not occupied by the sign – concerns not a just a typology, but also some form of process.

Third, almost exactly a year after the 12 October 1904 letter to Lady Welby discussed earlier in which he described a six-division relational classification, Peirce had begun to construct ten-division typologies. These were capable of yielding sixty-six classes of signs, although this possibility, to the best of my knowledge, doesn't seem to have been explicitly pursued in the Logic Notebook in this period. What is interesting about such a development, though, is that in order to produce ten divisions, Peirce now introduces, in addition to the five relational 'facet' divisions he had already established in 1904, divisions based upon the five correlates he was associating with the sign, namely the two objects and the three interpretants. This development was crucial to the way the logic evolved over the following two years.

Finally, these classificatory projects offer an interesting insight into Peirce's evolving conceptions of the interpretants. We see from the table that what were later standardized as the immediate and the dynamic interpretants are relatively stable, although we find *intentional* and *intended* for the immediate in two typologies from March 1906. On the other hand, as a reflection, no doubt, of Peirce's claim that his conception of the final interpretant was not entirely clear, this interpretant – identified in bold in Table 3.3 – receives, as in later typologies, a variety of different designations: *rational, significant, representative* (x2), *communicational, normal, eventual* plus the *habitual* interpretant.

1907

The year 1907, in which Peirce was much preoccupied by his personal conception of pragmaticism, is important for many reasons: he introduced a new range of interpretants, he offered a different conception of the object of the sign, required collateral observation of the dynamic object in the interpretation of signs and, above all, defined (or redefined) semiosis, and thus paved the way in part for the theoretical innovations of 1908 to be discussed in the chapter to follow. Conveniently, these innovations are all to be found in one long manuscript, R318. The disparate sets of texts composing the manuscript are versions of a projected article canvassing Peirce's particular brand of pragmatism, an article which was never published (see the Editors' introduction, EP2: 398). Surprisingly, unlike his practice in the previous three years examined in detail above, the only classification system he offers in this important manuscript is through a sequence of verbal examples, for which he gives no terminological clues, in place of the more usual tabular arrangement with its six or ten carefully labelled typological divisions.

The series of variants of the projected paper is a continuation of the enormous output of published papers and unpublished manuscripts produced during the previous two years, and is testimony to the continuing influence of his symbolistic and his consequent preoccupation with the symbolic, conceptual elements of his theory of the sign: 'I understand pragmatism to be a method of ascertaining the meanings, not of all ideas, but only of such as I term "intellectual concepts," that is to say, of those upon the structure of which arguments concerning objective fact may hinge' (R318: 189). The variants are thus his unsuccessful attempt to have the public understand this new, logic-based version of pragmatism: 'The reader will please remember that proofs are forthcoming, on demand, of all the allegations I am about to make; but they are not suitable to this journal nor to this article, in which my only purpose is to explain in what pragmatism consists, not to prove it to be true' (R318: 251).

The manuscript being composed of several attempts at the same paper, there are discrepancies between versions and even apparent contradictions in Peirce's statements. The important points discussed below are best considered as examples of Peirce trying to work out a logical proof of his pragmaticism by describing it in detail, unlike the confident statement to be found in the Prolegomena text published the year before. With its frequently repeated definitions and many examples of signs in action, R318 offers an important range of theoretical decisions contributing to Peirce's evolving conception of signification and the sign. This immense manuscript is a document composed of nearly 700 sequences, parts of which are reproduced in CP: 5.465–96 and parts in EP2: 398–433. This is a delicate situation as it tends to highlight, as in the case of the CP selection, concepts which the editors thought were important but which never appear again after 1907, namely a much-commented series of interpretants and the important concept of semiosis. Nevertheless, the several variants in the manuscript show that Peirce now saw the nature of the association of what he must still have considered to be the three foundational constituents of semiosis or 'semeiosy or action of a sign', as he also called it (R318: 55), as being the dynamic action involving the 'coöperation' of three subjects, namely a sign, its object and its interpretant:

> It is important to understand what I mean by *semiosis*. All dynamical action, or action of brute force, physical or psychical, either takes place between two subjects [whether they react equally upon each other, or one is agent and the other patient, entirely or partially] or at any rate is a resultant of such actions between pairs. But by 'semiosis' I mean, on the contrary, an action, or influence, which is, or involves,

a coöperation of *three* subjects, such as a sign, its object, and its interpretant, this tri-relative influence not being in any way resolvable into actions between pairs.

(CP: 5.484, 1907)

Similarly, Peirce, no doubt aware of the immensity of the task before him, defines 'semiotic' in a novel manner, and announces the need for future research into the identification in logic of what he saw as all possible varieties not so much of classes of signs, but of varieties of possible semiosis, thereby establishing a necessary theoretical relation between class of *sign* and class of *semiosis*: 'I am, as far as I know, a pioneer, or rather a backwoodsman, in the work of clearing and opening up what I call *semiotic*, that is, the doctrine of the essential nature and fundamental varieties of possible semiosis; and I find the field too vast, the labor too great, for a first-comer' (R318: 119).

Such a move would have been impossible in 1903, since, as seen in Chapter 2, classes of signs were not directly linked to the action in which the sign was engaged or to the definition of the sign: the only correlate so linked was, necessarily, the sign itself, since at this time it was both the determination of the object and the determinant of the interpretant, whereas the classes of signs involved neither of the other two correlates but, rather, relations between them and the sign. This statement is important, then, in two ways: first, it establishes that there is not one form of semiosis, but many different types. Second, it implies that to each distinct type of semiosis there corresponds a distinct class of signs; conversely, each distinct class of signs is necessarily the determination of a distinct type of semiosis.

With this in mind, consider, now, this example – one of many involving this particular military command – which takes the reader through what is, in essence, a case of semiosis:

Suppose, for example, an officer of a squad or company of infantry gives the word of command, 'Ground arms!' This order is, of course, a sign. That thing which causes a sign as such is called the object (according to the usage of speech, the 'real,' but more accurately, the *existent* object) represented by the sign: the sign is determined to some species of correspondence with that object. In the present case, the object the command represents is the will of the officer that the butts of the muskets be brought down to the ground. ... For the proper outcome of a sign, I propose the name, the *interpretant* of the sign.

(R318: 51–5)

In the ten-class system of 1903 the dynamic object was, typically, the determinant of a photograph, namely the entity reflecting light back onto the film in the camera; as seen in the discussion of informational signs, this was an object in no theoretically defined way related to human intention or volition: 'A better example [of a dicent, i.e. informational, index] is a photograph. The mere print does not, in itself, convey any information. But the fact, that it is virtually a section of rays projected from an object otherwise known, renders it a Dicisign' (EP2: 282, 1903). In the description of the military command, however, the object represented is explicitly identified as the 'will of the officer'. See too, this remark: 'The attitude of the officer and all the surrounding circumstances shows that the utterance is the expression of his present will. That present volition is the object represented' (R318: 255). This implies that intention and volition – sources of motivation unavailable in the 1903 system, in spite of their being implied by the definition of the sign at the time – are now seen as potential determinants of signs and, consequently, as the origins of semiosis. In this context the following extract from manuscript R299, 'Phaneroscopy: Or, the natural history of concepts', 1906, offers insights into what we are to understand by the officer's 'will':

> Experience is that state of cognition which the course of life, by some part there of, has forced upon the recognition of the experient, or person who undergoes the experience, under conditions due usually, in part, at least, to his own action; and the Immediate object of the cognition of Experience is understood to be what I call its 'Dynamical', that is, its real object ... By a 'cognitive' state, as opposed to a state markedly involving only elements of feeling and volition, I mean a state which, as it is in itself, and not as it may be represented reflectively, is a sign of an object for an interpretant state, which last may involve feeling, volition, or cognition, alone or in combination with either of the other of these elements of mental life.
>
> (LI: 344–5, 1906)

Now, strictly speaking, within Peirce's definition of experience, the officer's volition is the second, 'dual', member of the feeling-volition-cognition triad of experience, but since the vocal command is a specific instance or occurrence of a general type, and since it is uttered in a context seeking to inculcate uncontested habitual behaviour, we can consider it to be on a par with cognition and to be the vector of intentionality. However, this is a different conception of the dynamic object – here referred significantly to as 'the "real," but more accurately, the existent object' – to be found elsewhere in the manuscript. It was in this text that Peirce began to insist upon the need for collateral *observation* of the object in the interpretation of the sign:

> The Object of a sign, then, is necessarily unexpressed in the sign, taken by itself. Indeed, we shall soon see that whatever is so expressed comes under quite a different category. But the above examples show that that idea which though essential to the functioning of a sign can only be attained by collateral observation is the idea of a strictly individual thing, or individual collection or series, or an individual event, or an individual *ens rationis*.
>
> (R318: 623)

The requirement of collateral observation of the dynamic object seems to have been first introduced in a late variant of the paper (see, too, sheets 601, 611, 613), but see this earlier statement:

> In order that a thing may be a true sign its proper significate mental effect must be *conveyed* from another object which the sign is concerned with indicating and which is by this conveyance the ultimate cause of the mental effect. In order to be the cause of an effect, —or *efficient cause*, as the old phrase was, —it must

either be an existent thing or an actual event. Now such things are only known by observation. It cannot be itself any part of the mental effect, and therefore can only be known by collateral observation of the context or circumstances of utterance, or putting forth, of the sign.

(R318: 247–9, 1907)

On the other hand, 'collateral experience' (EP2: 480, 493, 495 and 498, 1908) and 'collateral acquaintance' (EP2: 496, 1908) figure in later definitions of the sign, and reflect a less restricted, more 'processual' conception of the object. Recourse to an observation-based collateral experience in order to identify the dynamic object suggests that Peirce is hesitating between conceiving the object of the sign as an existent visible dynamic object such as the model determining the photograph and the realization that the object of the sign can also, as in the case of the officer's command, be the locus of volition, agency, intentionality and purpose as the determinants of signification. This hypothesis is borne out by the following long extract from an earlier variant, one of several passages in which Peirce associates the two objects with the new series of interpretants that he introduces to explain pragmaticism's necessary restriction to the meaning of concepts:

> But all logicians have distinguished two objects of a sign; the one, the Immediate object or object as the sign represents it, (and without this sign would not be a sign); the other Real object, or object as it is independent of any particular idea representing it. Of course, many signs have no real objects. We turn to the interpretant, to see whether there is any corresponding distinction; and we find that in place of two, there are three different interpretants. First, there is the 'emotional interpretant', which consists in a feeling, or rather in the quality of a feeling. It is sometimes formed into an image, yet is more usually merely a feeling which causes the interpreter of the sign to believe he recognizes of [sic] the import and intention of the sign. A concerted piece of music, for example, brings a succession of musical emotions answering to those of the composer. This is an extreme case; usually the emotional interpretant consists merely in a sense, more or less complex, perhaps amounting to an image, perhaps not, of the meaning of the sign. All signs whatsoever must, in order to fulfil their functions as signs, first of all produce such emotional interpretants. Next, many signs bring about actual events. The infantry officer's word of command 'Ground arms!' produces as its existential interpretant, (the sign having been first apprehended in an 'emotional interpretant',) the slamming down of the musket-butts. The less thought intervenes between the apprehension and this act, the better the sign fulfills its function. All signs that are not to evaporate in mere feelings must have such an existential interpretant, or as I might perhaps better have called it, such an energetic interpretant. These two interpretants correspond to the two objects of a sign. The emotional interpretant, immediately produced by the sign, corresponds to the immediate object. The existential, or energetic, interpretant, corresponds to the real object whose action is obscurely and indirectly the active cause of the sign. But now there is a third interpretant, to which no object of the sign corresponds.

It is what we commonly call the *meaning* of the sign; but I call it the logical interpretant, or logical meaning of the sign.

(R318: 373–9)

Here Peirce first defines the two objects, designated as 'immediate' and 'real'. He then turns to the interpretants, identifying them in ordinal position as the emotional, the existential or energetic and, finally, the logical. In the course of this description, he establishes correspondences between the emotional interpretant and the immediate object, and between the energetic interpretant and the real object. This in itself is surprising as it suggests that a piece of concerted music – or an air played on a guitar, another example Peirce gives – has no real object, only an immediate one, and can only produce or generate an immediate interpretant in the form of a feeling, whence, in 1907, the term 'emotional' interpretant. Similarly, commands such as the well-known 'Ground arms!' example are determined by a 'real' object and determine both an emotional and an energetic interpretant, in this case the slamming-down of the musket butts.

At this point, as was noted earlier in the chapter, he introduces the even more surprising notion that there is a third interpretant 'to which no object of the sign corresponds': concepts, at this stage of the logic, have neither dynamic nor immediate objects but as complex general signs they determine all three interpretants. This is surely evidence that Peirce was still feeling his way through the problem of the interpretant sequence that he had introduced at least three years earlier, and that his thoughts on the problem were far from complete: he realized that a concept couldn't have an existent object but, rather, a class, and he presumably began to think in terms of necessitant objects. In the case of the logical interpretant his explanation is as follows: 'Of what kind are signs which determine "logical interpretants"? They are exclusively such as embody and convey thought proper, whether in the form of the concept, or in that of the meaning of a proposition, or in that of the force of a reason, or argument' (R318 385–7). At this time, then, Peirce was restricting the third interpretant, whether we call it signified, representative or logical, to determination by thought, a type of sign which determined the 'intellectual' logical interpretant. The resultant hierarchical relations between object, sign and interpretant as conceived by Peirce in at least one variant of the intended article are set out according to Table 3.4, in which signs are indicated in italics, concepts are shown to have no object at all and the term 'sonata' stands for concerted music.

The relations Peirce establishes between the two objects, the existential and the immediate, and the energetic and emotional interpretants – these two interpretants correspond to the two objects of a sign – are interesting as they seem to anticipate later developments in the way Peirce classified signs. Hitherto, subdivisions of signs were determined by the categories of phenomenology/phaneroscopy, but Peirce's insistence on referring to an existential object that has to be identified by observation makes such an existential entity a concrete source of causation when he later describes the process of semiosis as being initiated by such an object.

What, too, if the explanation is to be accepted, do we make of references to 'first' and 'second logical interpretants' and the 'ultimate' logical interpretant? This was, after

Table 3.4 Signs distributed according to object and interpretant type in R318: 373–9

Objects		Interpretants		
Real	Immediate	Emotional	Energetic	Logical
—	—	*concept*	*concept*	*concept*
command	*command*	*command*	*command*	
	sonata	*sonata*		

all, an attempt to expound his version of pragmatism: 'Moreover, since pragmatism, in my view, relates to intellectual concepts exclusively, and since these are all general, the mental element we seek must be general. The principal general constituents of the mind are desires and habits' (R318: 409). The only possible conclusion to any sequence of interpretants of the logical type is a habit or change in existing habits, and this is the role Peirce attributed at this time to what he conceived as the ultimate logical interpretant:

> Shall we say that this effect may be a thought, that is to say, a mental sign? No doubt, it may be so; only, if this sign be of an intellectual kind – as it would have to be – it must itself have a logical interpretant; so that it cannot be the ultimate logical interpretant of the concept. It can be proved that the only mental effect that can be so produced and that is not a sign but is of a general application is a habit-change; meaning by a habit-change a modification of a person's tendencies toward action, resulting from previous experiences or from previous exertions of his will or acts, or from a complexus of both kinds of cause.
>
> (R318: 67–9)

This curious series of interpretants – the logical/intellectual, the energetic/existential and the emotional – became the source of much debate in later commentaries. The logical in particular was not only the object of much discussion, but became a basic theoretical concept in many semiotic and philosophical studies. However, the concept has rarely been taken to its extreme, for authors, if they have relied on the published extracts, have necessarily been unable to engage with the full list: there is not one logical interpretant, but at least four different types.[22] These are scattered through the manuscript: first logical interpretants, that is, conjectures, hypotheses (R318: 91, 513), second logical interpretants (R318: 507) and third logical interpretants (R318: 509), and an ultimate logical interpretant that has fared better than the other three. It seems that such a proliferation of logical interpretants has either presented authors with intractable theoretical difficulties or, more perversely, that the authors themselves may have restricted their research to the passages from the manuscript to be found in the *Collected Papers* and *Essential Peirce* volume two, neither of which mentions the series.

For such studies to have authority any discussion of concepts from this manuscript surely requires it to be read in full.

The emotional, energetic/existential and logical interpretants *as a group* also became a thorny theoretical issue, being thought by some to correspond to subdivisions of the dynamic interpretant, or for others a supplementary series that somehow runs parallel to the later standard immediate, dynamic and final series established during the following years. The fact is, it is unlikely that there would be three subdivisions of the dynamic or final interpretant as has been suggested. In his classifying quest, Peirce was principally interested in, and consequently only subdivided, the sign; and in this transitional period at least, he still subdivided the sign according to its phenomenological value. For example, a sign can be classified as a sinsign if, in itself, its phenomenological value is Secondness, or as a symbol if the relation between the sign and the object is a general convention, that is, has to be learned and thus partakes of Thirdness. But nowhere in the Peirce canon, again to the best of my knowledge, are the interpretants subdivided and named in the way in which a sign is in a classification; nor is there any reason for them to be. This was not, however, Peirce's final word on the interpretants, and as suggested earlier, these concepts are not to be found elsewhere either in an earlier or later text. They were simply the temporary consequences of his attempt to work out and describe his pragmaticism by means of a theory of the sign, and they belong, with the others from previous taxonomies, to this transitional period between 1903 and 1908.

Summary and discussion

The major points developed in the transitional stage in Peirce's developing conception of the sign hypothesized in the chapter were, to begin with, the introduction of a hexad of correlates in 1904, which enabled Peirce to posit a more complex typology than in 1903. This new typology was composed of the sign plus five relational trichotomies. Reasons for such an expansion will be suggested in Chapter 6, when other stages in Peirce's evolving conception of the sign will be examined. A further development in 1904 was the redefinition of phenomenology as phaneroscopy in the classification of signs. The system of iconic subclasses was redefined in 1905, characterized by the disappearance of metaphor and by the diagram now being identified as the most complex of the three, no doubt for consistency with Peirce's development of the Graphs as expounded in the Prolegomena text of 1906.

Another important feature of the transitional period was the definition of the sign as a medium for the communication to the interpretants of a form originating in the dynamic object. Significantly, this new definition of the sign was accompanied by three further developments: the redefinition of the diagram as an icon being 'made for the purpose' mentioned above, the introduction of the concept the quasi-mind, and the identification of the source of the immediate and dynamic interpretants as being respectively the determination of the utterer and the determination of the interpreter. The introduction of the quasi-minds is significant as these supply an abstract context, but not for representation as defined in 1903, as a context for relationally derived representation would be illogical. Rather, they provide a context for process: a source and a receiver of a communication. Peirce's thinking on signs – his logic, therefore – was developing into a logic of process, with the explicit notion that all sign activity, language to the fore, is dialogic in nature. This culminates in 1907 with the definition of semiosis.

Finally, one has the impression that throughout this transitional period, while not becoming more materialistic, Peirce's pragmaticism was now growing closer to the 'things of life' – τα πράγματα της ζωής – even as he enquired endlessly into the caprices of meaning. For example, as we see in the next chapter, in 1908 existence was to replace Secondness in the criteria employed in the investigation of signification.

4

The System of 1908

When considering the late systems the reader should bear in mind two things. First, the meaning of the general title of the book: *Developing a Neo-Peircean Approach to Signs*. Since it is in this chapter that the neo-Peircean approach is stated most clearly, it is the most important chapter in the book. Second, by 'system' or 'sign-system' is understood a definition of the sign *and* such typologies as the definition yields. This chapter deals principally with a conception of the sign which now contextualizes it with respect to the process in which it is assigned a particular status, and to a lesser extent with the typologies this new conception yields.

As its title states, the chapter deals almost exclusively with the period between 1908 and 1909, in other words with the period principally involving a letter and drafts to Lady Welby late in 1908 and 1909 and letters and drafts to William James in 1909. Why, the reader is probably wondering, stop at 1909 and not later, since Peirce was still writing about signs in 1913? Although Peirce makes further remarks on phaneroscopy (R611, 1908; R645, 1909–10), logic (R645, 1909–10), on the existential graphs (SS: 94–108, 1909; R669, 1911) and sporadic references to the icon-index-symbol trichotomy in the period after 1909 (e.g. CP: 2.230–2.232, 1910; R675, 1911), he doesn't propose a completely new system with definitions and typologies that might contribute to the approach to signs being developed in this book. It is indeed symptomatic of the state of our knowledge of Peirce's thinking on signs in this period that Bellucci's recent timely and otherwise comprehensive selection of Peirce's semiotics writings until 1912 (Bellucci 2020), is singularly lacking in evidence of such a new system in the period after 1907: there is no reference to the process of semiosis as the action of the sign, for example, in Bellucci's selection of texts from the period after 1908. There are no new typologies other than two drafts from 1908 (2020: 316–17), no new descriptions of the interpretants, although the sign and the object are reviewed in certain manuscripts, as is the discipline of logic.

There are several reasons for such a situation. There is no manuscript evidence of Peirce developing new directions in his approach to signs, but, rather, fresh unfulfilled attempts to produce a comprehensive book on logic (EP2: 500–2, 1909; R675, 1911). Consequently, what we know of the late systems comes essentially from a restricted set of correspondence and drafts. In short, Peirce seems not to have attempted to develop the ideas he had expressed in the letter to Lady Welby dated 23 December 1908, opting instead to try to consolidate, or remind his reader of, previous theoretical positions. As he was too old, too fragile and too poor to complete such a project, there is no Syllabus-like general text to exploit, only a set of letters and drafts composed in 1908 and the James correspondence of 1909, in which, moreover, the terminology raises problems of interpretation. It follows from this that the chapter will, like any other attempt to chart and interpret the stages in the emergence of the systems in the years 1908–9, involve much of what might rather pointedly be considered as Peircean abduction …

The period covered by the chapter might easily be subtitled as the period of controversial topics: problematic, debateable issues stemming essentially from the paucity and fragmentary nature of the information available, and to a lesser extent, from the deleterious effect of the very mixed critical reception of these sparsely documented late systems already discussed in Chapter 1. One such issue is the critical confusion as to whether Peirce is using phaneroscopy or some other quite different theoretical background to his descriptions of the sign, its correlates and its associated typologies. Yet another concerns the scope and theoretical status of the typology described in the letter to Lady Welby of 23 December 1908, the typology in which it will be contended in the following paragraphs that the process of semiosis is described. Finally, in addition to providing scholars with a thorny theoretical problem, the constituents of the typology and above all, the order of the interpretants composing it has brought its share of critical discussion, debate and disagreement.

Resolving these 'controversies' should not be considered as yet another form of, or attempt at, exegesis: any attempt to resolve them is, on the contrary, crucial to the understanding of the central topic of this chapter, namely semiosis, and to our understanding of what semiosis is in what is posited here as its Peircean guise, and of how it functions. The topics are ordered as they occur in the letter to Lady Welby. Bearing in mind that what I and others have to say on such issues necessarily reduces to matters of opinion, it is nevertheless to be hoped that such a thematically organized 'controversy approach', which is inescapably polemical at times, will give the reader a clear idea of what is at stake theoretically. As the central sections of the chapter seek to refute what may be considered the standard interpretation of certain contents of the letter, one which is totally at odds with the conception of semiosis advanced in this study, the reader is advised that the discussion will perforce involve examination of the letter in considerable detail. One aspect of Peirce's late work in logic that I won't be dealing with in detail is his pursuit of new classes of signs in his numerous ten-division classifications (six at least in 1908 alone!). There is much interesting work that has been undertaken by Peirce scholars interested in resolving ordering problems that seem to have been left unfinished by Peirce. But deriving sixty-six different classes of signs is not a priority in this study.

Category or universe: From categorial to modal subdivisions

After a discussion of various topics including truth, faith, belief, the origin of the term 'corollary' and others, Peirce turns to Lady Welby's concept of significs, which he sees as possibly equivalent to his own enquiries into the relations holding between signs and their interpretants – it would thus investigate rhemes, dicents and arguments

(SS: 80). In this case, he suggests, to be conducted in a truly scientific fashion it would require the extension of the investigation to include 'other questions of semeiotic'. This is the cue for him to begin the description of the theory of signs that he held at that particular time, and it begins with the well-known 'sop to Cerberus' statement, but more importantly, announces the theoretical background to this latest definition of the sign, namely three universes:

> I define a Sign as anything which is so determined by something else, called its Object, and so determines an effect upon a person, which effect I call its Interpretant, that the latter is thereby mediately determined by the former. My insertion of 'upon a person' is a sop to Cerberus, because I despair of making my own broader conception understood. I recognize three Universes, which are distinguished by three Modalities of Being.
>
> (SS: 80–1, 1908)[1]

At which point Hardwick, the editor, adds the footnote: 'See Peirce's statement on the cenopythagorean categories in the letter dated 12 October 1904', the reference to the categories in a statement explicitly citing universes being characteristic of much commentary of the contents of the letter, an initial debateable topic to which we return below.[2]

Thus, true to his principle of supplying the background theoretical framework to his classifications, as was the case with phenomenology in the Syllabus (EP2: 267–72) and the letter to Lady Welby of 12 October 1904 (SS: 23–32), Peirce prefaces his description of his new classifications and his analysis of the nature of the sign with an introduction to the highly innovative theoretical background that underwrites them, here a system of three universes. This is how Peirce goes on to describe them to Lady Welby:

> One of these Universes embraces whatever has its Being in itself alone, except that whatever is in this Universe must be present to one consciousness, or be capable of being so present in its entire Being. It follows that a member of this universe need not be subject to any law, not even to the principle of contradiction. I denominate the objects of this Universe *Ideas*, or *Possibles*, although the latter designation does not imply capability of actualization. On the contrary as a general rule, if not a universal one, an Idea is incapable of perfect actualization on account of its essential vagueness if for no other reason. For that which is not subject to the principle of contradiction is essentially vague. For example, geometrical figures belong to this Universe.
>
> (SS: 81)

There are two related points to be mentioned with respect to this definition. First, such universes contain 'objects', here in the more general sense of entities as opposed to the technical sense of object of a sign, though all three universes can contain these, too. Second, as if to emphasize the point, Peirce affirms that geometrical figures 'belong' in the Universe of possibles. The terminology is clear: like that of class membership, universes are receptacles for possible entities. I repeat what Peirce said of the distinction he established between categories and universes in the *Monist* 'Prolegomena' text:

> Oh, I overhear what you are saying, O Reader: that a Universe and a Category are not at all the same thing; a Universe being a receptacle or class of Subjects, and a Category being a mode of Predication, or class of Predicates. I never said they were the same thing; but whether you describe the two correctly is a question for careful study.
>
> (CP: 4.545, 1906)

And here:

> Let us begin with the question of Universes. It is rather a question of an advisable point of view than of the truth of a doctrine. A logical universe is, no doubt, a collection of *logical subjects*, but not necessarily of metaphysical Subjects, or 'substances'; for it may be composed of characters, of elementary facts, etc.
>
> (CP: 4.546, 1906)[3]

In the letter to Lady Welby he goes on to describe the two remaining universes in the same vein, with reference again to a membership relation:

> Another Universe is that of, 1st, Objects whose Being consists in their Brute reactions, and of, 2nd, the Facts (reactions, events, qualities etc.) concerning those Objects, all of which facts, in the last analysis, consist in their reactions. I call the Objects, Things, or more unambiguously, Existents, and the facts about them I call Facts. Every member of this Universe is either a Single Object subject alike to the Principles of Contradiction and to that of Excluded Middle, or it is expressible by a proposition having such a singular subject.
>
> The third Universe consists of the co-being of whatever is in its Nature necessitant, that is, is a Habit, a law, or something expressible in a universal proposition. Especially, continua are of this nature. I call objects of this universe Necessitants. It includes whatever we can know by logically valid reasoning.
>
> (SS: 81–2)

Furthermore, in a draft dated 25 December 1908 Peirce discusses the ordering of three trichotomies in a new typology, and here too, he attributes a universe membership relation to the sign and the immediate object:

> The inquiry ought, one would expect, to be an easy one, since both trichotomies depend on there being three Modes of Presence to the mind, which we may term The Immediate, – The Direct, – The Familiar Mode of Presence.
>
> The difference between the two trichotomies is that the one refers to the Presence to the Mind of the Sign and the other to that of the Immediate Object. The Sign may have any Modality of Being, i.e., *may belong to any one of the three Universes*; its Immediate Object must be in some sense, in which the Sign need not be, Internal.

To begin, then, it is evident that an Actisign, or *one that belongs to the Universe of Experience,* which Brutely acts on the person, can also be a Denominative, that is, that its Immediate Object is represented as belonging to the same Universe; so that 12·22, the central class of our block of nine, is possible. Indeed, a pointing finger is a familiar example of a Sign of that class.

(CP: 8.354–8.355, 1908, emphasis added)

We note, too, that in an earlier text from this same year he offers a more precise description of what, for the examples examined later in this study, is the most important universe, namely the universe of necessitant entities, and describes what he refers to as three 'universes of experience' that can host logical entities, namely, possible, existent and necessitant entities.[4] In this text, 'The Neglected Argument for the Reality of God' (EP2: 434–50, 1908), Peirce offers the following brief but thought-provoking inventory of the sorts of entities that are members of the universe of necessitants:

The third Universe comprises everything whose Being consists in active power to establish connections between different objects, especially between objects in different Universes. Such is everything which is essentially a Sign, – not the mere body of the sign, which is not essentially such, but, so to speak, the Sign's Soul, which has its Being in its power of serving as intermediary between its Object and a Mind. Such, too, is a living consciousness, and such the life, the power of growth of a plant. Such is a living institution, – a daily newspaper, a great fortune, a social 'movement.'

(EP2: 435, 1907)

Thus, what must be borne in mind when discussing Peirce's theory of the sign in 1908 is that the universes he employs in the definition and classifications to which we turn below are *logical* concepts. Phaneroscopy, which Peirce was still working on concurrently with the classification of signs in 1908–9, is independent of logic, for, as we saw in Chapter 1, phenomenology precedes and 'feeds' logic in the classification of the sciences. Now, if he was maintaining this classification of the sciences – and we have no reason to suppose that he wasn't – logic would still be dependent upon phaneroscopy. There is, therefore, potentially, a traceable derivation of the three universes from the categories, but the derivation is indirect – phaneroscopy may determine the triadic distribution of the three universes, but a category itself is not a receptacle, it has no materiality and it has no 'members' that can trigger the action of the sign physically or otherwise. That these universes should have been derived from the categories, there is no doubt; but they are not the same and they are employed in a very different manner in very different semiotic contexts. On first encountering these universes, the temptation is to see them, as certain commentators have, as varieties of universes of discourse, and as therefore being of an essentially logical nature. However, as Peirce maintains in footnote 12 of the 1906 'Prolegomena', these 1908 universes have little to do with the more familiar universes of discourse:[5]

I use the term Universe in a sense which excludes many of the so called 'universes of discourse' of which Boole, De Morgan, and many subsequent logicians speak, but which, being perfectly definable, would in the present system be denoted by the aid of a graph.

(LI: 320n, 1906)

A universe of discourse would logically only pertain to propositions, it cannot concern the earlier non-discursive icons and indices (a characteristic reminiscent of the scope of pragmatism being limited to concepts), which Peirce includes in the four further subdivisions added to the six-division typology described in the letter and to be discussed below.

Worse, in the discussion of these universes, is that a depressing number of specialists continue to promote the idea that the universes are just another name for the phaneroscopic categories, which is poor, very un-Peircean theorizing. As we saw in Chapter 1, his late semiotics has generated incomprehension and dismay among such specialists, so when these scholars read of universes, we have to imagine that they think that Peirce was simply mistaken or was employing imprecise terminology. It seems to me that the only way forward is to try to understand what new approach Peirce was testing with these new concepts; to accept that his theory of signs and the way they function was evolutionary, in continuous development; and to adopt his characteristically carefully chosen terminology, if only for the simple reason that there might in fact be an important distinction being made even if we can't immediately see it. Replacing Peirce's choice of words by a terminology with which one is more familiar, as many commentators prefer to do, seems very lazy thinking, and a rejection of his ethics of terminology, in which he advises researchers to make up a new term for a new concept, as here, where 'universe' clearly constitutes a new, innovative concept.

Semiosis and the 23 December 1908 typology[6]

After having introduced the three universes as the theoretical background, Peirce presents and illustrates the first three of the six divisions in this particular twenty-eight-class typology, with a brief arrangement of the interpretant divisions to follow the description of the typology. We understand this to be the beginnings of the presentation of a new typology at this point in the letter, as, characteristically, all Peirce's typologies begin with the sign division, followed by those pertaining to the object and, finally, those pertaining to the interpretants. This is his presentation of the three divisions, beginning as per usual with the sign and its denominations:

> A Sign may *itself* have a 'possible' Mode of Being hexagon inscribed in or circumscribed about a conic ... Its Mode of Being may be Actuality: as with any barometer. Or Necessitant: as the word 'the' or in any other in the dictionary. For a 'possible' Sign I have no better designation than a *Tone*, though I am considering replacing this by 'Mark' ... An Actual sign I call a *Token*; a Necessitant Sign a *Type*.[7]

Peirce then continues to present Lady Welby with the divisions concerning the two objects:

It is usual and proper to distinguish two Objects of a Sign, the Mediate without, and the Immediate within the Sign. Its Interpretant is all that the sign conveys: acquaintance with its Object must be gained by collateral experience. The Immediate Object is the Object outside of the sign; I call it the Dynamoid Object. The sign must indicate it by a hint; and this hint, or its substance, is the Immediate Object. Each of these two Objects may be said to be capable of either of the three Modalities, though in the case of the Immediate Object, this is not quite literally true. Accordingly, the Dynamoid Object maybe a Possible; when I term the Sign an *Abstractive*; such as the word 'beauty'; and it will be none the less an Abstractive if I speak of 'the beautiful' since it is the ultimate reference and not the grammatical form, that makes the sign An [*sic*] Abstractive. When the Dynamoid Object is an occurrence (Existent thing or Actual fact of past or future), I term the sign a *Concretive*; any one barometer is an example; and so is a written narrative of any series of events. For a *Sign* whose Dynamoid Object is a necessity I have at the present no better designation than a '*Collective*,' which is not quite so bad a name as it sounds to be until one studies the matter. If the Immediate Object is a 'Possible,' that is, if the Dynamoid Object is indicated (always more or less vaguely) by means of its qualities, etc., I call the Sign a *Descriptive*; if the Immediate [Object] is an Occurrence I call the sign a *Designative*; and if the Immediate Object is a Necessitant I call the Sign a *Copulant*; for in that case the Object has to be so identified by the Interpreter that the Sign may represent a necessitation.

(SS: 83–4)

This passage calls for a number of remarks. He first reiterates the distinction between the two objects, defining the mediate, that is, dynamic (often 'dynamical' in Peirce's notes, but here 'dynamoid' and elsewhere 'real') object as the object 'outside' the sign, the object which determines the sign to representation in the first place, but reaffirming the principle announced in the 1907 Pragmatism 'Prag' manuscript (R318: 613, 623, for instance, including collateral observation of the *utterer*, 318: 611), whereby the dynamic object requires, to be identified, the interpreter's collateral experience of it independently of its representation by the sign (remember that Peirce also writes of 'collateral acquaintance with', and 'collateral observation of' the object). It is the function of the immediate object, here described as the object within the sign, to represent the dynamic as a hint or its substance, this hint thus being the immediate object. For completeness, note a later definition which repeats the indicating function of the immediate object:

We must distinguish between the Immediate Object, – i.e. the Object as represented in the sign, – and the Real (no, because perhaps the Object is altogether fictive, I must choose a different term, therefore), say rather the Dynamical Object, which, from the nature of things, the Sign *cannot* express, which it can only *indicate* and leave the interpreter to find out by *collateral* experience.

(CP: 8.314, 1909)

The extract calls for a further remark. In the passage, Peirce uses the example of the common noun 'beauty' as an example of an abstractive sign, namely a sign which represents its 'possible' object by virtue of its qualities. This suggests that Peirce was considering this presentation of the sign and its two objects as forming the first three trichotomies of a *typology*, as all his typologies begin, as in the letter and as mentioned above, with the sign division. This presents us with a problem, for if, as the passage suggests, the sign 'beauty', which as a linguistic unit is necessarily an instance of a type (an occurrence of a necessitant entity, therefore), determines a *possible* dynamical object, then any following interpretants would necessarily be possibles, too, namely effects or reactions of the nature of qualities, beginning with what Peirce later calls the sign's interpretability, which is its immediate interpretant.[8] In this case, the noun's only possible interpretation would be the quality of a feeling, whereas we know that as a type it must have a conventional 'dictionary' meaning without which it wouldn't function as a linguistic unit. The problem is dealt with in greater detail in Jappy (2016: 93–7).[9]

In the following section of the letter he expand the triadic 'cooperation' of semiosis holding between three subjects such as sign, object and interpretant as defined in 1907, into one involving the sign and its five correlates in the following formulation, which is advanced here as both a new classification and an expression of the dynamism in semiosis, but, unfortunately for posterity, also appears to be the only mention of such an object-initiated twenty-eight-class, six-division typology in the Peirce canon. This formulation, too, has attracted its debateable issues, which we deal with below. In stark contrast to the presentation of sign and objects in 'classification' order, this hexadic 'system' begins with the dynamic object in an order which can be seen to correspond, in an expanded state, to the numerous general definitions of the sign:

> It is evident that a possible can determine nothing but a Possible, it is equally
> so that a Necessitant can be determined by nothing but a Necessitant. Hence it
> follows from the Definition of a Sign that since the Dynamoid Object determines
> the Immediate Object,
> which determines the Sign itself,
> which determines the Destinate Interpretant,
> which determines the Effective Interpretant,
> which determines the Explicit Interpretant,
> the six trichotomies, instead of determining 729 classes of signs, as they would if
> they were independent, only yield twenty-eight classes; and if, as I strongly opine
> (not to say almost prove) there are four other trichotomies of signs of the same order
> of importance, instead of making 59049 classes, these will only come to sixty-six.
> (SS: 84, 1908)

What makes this statement problematic is, first, the nature of the formulation – is it simply a typology or does it also represent some sort of progression regulated by the signification of the term 'determine'? If so, can we reconcile determination with semiosis? Second, what is the order of the three interpretants given here, as Peirce introduces not only a new kind of typology but very frustratingly describes it by engaging a terminology – 'Destinate' and 'Explicit' – not to be found anywhere else in his classifications? If he had employed the standard terms 'immediate', 'dynamic' and 'final' there would be no issue or debate.

The universe hierarchy principle

The determination sequence begins with what we might call the universe hierarchy principle. Being composed of qualities, the elements belonging to the universe of possibles, for example, can only 'determine', in a sense to be defined below, elements from the same universe. Similarly, elements from the universe of existents can only determine – be associated, combined with, to put it simply at this stage – with elements from their own universe or with those of the less complex universe of possibles. Necessitant elements can be combined with elements from all three universes. This terse but elegant formula thus regulates the various combinations of the three universes, yielding not 729 potential classes of signs but the twenty-eight mentioned by Peirce. Having announced this principle, Peirce proceeds to set out the six divisions that will yield the desired classification.

Interpretant order

For convenience we replace the terminology proposed by Peirce by what is the standard usage: immediate, dynamic and final interpretants. This gives us two possible options for the identification of the interpretants named in the formula, of which only the interpretant sequence is repeated as follows: 'the Sign itself which determines the Destinate interpretant, which determines the Effective interpretant, which determines the Explicit interpretant'. As 'effective' had already been used in 1906 to identify the dynamic interpretant, the problem, then, is the identification of the immediate and final interpretants. There are thus two possibilities, (A) and (B) below, on which the correlates Od, Oi, S, Ii, Id and If represent respectively the dynamic object, the immediate object, the sign, the immediate interpretant, the dynamic interpretant and the final interpretant. One order, (A), the 'Savan' order, is where the immediate interpretant (Ii) is last in the sequence, and the other, (B), advanced here as the order of semiosis, where the final intepretant (If) is indeed final in the interpretant sequence, and where the arrow → represents the relation 'determines':

A) Od → Oi → S → If → Id → Ii
B) Od → Oi → S → Ii → Id → If

We deal with this problem by starting with remarks by David Savan (1988). Savan is not to be seen as a whipping-boy or a strawman to be taken to task for what he wrote; on the contrary, it is to his enormous credit that he took up the description of the determination sequence and tried to show how it worked as a typology. It is just that his interpretation of Peirce's statements in the letter has been taken up by other scholars, and has assumed the status of orthodoxy. The problem, then, concerns what Peirce meant as the order of the interpretants in the sequence described in his letter. The sequence (A) is the one preferred by most Peirce scholars, following Savan, who takes issue himself with earlier commentators such as Lieb, and Burks and Weiss, who proposed the interpretant order (B) defended in this study. As can be seen from schemas (A) and (B), the position adopted here is quite the opposite of Savan's, and as he was a pioneer in the interpretation of the sequence, the discussion naturally takes his position as the one to dismiss.

When he claimed that the Explicit interpretant was another name for the immediate (1988: 52),[10] Savan was drawing on the Buchler edition[11] of paragraph CP: 5.473 in which Peirce explains what he means by the interpretant of a sign. Initially, Peirce writes: 'For the proper significate outcome of a sign, I propose the name, the *interpretant* of the sign.' Later in the same paragraph he writes: 'On these terms, it is very easy (not descending to niceties with which I will not annoy your readers) to see what the interpretant of a sign is: it is all that is explicit in the sign itself apart from its context and circumstances of utterance' (CP: 5.473; R318 57). Now, Peirce does indeed mention the immediate interpretant in the passage, but this is in a discussion of purely mechanical processes, e.g. a change in the height of the column of mercury in a thermometer, not of semiosis in general.[12] Moreover, in the course of the later discussion of semiosis in CP: 5.484, he is clearly associating the interpretant in semiosis with what, at the time, he called the 'logical interpretant', the most complex of the three: 'But by "semiosis" I mean, on the contrary, an action, or influence, which is, or involves, a coöperation of *three* subjects, such as a sign, its object, and its interpretant'. Since, on the occasions when Peirce refers simply to the triadic combination of sign, object and interpretant, he typically means the dynamic object and the final interpretant, it is most probably the logical interpretant which is the manifestation of all that is explicit in the sign, not, as Savan and others have claimed, the immediate. Unfortunately for Peircean semiotics, this mistake has given rise to a hard-held, conservative orthodoxy.

There are a number of reasons which justify the choice of sequence (B) as the correct order. The rebuttals of Savan's position, held, too, by other Peirce scholars[13] will be as follows: terminological considerations, the theoretical implications of this position and evidence adduced from the examination of Peirce's many typologies.

Implications of Savan's order

The immediate interpretant

First, consider these two dictionary entries, one British, one American:

Destinate
† 'destinate, ppl. a. (n.) Obs. or arch. Destinate
2.2 Set apart for a particular purpose; ordained; intended (OED)

Destinate adjective
Definition of destinate
1: archaic: ordained by fate
2: set apart for; intended (Merriam-Webster)

It is surely unmistakable from these definitions that the 'Destinate Interpretant' in Peirce's formula is likely to be the immediate interpretant, identified by Peirce in earlier typologies as the intentional, or the intended interpretant as can be seen from the entry (in bold) for 31 March 1906 in Table 4.1.

Second, in the Logic Notebook, as seen in the previous chapter, Peirce offers the following very clear definition of the term 'immediate': 'to say that A is immediate to B means that it is present in B' (R339: 243Av, H460, 1905). This corresponds to descriptions Peirce gives of the immediate interpretant as being the interpretant 'in the sign': 'It is likewise requisite to distinguish the *Immediate Interpretant*, i.e., the Interpretant represented or signified in the Sign, from the *Dynamic Interpretant*, or effect actually produced on the mind by the Sign' (EP2: 482, 1908). Cf., too, the following descriptions of the two objects and three interpretants:

> It is usual and proper to distinguish two Objects of a Sign, the Mediate without, and the Immediate within the Sign. Its Interpretant is all that the Sign conveys: acquaintance with its Object must be obtained by collateral experience. The Mediate Object is the Object outside of the Sign; I call it the *Dynamoid* Object. The Sign must indicate it by a hint; and this hint, or its substance, is the *Immediate* Object.
>
> (SS: 83, 1908)

> For when we speak of the object of a sign, we may mean the *object* in its independent being, or as we may call it the *dynamic* object as something which really acts upon the sign and determines it or, on the other hand, we may mean the *immediate* object, the object as the sign represents it.
>
> (R284: 54, 1905)

> ... the Immediate Interpretant is what the Question expresses, all that it *immediately* expresses.
>
> (CP: 8.314, 1909; emphasis added)

Given Peirce's definition of immediacy and the definitions of the immediate interpretant in which it is defined to be 'represented or signified in' the sign (as is the immediate object), the vigilant reader is going to wonder why, in Savan's scheme, the immediate interpretant should now find itself at several removes from the sign, in which it is defined to inhere, to be 'present'. Consider now, a later statement in a letter to Lady Welby in 1909:

> My Immediate Interpretant is implied in the fact that each Sign must have its peculiar interpretability before it gets any Interpreter. My Dynamical Interpretant is that which is experienced in each act of Interpretation and is different in each from that of any other; and the Final Interpretant is the one Interpretative result to which every Interpreter is destined to come if the sign is sufficiently considered. The Immediate Interpretant is an abstraction, consisting in a Possibility. The Dynamical Interpretant is a single actual event. The Final Interpretant is that toward which the actual tends.
>
> (SS: 111, 1909)

Since the sign has to have an immediate interpretability before it even reaches an interpreter, if we followed Savan's schema, in any sequence of reactions formed in the interpretation of a sign the final interpretant would be enacted before the interpreter had understood the tenor of the sign (theoretically communicated to the immediate interpretant). For example, the squad of soldiers, in Peirce's many versions of the 'Ground arms!' command, would have downed the musket-butts before they had actually understood the order that the officer had shouted at them.

Third, given the situation represented by schema (A), where the sign would immediately determine its final interpretant, in turn determining the dynamic interpretant which would then determine the immediate, that is, the sign's interpretability, one has to wonder what space is left in such a sequence of relates for chance, spontaneity, misinterpretation, etc. Returning briefly to a discussion in Chapter 3 of the draft to Lady Welby from March 1906 in which Peirce introduced new names for the three interpretants, in particular the intentional and effectual interpretants (RL463: 29, 1906), it was shown that this logical disjunction distinguished functionally the intentional (i.e. immediate) interpretant as a determination of the mind of the *utterer* from the effectual (i.e. dynamic) interpretant as a determination of the mind of the *interpreter*. Such a disjunction is highly significant as it introduces the interpretive differential between the utterer and the interpreter discussed in Chapter 3. If the utterer and interpreter involved in the communication have widely differing experiences of the world, then the anti-necessitarian, non-deterministic basis of Peirce's conception of interpretant order would explain those cases where the effectual/dynamic interpretant is not congruent with the intentional/immediate; in other words, where the reaction of the interpreter is not congruent with interpretability inherent in the immediate interpretant. If determined immediately, the final interpretant would inevitably close interpretation by mediately predetermining the sign's interpretability, its meaning in other words, this being the function which logically devolves to the sign.[14] If this interpretability/meaning communicated by the immediate interpretant – in theory determined by the dynamic object through the immediate object and the sign as 'a determination of the utterer' – derived from the final interpretant via the dynamic, it would necessarily neutralize all possibility of confusion, misapprehension, misinterpretation or freedom of interpretation of the sign by the interpreter: there would be no logical way of explaining the oft-encountered non-congruity of interpreters' responses to the intentionality expressed by signs.

Savan's proposed schema would suggest that it is the habit (the final interpretant immediately determined by the sign and subsequently determining the dynamic interpretant) that produces the single dynamic action of a percussive sign, for example, whereas for Peirce it is only repeated actions that bring about self-control and habit. No habit is instantaneously or immediately acquired. Any order of semiosis other than the one postulated in this study has the potential to leave chance, tychism and fallibilism – the possibility of making errors of reasoning and correcting them – in tatters, has the potential to reinforce the necessitarianism he combated and to encumber the semiotics with the embarrassing determinism of a final interpretant, a habit, say, determining first all the actions that produced it and ultimately the interpretability that gave rise to these actions. On the contrary, for Peirce, habits are formed by reiterated patterns of behaviour, that is, dynamic interpretants, which are a function of the interpreter's understanding of the meaning imparted by the sign.[15] Consider Peirce's statement: 'I propose here to examine the common belief that every single fact in the universe is precisely determined by law' (W8: 251). This was the belief that Peirce challenged in his 1892 *Monist* paper 'The doctrine of necessity examined'. Were the final interpretant to determine all occurrences of the dynamic interpretant, thereby excluding all chance of purely spontaneous occurrences, we should have the situation specifically rebutted by Peirce in the paper. On the other hand, if, as in the order on schema (B), the sign determines first the immediate interpretant, there is space for chance, misinterpretation, error, spontaneity, as the immediate determines the dynamic. In this case, the usual, percussive or sympathetic nature of the sign will be a function of the infinitely varied field of interpreters' experience. In other words, it is the transition from the intentionality expressed by the immediate interpretant to the actuality of the response expressed by (produced as) the dynamic interpretant that offers space for spontaneity, chance, misinterpretation, etc.

The final interpretant

While the problem raised by the position of the immediate interpretant takes on almost metaphysical proportions, the necessary final position of the final interpretant in the sequence is a matter of definition, for examination of Peirce's definitions of the final interpretant yields further evidence that schema (A) cannot be correct. If we consider just three, from a pragmaticism draft entitled 'Phaneroscopy' from 1906, a draft letter to William James early in 1909 and the letter to Lady Welby of March 1909, we see that expressions such as 'eventually to be reached', 'that towards which' and 'that which *would* finally', we find that the three have in common the notion that the final interpretant has a value involving futurity, a value which is surely incompatible with its being placed arbitrarily in a position immediately following the sign:

> That ultimate, definitive, and final (i.e. eventually to be reached), interpretant (final I mean, in the logical sense of attaining the purpose, is also final in the sense of bringing the series of translations [to a stop] for the obvious reason that it is not itself a sign) is to be regarded as the ultimate signification of the [sign].
> (LI: 356–7; 1906)

> The Final Interpretant is the one Interpretative result to which every Interpreter is destined to come if the Sign is sufficiently considered ... The Final Interpretant is that toward which the actual tends.
> (SS: 111, 1909)

But we must note that there is certainly a third kind of Interpretant, which I call the Final Interpretant, because it is that which *would* finally be decided to be the true interpretation if consideration of the matter were carried so far that an ultimate opinion were reached.

(EP2: 496; 1909)

Correlate order in classifications

A further reason for rejecting the (A) sequence is provided by Peirce's own ordering conventions in his many six – and ten-division typologies. Consider Table 4.1, which displays fourteen such typologies constructed by Peirce between October 1904 and December 1908, with the final interpretants indicated in bold. We note that only two classifications – both italicized – actually use the interpretant order of schema (A) above, namely the first typology tentatively dated August 1904, and the correlate order given, though not formally in a table, by Peirce in the letter to Lady Welby of 12 October 1904, the third in the list.[16] We note, too, that the other twelve all place the final interpretant, or its equivalent appellation, in final position, and that all the typologies in the table, barring the one under discussion with the date in bold in Table 4.1 and represented by (B) above, begin with the sign division. Although the typology under discussion here begins with the dynamic object, there is nevertheless no reason to suppose that Peirce would change the order of the interpretants, and he certainly never mentions such a change.

If we now examine the four supplementary trichotomies Peirce added to the determination sequence beginning with the dynamic object we note, and this can be seen clearly in Table 4.1, that the trichotomies yielding suggestive, imperative and indicative signs, must be relational divisions associating sign and dynamic interpretant (EP2: 490), while the final trichotomy distinguishes semes, phemes and delomes, new names for the signs identified in the 1903 relational trichotomy holding between the sign and the final interpretant, as rheme, dicisign and argument (EP2: 490).

> The additional 4 trichotomies are undoubtedly 1st, Icons (or Simulacra Aristotle's
> Indices   Symbols   ὀνοίωμητα)
> and then 3 referring to the Interpretants. One of these I am pretty confident
> is into: Suggestives, Imperatives, Indicatives, where the Imperatives include
> Interrogatives. Of the other two I think that one must be into Sign assuring the
> Interpretants by
> Instinct   Experience   Form
> The other I suppose to be what, in my Monist exposition of Existential
> Graphs, I called
> Semes   Phemes   Delomes
>
> (SS: 84–5)

After 1904 Peirce never employed sign-to-immediate object and sign-to-immediate interpretant relational divisions, as the immediate object and immediate interpretant were defined, as seen before, to be already 'present in' the sign. This being the case, the absence of any subclass of signs yielded by a putative Sign-Destinate Interpretant

Table 4.1 Fourteen six- and ten-division typologies established between 1904 and 1908

	Typology order	
	Divisions	
Date		
Aug? 1904	(S); S-Od, Oi; **Isignified** (=If), Id, I(i)	(R339 450, 239v)
07-08-1904	(S), Oi, S-Od, Ii, Id, **Isignified**	(R339 451, 240r)
08/10/1905b	S, S-Od, S-Oi, S-**Isignified**, S-Id, S-Ii	SS 32-34
07-07-1905	S, S-Oi, S-Od, A-Ii, A-Id, A-**Irational**, where A = appeal to,	247r
08-10-1905	S, Oi, Od equiv. (S-Od), Ii, Id, **Isignificiant** equiv. (S-If)	252r
08/10/1905b	S, Oi, Od, S-Od, Ii, Id, S-Id, **Irepresentative** (=If), S-Irep, S-O-Irep	253r
09-10-1905	S, Oi, Od, **Irepresentative** (incomplete)	255r
13-10-1905	S, Oi, Odα, Odβ, Ii, Idα, Idβ, Ifα, Ifβ, Ifγ (If=**representative**)	262r
06-03-1906	Od, Oi, S, Iintentional, Ieffective, **Icommunicational**	EP2 278
31-03-1906	S, Oi, Od, S-Od, I**intended**, Id, S-Id, If, Pass(If), **normal**(If)	275r
31-08-1906	S, Oi, Od, S-Od, Iinit, Imid, S-Imid, purpose(**Ieventual**), influence(S on Iev), Ass(S to Iev)	285r
10-07-1908	S, Oi, Od, S-Od, Ii, Id, S-Id, **Iultimate**, S-Iult, S-O-Iult (letter to Russell) Robinson	579-580
23-12-1908	Od, Oi, S, Idestinate, Ieffective, **Iexplicit**; *plus* S-Od, S-Ieff, S-O-Iexpl, S-Iexpl	EP2 480-481
24-12-1908	S, Oi, Od, S-Od, Ii, Id, S-Id, **Inormal**, S-Inor, S-Od-Inor	EP2 481-482
25-12-1908	S, Oi, Od, S-Od, Ii, Id, S-Id, **Ieventual**, S-Ieventfulf, S-O-Ieventual	EP2 483-490

division in the final four, and not identifiable in any of the subsequent typologies in later draft letters to Lady Welby, further suggests that the destinate is the immediate and the explicit another designation for the final.

Part of the problem lies in certain authors' eagerness to see a hierarchy among the interpretants themselves, as though the immediate is somehow degenerate with respect to the dynamic, and doubly degenerate with respect to the final. Whatever Morand (2004) and Diversey (2014), for example, suggest, namely that the process and correlate order are established by the categories, there is nothing of this in Peirce in 1908, as the various correlates involved in the extended definition of a sign are just that – specific 'genuine' stages in an ordered process, stages that also provide the trichotomies of a hexadic typology; and the only degeneracy that might possibly apply would concern the 'vertical' hierarchy governing relations between subdivisions of the various six trichotomies. Peirce does explain that the three interpretants were given by the categories (R318: 281, 1907), but looking at the various ten-division typologies in which the interpretant order is very clearly Ii, Id If, it must be obvious to even the staunchest Savan follower that a necessitant Ii can determine an existent and a possible Id, and through these an existent and a possible If. The relations between the trichotomies are governed not by phaneroscopy, but by the universe hierarchy stated at the beginning of the description of the determination sequence. Within the typology no subdivisions of necessitant correlates can be determined by those of existent or possible correlates, and the subdivisions of possible correlates can only determine subdivisions of possible correlates. With a rule as simple as the one Peirce gives in the 23 December letter appeal to degeneracy is both irrelevant and misleading.

The determination sequence

Having hopefully resolved the ordering problem, we now need to examine in detail the relation of determination holding between the six relates identified in the formula. The term 'determine' is important in his logic as it occurs, for example, in most of his definitions of the sign. This is the thorny theoretical problem that the determination sequence raises. First, what does Peirce mean by the term? Herewith a number of definitions ordered chronologically and culled from diverse Peircean sources:

> To determine means to make a circumstance different from what it might have been otherwise.
> (W1: 245, 1865)

> A sign is supposed to have an object or meaning, and also to determine an interpretant sign of the same object. It is convenient to speak as if the sign originated with an utterer and determined its interpretant in the mind of an interpreter.
> (R11: 1, 1903)

> I propose to extend the meaning [of 'determination'] so as to cover any state of a man having an accidental cause in which he would behave upon occasion in a way more special than men in general or even the person in question would usually be at all certain to behave in the absence of the special cause.
> (R298, 1906: LI; 357)

> The proper way to pursue the inquiry is to start from the definition already given of the triadic relation of Sign-Object-Interpretant. *We thus learn that the Object determines (i.e. renders definitely to be such as it will be,) the Sign in a particular manner.* Now it is of the essence of the Sign to determine certain Ideas, i.e. certain Possibles; and it is the essence of any Tendency to determine Occurrences. Therefore, an Actisign or a Potisign may be a Copulative. But no Occurrence or collection of occurrences can logically determine a Habit or other Tendency.
> (CP: 8.361, 1908; emphasis added)

> A Sign is a Cognizable that, on the one hand, is so determined (i.e., specialized, *bestimmt*) by something *other than itself,* called its Object
> (CP: 8.177, 1909)[17]

What these definitions have in common is the idea that in the process of determination one entity has such an influence on another that it causes this second entity to be different from what it might otherwise have been, causes it to be different from what it would have been, had there been no determination process. This means, for example, that the 'association' or combination between elements of the three universes can only determine, can only cause to be other than they might otherwise have been, elements from similar or less complex universes. Although the principle was stated explicitly in 1908, Peirce had already applied it in the ten-class typology of 1903 and the hexad of 1904.

The theoretical issue concerns the identification of the 23 December sequence as a process, if it is one. In other words, if it is a process and not simply a novel object-initiated typology, what sort of process might it be? The order is given again below in Figure 4.1, where the arrow simply stands for the expression 'determines'.[18]

The problem is thus to determine whether the sequence is a case of semiosis or simply a set of elements ordered by some other sort of relation. It is the position adopted here that this is a case of semiosis, but to justify the decision we need to examine the facts. First, Peirce, remember, defines semiosis in a very precise manner: 'But by "semiosis" I mean, on the contrary, an action, or influence, which is, or involves, a coöperation of *three* subjects, such as a sign, its object, and its interpretant'. The formula he sends to Lady Welby contains six 'subjects', but from what we now know of Peirce's conception of immediacy with immediate object and immediate interpretant present in the sign by definition, we can rewrite the whole system to be collapsible to three (with the immediate object and interpretant 'included' in, 'present' in the sign) and, as in Figure 2.4 from Chapter 2, represent the potential of the formula with the three subjects of semiosis as Figure 4.2.

Since we can assume that for Peirce the 'determination flow', or the 'flow of influence'[19] from dynamic object to final interpretant is rational, purpose-driven and not random, we have to examine just what he means exactly by the expression 'determines'. The definitions all correspond to the action or influence of one entity upon another in such a way that it effects the second entity's subsequent conduct or nature. However, returning to Figure 4.1, the problem is to decide whether it represents

$$Od \rightarrow Oi \rightarrow S \rightarrow Ii \rightarrow Id \rightarrow If$$

Figure 4.1 The six correlates set out in 'determination' order.

Figure 4.2 The three principal subjects of semiosis set out in determination order.

genuine semiosis or simply an inorganic sequence of five dyadic relations. Consider another of Peirce's definitions of 'determination' from the Logic Notebook:

> Notes on my Provisional Classification of Signs
> I thought of the Object of a Sign as that which determines the sign; and this is well thought. I have thought of the Interpretant is that which the Sign determines or might determine or should determine, but this is not so well. *For my idea of determination is dyadic while the idea of the relation of the interpretant to the Sign is triadic.*
>
> (R339 276r, H522,1906; emphasis added)

What the italicized statement suggests is that the determination sequence is a series of dyadic relations, a sort of logical domino or 'knock-on' effect initiated by the dynamic object, whatever that might be. A definition of the sign employing the term 'determine' such as this one from the Syllabus of 1903 and already discussed in Chapter 2 is notable in that the determination is, unlike that of the 1908 sequence, associated with an indication of degree, 'such'; besides, the whole relation is defined to be triadic:

> A *Sign*, or *Representamen*, is a First which stands in such a genuine triadic relation to a Second, called its *Object*, as to be capable of determining a Third, called its *Interpretant*, to assume the same triadic relation to its Object in which it stands itself to the same Object. The triadic relation is *genuine*, that is its three members are bound together by it in a way that does not consist in any complexus of dyadic relations.
>
> (EP2: 272–3, 1903)

Is it possible that Peirce is using the term in a broader sense in the determination sequence sent to Lady Welby? We note from a later draft that he states that the sign can determine the dynamic object, a surprising remark in view of the general definitions of the sign, until one realizes that he is talking about relations within a typology, not within a process: 'Adopting this enumeration [i.e. presentation of the signs in three ways, as a trichotomy] as a basis of a division of Signs, I obtain: A. *Descriptives*, which *determine* their Objects by stating the characters of the latter' (EP2: 484; final emphasis added). In the ten-class system of 1903, the phenomenological status of the sign itself governs how it can be associated with its 'facets' derived from the sign-object and sign-interpretant divisions: if the sign is a sinsign, it can only be either indexical or iconic from the point of view of its relation to its object, for example. And it is the necessarily static hierarchical structure of these association rules which governs the nature of the determination process involved in the typology: it determines, that is, governs the permissible selection of supplementary features of one and the *same* sign. This is the case, of course, in all subsequent typologies, with the notable exception of the one from 23 December 1908. As suggested earlier, however, in this latter case the sequence of seemingly dyadic determination relations in fact forms a purposive, rational whole, where determination assumes a dynamic character involving not different aspects of the same sign but different correlates participating in the same process, all of which being capable of belonging to one or other of three different universes of existence.

Although Peirce seems not to have been entirely consistent in the meaning he attributes to the concept of determination, this, I contend, is the process of semiosis: schema (B) and Figures 4.1 and 4.2 diagram in skeletal fashion the basic structure of a step-by-step realization of the process, of a process in which the logical and the chronological coincide. The diagrams do NOT, nor are intended to, represent any form of definition of the sign: although dyadic the relation of determination represented by the arrows in sequence is dynamic, but is in no way associated with any measure of degree; and in any case, Peirce had already defined the sign in his conventional manner earlier in the letter: 'I define a Sign as anything which is so determined by something else' (SS: 80). What makes the sequence all the more distinctive is that the order of semiosis also corresponds to the ordering of divisions within the typology. Table 4.2 sets out the divisions 'down the page' as Peirce might have done.

Unlike the table of the ten-class system of 1903 described in Chapter 2, in which discrimination between subclasses was effected by reference to the one or other of the three phenomenological categories, by 1908 the categories had been replaced in Peirce's classification of signs by the three universes discussed earlier in the chapter, although Peirce continued to work upon phaneroscopy, his still embryonic incomplete 'science-egg',[20] independently of the classification of signs after 1908. The designations of the sign subclasses in Table 4.2 (and Table 4.3) have been obtained from subsequent drafts intended for Lady Welby (EP2: 481–90). Although neither the chapter nor, indeed, the study, is concerned with Peirce's classifications as being the objects of further 'development', it will be useful for subsequent chapters if some of these divisions are explained at this point. In order to make this more evident, the content of Table 4.2

Table 4.2 The 1908 six-division 28-class typology

	Universe		
	Possible	Existent	Necessitant
Subject			
Od	abstractive	concretive	collective
Oi	descriptive	designative	copulant
S	mark	token	type
Ii	hypothetical	categorical	relative
Id	sympathetic	percussive	usual
If	gratific	to produce action	to produce self-control

Table 4.3 The order of divisions yielding 28 classes of signs

	Subject									
(*semiosis*)	Od	→	Oi	→	S	→	Ii	→	Id	→	If
Universe										
Necessitant	collective		copulant		type		relative		usual		to produce self-control
Existent	concretive		designative		token		categorical		percussive		to produce action
Possible	abstractive		descriptive		mark		hypothetical		sympathetic		gratific

has been reformatted in a 'horizontal' table reading across the page, and to make the determination sequence clearer arrows have been added between successive correlates. Note, however, that Peirce never set out his typologies across the page as in Table 4.3.

As can be seen clearly in Tables 4.2 and 4.3, the twenty-eight classes yielded by the hexadic formula described in the letter of 23 December 1908 do *not* derive from any relational divisions. Such divisions were added later in the letter with reference to sixty-six classes of signs. Examining Table 4.3, we see that if the dynamic and immediate objects are necessitant, for example, and the sign a token, then the subsequent interpretant divisions can only be either existent or possible. If the final interpretant is an existent then the sign produces an action; and if the final interpretant is a 'possible' then the sign produces the quality of a feeling. In the first case, if we were intent on classifying signs, the class obtained, avoiding redundant information, would be an action-producing copulant token (this, for anyone wishing to use such a system, is surely a more congenial appellation than a categorical, percussive, action-producing collective, copulant token, since, as shown in Table 4.3, certain redundancies can be avoided. If the sign is copulant it is necessarily collective, and if it is an action-producing token, it is necessarily also categorical and percussive). This is a far more complex and sophisticated system than the one from 1907 examined in the previous chapter, where we had a disjunction in the types of signs capable of producing the final (logical), dynamic (energetic) and immediate (emotional) interpretants. The system in Tables 4.2 and 4.3 also shows how placing the final interpretant in the position immediately following the sign and the immediate in the final division, as Savan and others proclaim, would exhaust the possibility of alternative interpretations and stifle any form of spontaneity.

The correlates and their function

Having proposed the ordering of the correlates in Peirce's formula as the model of semiosis, and having set out the equivalent typology as two tables (Tables 4.2 and 4.3), the present section examines aspects of the correlates contributing to semiosis and the divisions they form in the tables. For discussions to be conducted in the following chapters, the most important of these divisions concern the two objects, the sign and the final interpretant. This is not to say that the others are not important within the scheme, but, as the purpose of the study is not to promote an extensive classification of signs according to the 1908 model or, as others have done, to evaluate possible orderings of Peirce's several ten-division taxonomies, full description of the system in Table 4.3 is unnecessary.

As the entity triggering semiosis, the dynamic object division obviously requires close examination. To render the terminology in Table 4.3 a little less abstract, we consider two sets of examples from a draft composed two days after the letter to Lady Welby. In it, amongst other things, Peirce writes that objects may be presented by their signs in three ways: first as mere ideas, second as brutally compelling attention, third as rationally recommending themselves or as a habit. Describing the nature of their dynamic objects he states that signs are either (1) signs of possibles, that is abstractive signs such as colour, mass, whiteness; (2) signs of occurrences, that is 'concrete' signs, concretive, such as 'man', 'Charlemagne', that is, a specific individual; and (3) signs of collections, generic terms such as 'mankind', 'the human race', that is, the necessitant signs in the dynamic object division in Table 4.3, identified as collective signs (EP2: 489).

In the same draft he describes signs identified according to their immediate objects in order of increasing complexity as (1) descriptives, which describe the characters of the object; (2) designatives, such as demonstrative pronouns or a pointing finger; (3) copulants, 'which neither describe nor denote their objects but merely express universally the logical sequence of these latter upon something otherwise referred to'. Among examples of such signs he gives '"If__then__" or "__is relative to__"' (EP2: 484). This restriction to the purely verbal here and in the case of the dynamic object is in no way surprising. For one thing, he was a logician, and the examples, particularly of signs determined by virtue of the nature of the immediate object, are typical logical formulae. Moreover, although often expressing a preference for reasoning by diagrams, he must have found verbal examples far easier to employ in correspondence (although he does send examples of his Existential Graphs, his '*icons* of thought', to the hapless Lady Welby, who was invited to interpret them. See, for example, his letter of 21 January 1909 (SS: 94–108)).

However, not all Peirce's examples are drawn from logic. As seen in the previous chapter, in one of his analyses of the 'Ground arms!' examples, he states that the object of the command was the officer's 'will': 'In the present case, the object the command represents is the will of the officer that the butts of the muskets be brought down to the ground' (CP 5.473, 1907). It was shown in Chapter 3 that with respect to the ten-class system of 1903 the dynamic object was, typically, the determinant of a photograph, namely the entity reflecting light back onto the film in the camera, in other words an object in no theoretically defined way related to human intention or volition (EP2: 282, 1903). In such a case, as the sign is determined solely by the object being photographed, the intentions or wishes of the photographer or client are irrelevant to the definition of the sign. In the description of the military command, however, the object represented is explicitly identified as the 'will of the officer'. This implies that intention and volition – sources of motivation irrelevant to the classification criteria used in the 1903 ten-class system in spite of their being implied by the definition of the sign at the time – are now seen as potential determinants of signs and, consequently, as the origins of the action of the sign, namely semiosis. See, too, this definition of the sign from the Pragmatism manuscript in which the concept of semiosis is introduced: 'A *sign* is whatever there may be whose intent is to *mediate between* an *utterer* of it and an *interpreter* of it, both being *repositories of thought*, or *quasi-minds*, by *conveying* a *meaning* from the former to the latter' (R318: 421, 1907): by 1907 Peirce was including a purposive 'ingredient' – intent, here – in the definition of the sign.

Since they are general and of a cognitive nature – elements of mental life – intent, intention, intentionality, unlike volition,[21] belong in the universe of necessitant entities, amongst whose other members we have already found 'a living institution, – a daily newspaper, a great fortune, a social "movement"' (EP2: 435, 1907). Although Peirce doesn't phrase the problem in this way, the post-1903 broadened conception of the dynamic object that he advanced in the 'Prolegomena' text of 1906, allied with the hexadic process of semiosis, offers the means of distinguishing logically between intention, or purpose[22] – both being varieties of final causes – in living organisms, and physical causation in the case of inanimate agencies. Remember from Chapter 1 that Peirce divided the idioscopic sciences into physics and psychics, of which latter a neo-Peircean semiotics is offered here as an example, and, as we saw there, he distributed the two types of cause as follows:

> Class III is Bentham's *idioscopic*; that is, the special sciences, depending upon special observation, which travel or other exploration, or some assistance to the senses, either instrumental or given by training, together with unusual diligence, has put within the power of its students. This class manifestly divides itself into two subclasses, the physical and the psychical sciences .... Under the former is to be included physics, chemistry, biology, astronomy ... ; under the latter, psychology, linguistics, ethnology, sociology, history, etc. [Physics] sets forth the workings of efficient causation, [psychics] of final causation.
>
> (CP 1.242, 1902)

Since in Peircean logic semiosis is always initiated by the object, necessitant objects such as those already mentioned are 'exponents' of intention, and appertain to the realm of the organisms with which the various disciplines of 'psychics' are concerned, whereas existent objects are exponents of efficient causation enacted by the non-animate entities studied in physics. This latter type of causation is surely not far removed from John Deely's concept of physiosemiosis (Deely 2001, 2009b). What both necessitant and existent objects demonstrate, of course, is the importance of the switch from phenomenology/phaneroscopy to what, given their denominations in the letter as 'universes of existence', is presumably a type of ontological system the members of whose three universes can be general, particular or qualitative. Taken as a classification which additionally exhibits the processual structure of semiosis, Table 4.3 thus yields twenty-eight classes both of signs and of possible semioses: one of qualitative semiosis, six of existential semiosis and twenty-one of necessitant semiosis. Twenty-one classes of necessitant causation, including intention, volition, purpose, etc., might seem restricted in view of the enormous variety of extant organisms, their various behaviours and the signs they produce and engage with, but it is important here to bear in mind the scope of the second relational division of 1903: the different cases of icon, index and symbol are practically innumerable. A similar inexhaustibility applies to the twenty-eight classes of signs and of semioses.

The sign division is less complex; we simply note that Peirce was not convinced by his choice of terminology. In the letter to Lady Welby he announces *tone* (or mark, a term from the 1860s: W1: 307), *token* and *type*, but in a later draft (25 December: EP2: 483) opts instead for *potisigns*, signs of qualitative possibility, *actisigns*, signs of actuality such as photographs, thermometers and windsocks on aerodromes, and *famisigns*, signs of generality.[23] The latter term is an interesting choice as it underlines the fact that the general is not necessarily the inaccessible world of invisible entities, concepts and relations, but composed of the very familiar signs of life, the English definite article being a case in point. He had introduced this particular trio of terms in the 'Prolegomena' article of 1906 and formulated the type-token ratio (TTR) distinction that has since been adopted as a basic but effective measure of lexical density in natural language corpora. Note, however, that the sign is considered now as any medium capable of being inscribed with a form emanating from the dynamic object and capable of communicating that form to a series of interpretants, in other words, capable of activating a specific series of reactions in an interpreter.

The final interpretant division is of particular interest as it restricts the scope of what the final interpretant was defined to be in 1903. Although indicated simply at that time as the interpretant that was mediately determined by the object, it was labelled 'signified' (final) in its relation to the sign in the letter to Lady Welby dated 12 October 1904 (SS: 33), and yielded the familiar rheme, dicent and argument, which corresponded to, he states, 'the old division Term, Proposition, & Argument, modified so as to be applicable to signs generally' (SS: 33). Within the hexadic universe-governed system described in the letter to Lady Welby four years later, the final interpretant functions as an independent correlate: it doesn't enter into a sign-classifying relation with the sign, but constitutes the final stage of the 'determination flow' initiated by the dynamic object, and in this respect completes classification both of the telic nature of semiosis and the precise purpose of the sign.

A brief attempt at classification will clarify the contribution of the final interpretant to both semiosis and Peirce's wish to classify signs, and can be followed in Table 4.3. If the final interpretant is a possible, then the sign produces the quality of a feeling (in R318 Peirce suggests that a concerted piece of music conveys this quality from the composer to the members of the audience (R318: 665–7, 1907)).[24] Since such a concerted piece of music is not a random occurrence, the dynamic object is an intentionality, and although gratific at the final interpretant division of a classification, the sign would be collective in the dynamic object division and necessarily a token as a sign as it has to be existent to be heard.

The sign qualifies as 'action-producing' if the final interpretant is a member of the universe of existents. The 'Ground arms!' example is a good example: the sign is necessarily collective in the dynamic object division, as this dynamic object, as seen above and in Chapter 3, is the 'wish of the officer', an intentionality. As a sign, in order to be audible it must be a token, though as a token it is the instance of a verbal type. Finally, the sign, assuming it has been understood at the immediate interpretant stage, produces the grounding of the musket-butts as the existent action-producing final interpretant.

Finally, when the final interpretant is necessitant, it is obligatorily the effect of or a reaction to, a collective sign at the dynamic object stage. Pierce describes such a sign as producing self-control, sustaining a habit or forming a new one. What is particularly interesting in this new classification and the semiotic process that underwrites it is that the necessitant final interpretant is the only interpretant that might conceivably support the sort of semiotic continuity mentioned in 1902, namely what Eco (1984), for example, referred to as 'unlimited semiosis': 'Genuine mediation is the character of a *Sign*. A *Sign* is anything which is related to a Second thing, its *Object*, in respect to a Quality, in such a way as to bring a Third thing, its *Interpretant*, into relation to the same Object, and that in such a way as to bring a Fourth into relation to that Object in the same form, *ad infinitum*' (CP 2.92 1902).

At the time, there was only one interpretant, to be found unnamed only in definitions of the sign, but otherwise as part of the third trichotomy identified in 1903 as the sign-interpretant division. Much has been written on the subject of unlimited semiosis, which was rejected amongst others by T. L. Short (2007: 44–45). What the various authors who have weighed in on the subject have neglected to consider is that Peirce's thinking on signs didn't come to some sort of closure in 1903, but had renewed itself considerably, as this chapter has sought to show, by December 1908.

Summary and discussion

The chapter has shown that by defining the three modal universes and the sorts of entities they can contain, Peirce had changed significantly the theoretical framework within which he approached the process and circumstances that condition the way signs function. Moreover, since by 1908 the object is now explicitly defined to be the origin, the 'triggering agency' or initiator of semiosis, such an object can clearly be a source of volition and intentionality. In short, while the system of 1903, in which the identity of the object as the dynamic source of the determination of the sign is irrelevant, is unable to accommodate intentionality, the hexadic system of 1908 can show it to be the initiator of semiosis.

What many commentators seem not to want to notice is that Peirce is now replacing the phenomenological framework underwriting the classification of signs advanced in the Syllabus by what has, given the fact that these are 'universes of existence', now been referred to as an ontological one: a system of modally differentiated universes containing all that *is*, including possible and necessitant entities. Whereas the three-division ten-class typology displayed in Figures 2.3 and 2.4 and Table 2.2 in Chapter 2 used Peirce's three categories as the criteria in order to subdivide the sign and the two sign-correlate trichotomies, the later hexadic typology introduced in the 1908 letter, on the other hand, is now defined within a framework which employs three universes to establish what I take to be the subdivisions of the six correlates of semiosis, specifically, a universe of possible, one of existent and one of necessitant entities in order of increasing complexity (EP2: 478-9). Most importantly for present purposes, these universes now provide Peirce with a range of possible semiotic constituents – signs, objects, interpretants – that is logically inexhaustible.

The purpose of the phenomenology in 1903 had been to establish clearly the formal elements making it possible to describe the sign as a phenomenon. This was how Peirce employed the three categories of Firstness, Secondness and Thirdness to establish the various subdivisions described in Chapter 2, and although the sign was defined there as being determined by its object to produce an interpretant, there was no dynamism inherent in the classes defined by the resultant three-division typology: they involved no dynamism for the simple reason that the typology of 1903 provided no way of identifying the dynamic object that triggers the signifying process. Nevertheless, by 1908, with the definition of the sign as a medium and with Peirce's description of semiosis as a dynamic process, the three universes supplied the system with 'receptacles' of entities – possible, existent and necessitant entities – that could function as signs and interpretants, and, most importantly, as objects. As to why Peirce should have switched to this 'ontological' framework, we can only speculate: one possible reason was his growing awareness of the structure of semiosis that we saw burgeoning in the previous chapter with the introduction of quasi-minds in the process of communication.

Finally, the chapter has reviewed the order of determination presented by Peirce in the letter to Lady Welby. This can be shown to be both a typology as Peirce maintained in the letter, and also a process of which the dynamic object, of whatever nature, is the initiating agency, and the sign a medium capable of conveying the form emanating from the dynamic object: a medium, for example, capable of conveying the stimuli of habit, purposive action or the quality of a feeling. Whereas the definition of the sign involves an irreducibly triadic relation holding between sign, object and interpretant, semiosis as presented in the letter and as understood in this study is an ordered dynamic sequence of dyadic determinations, or influences, affecting six correlates in a process. Establishing the correct order of occurrence of the six correlates within the sequence is an indispensable prerequisite to employment of semiosis in research. What the chapter derived was one account of the Peircean version. There are other versions of the Peircean system, and versions defined within alternative semiotic theories. Reviewing these is irrelevant to the purposes of the present study.

5

Approaches to Semiosis

The last chapter sought to show that the letter to Lady Welby contained the description of the process of semiosis in the guise of the determination sequence beginning with the dynamic object and ending in the determination of the final interpretant. This was, of course, the present commentator's opinion, and not a view shared by (probably the majority of) other Peirce commentators. This chapter addresses two aspects of this conception of semiosis, with the aim both of consolidating the thesis advanced in the last chapter and of bringing to the fore certain characteristic features that render Peircean (idioscopic) semiotics a theory still to be reckoned with today. The first approach is from the inside, so to speak, since it seeks to adduce additional evidence to support the conclusion that the hexad of the 23 December letter to Lady Welby is both a typology and a representation of the process of semiosis. The second part of the chapter is, by contrast, 'external', in the sense that it compares and contrasts the pertinent features of Peircean semiotics with alternative conceptions of sign, language, mind and semiosis.

With the intention of confirming the conclusions of the previous chapter, the initial section investigates the skeleton representation of a ten-class typology to be found in a draft letter left as a 'scrap' for Lady Welby to work out for herself. My argument here is that it is an abridged version of the twenty-eight-class typology which, I contend, is also, an elementary model of the process of semiosis. Moreover, this particular ten-class skeleton typology, as an abridged model of semiosis, can be shown to correspond to the definitions that Peirce originally proposed for the sign in 1903. The discussion and its conclusions are proposed as further support of the position adopted in the previous chapter.

Thereafter, taking for granted that the model of semiosis advanced in the study is correct, the rest of the chapter returns, amongst other things, to the problem of 'looking' introduced in Chapter 1, and once more broaches the problem of relevance. There it was noted that the 'sciences' of cenoscopy and idioscopy as Peirce defined them involved observation. Now, these ideas were formulated over a hundred years ago within a specific idiosyncratic conception of scientific enquiry, and since then a number of different innovative approaches to observation, to 'looking', to the relation or, more precisely, to the relations that might hold between the observer and the object observed, between the analyst and the analysand, between an organism and its environment, have been advanced. Chief among these potentially conflicting conceptions of observation are the various strains of the enactivist movement in cognitive science and, also, an alternative Peirce-related theory of the sign developed within biosemiotics, initially by Thomas Sebeok and, more recently, by John Deely and other biosemioticians. Just how Peircean semiosis as described in this study relates to these more recent conceptions of observation is thus the focus of the second section of the chapter.

Deriving the post-scriptum diagram[1]

Since one of the ideas proposed in this study is that Peirce's conception of signs and the action of signs is evolutionary, developmental, in that he continually reviewed and reconsidered the theories he was expounding, and since I am suggesting that the two systems separated by five years are in one way quite distinct, it is of utmost importance that this theoretical difference be made manifest and my claim be justified. However, before discussing the post-scriptum table, I should like to quote a long passage from Freadman (2004) which crystalizes many of the misapprehensions concerning the very late systems I am interested in:

> I have suggested that the best way to read the second classification, the combinatory of the Syllabus, is as a 'grammar' of the sign, meaning by this what Peirce always meant by 'grammar', the study of the conditions fitting something to act as a sign. It is proper that this should comprise a trichotomy analyzing the sign itself, another analyzing the relation of the sign with its object, and a third analyzing the structural properties of the sign as they determine its interpretability. What is the function of the further classifications that analyze the 'two objects' and the 'three (or six …) interpretants'? Are they, respectively, a 'logic' and a 'rhetoric'? Why produce classification of kinds of object and kinds of interpretant, as if these two relata of the sign were theorizable outside the relation that gives them their function in the sign? And why, given that all three relata – the sign, the object, and the interpretant – are *signs*, why do we need special classifications to deal with each relatum? The question is troubling because it draws our attention to the silent assumption of the further classifications if each relate of the sign relation requires its own classification, this implies that each relatum is phenomenologically, or ontologically, or metaphysically, different from the others. This implication violates all Peirce's principles. For the difference between the object, and the sign, and interpretant, is a structural and functional one: there is no essence of objects, say, or interpretants, or even of signs, that requires its own theory. They act as they do, fulfill the function that they fulfill, because of the place they occupy in the relation. This relation is dynamic and ever-changing, but all its relata are signs.
> (2004: 167–8)

That Freadman should see the 1903 classification as a grammar corresponds broadly to what was said in Chapter 2: Speculative Grammar specifies the constraints determining whether some entity is or is not a sign. Although as defined the sign requires both an object and an interpretant with which it enters into a triadic relation, neither object nor interpretant is the immediate concern of Speculative Grammar, and thus, although Peirce devotes considerable energy in distinguishing their respective categorial and ontological statuses, neither is ever classified. However, the present study diverges considerably from Freadman's statements concerning the 'further classifications', namely the typology described to Lady Welby in the 12 October 1904 letter (e.g. see Freadman 2004),[2] but above all, the 1908 systems, including the ten-class post-scriptum table (Freadman doesn't reference the latter directly). For a start, it is scientifically indispensable to theorize, that is, specify the number, nature and functions of, the two objects and three interpretants. Freadman here succumbs to the sign=triadic relation fallacy, claiming that the 'sign relation' governing all three relates is a sign. Nor is it true that all three relata are signs. Such errors are due, I believe, to a recurrent resistance – illustrated for simplicity here by Freadman's otherwise exhaustively researched study, but there are many other such commentators – to the possibility that Peirce's conception of the sign, its scope for dynamic action and the new ways in which it can be envisaged and classified have undergone a significant evolution, and that in his later statements there was an implicit conception of semiosis developing in conjunction with his quest for as many classes of signs for logic as he could find. This is a refusal, too, to accept the universes of necessitant, existent and possible entities applied to the two objects and the three interpretants as the appropriate criteria for a very innovative but misunderstood system of classification. As Freadman concludes in the passage, the relation between the relates is dynamic, but after 1904 Peirce explicitly recognized six such relates and showed how they all functioned together. In view of the widely held rejection of the late systems as expressed by Freadman in the quotation above, it is imperative that the position advanced in this study be fully justified theoretically. Investigation of the ten-class post-scriptum table will examine from a different perspective the principal points of discussion of the hexadic typology examined in Chapter 4 and, concomitantly, will seek to validate the important differences in conceptions of the sign and its classification that were posited there to have developed between 1903 and 1908.

***

We know from a page in the Logic Notebook (R339: 339v, H636), dated 27 December 1908, and from various drafts intended for Lady Welby from 24 to 28 December, that Peirce didn't cease working on his ten-division typologies after the 23 December letter to his British correspondent. For example, at the end of the final draft of 28 December, he left a series of scraps, including an intriguing table simply composed of ten sets of three divisions of signs:

> P.S. 1908 December 28. Well, dear Lady Welby, you deserve this infliction, for having spoken of my having 'always been kindly [!!!] interested in the work to which my life is devoted', when I have myself have been entirely absorbed in the very same subject since 1863, without meeting, before I made you acquaintance, a single mind to whom it did not seem very like bosh. I add some scraps.
> (RL463: 143, 1908)

The four scraps set out on the following page of the manuscript were separated by short horizontal lines. These are rather intriguing remarks as they echo, sometimes almost to a word, parts of the letter sent earlier to Lady Welby on 23 December. The scraps themselves include a desire to read an encyclopaedia article that Lady Welby had written, a rather testy reference to British want of finesse occasioned by her misunderstanding of his term 'attractive fancy' (SS: 76), and a reference to a comical slip in her type-written letter concerning the term 'corollarial' (SS: 77). Moreover, the remarks in the scraps continue on the following page and include, in a different order, the same reference to the word 'play' (SS: 77). At first sight, the scrap seems to be some sort of written rehearsal for the letter, but Peirce has dated it himself as 28 December 1908, five days after writing and dating the letter. Furthermore, as we see below, there is evidence that Peirce was working towards the post-scriptum table in the days before he consigned it to the scrap. Whatever the case may be, at the top of the page he had also left the intriguing V-shaped diagram containing ten classes of signs (Figure 5.1), without any explanation of its purpose, only a note below the diagram indicating as to how the table was to be read.[3]

Owing, presumably, to the scant information provided by Peirce, the diagram seems not to have been much investigated, with the exception of the early discussion by Sanders (1970) and above all Farias and Queiroz (e.g. 2014a, 2014b, 2017), authors of original studies investigating the ways in which diagrams bring out the formal aspects of the relations between Peirce's various classifications, including the post-scriptum, referred to by Farias and Queiroz as the 'Welby' table. See also Borges (2010,

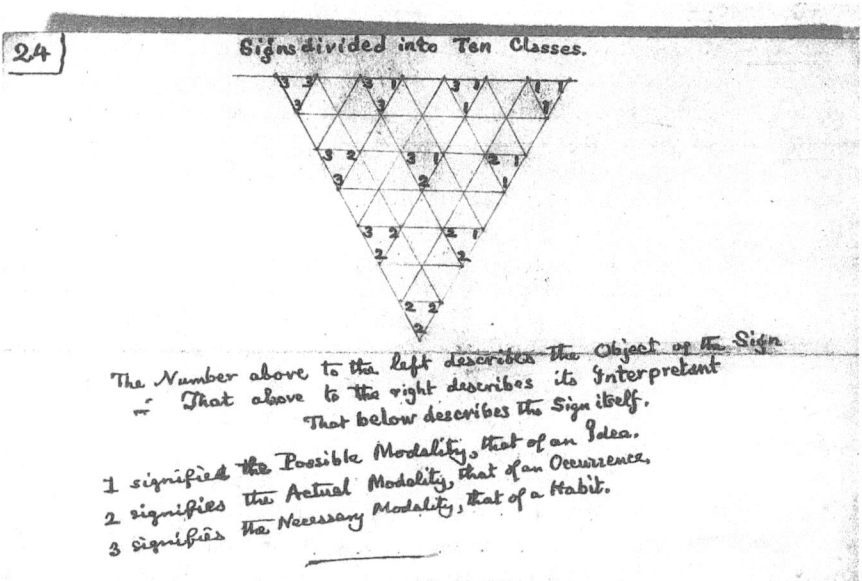

Figure 5.1 The first page of post-scriptum scraps. RL463: 144, 28 December 1908; MS Am 1632 (Box 45: L463), Houghton Library, Harvard University.

2016) and Romanini (2014); but see Liszka (2018) and Marty (2020) for two different assessments. Most interesting for present purposes is Farias and Queiroz (2014a), which specifically investigates ways in which Peirce employs diagrammatic methods to model two very different ten-class systems of signs. Towards their conclusion the authors note:

> However, we must remember that, in the *Welby* diagram, what we are calling Object is described as 'the mode of being of [the Sign's] Object' (and not the relationship of the Sign with its Object), and, similarly, that what we are calling Interpretant is described as 'the mode of being of [the Sign's] Interpretant'. The implication of this is that Peirce seems to be showing us here, with this diagram, is that the mode of being of the Sign's Object (immediate or dynamic) determines the mode of being of the Sign, which determines the mode of being of its Interpretant (immediate, dynamic or final). This is not the order of determination that generates the 10 classes of signs described in the *Syllabus*, but is also not in contradiction with it. This is the basic structure of the order of determination which gives rise to another classification, the 28 classes of signs.
>
> (2014a: 668)

The authors make an important point here, namely that the placing of the correlates in the classes corresponds to the order described by Peirce for the twenty-eight classes mentioned in the letter to Lady Welby. What must be added – and this justifies my taking the table as an abridged version of the twenty-eight-class typology described in the previous chapter – is that the numerical values accorded the correlates as they are placed in each cell correspond to the order of determination in all Peirce's numerous definitions of the sign, and this also justifies treating the schema as an abridged model of classes of semiosis.

Explaining just how he might have derived the post-scriptum table will involve reviewing the significance of a page from the Logic Notebook (Figure 5.2) dated a day earlier than the post-scriptum scraps, from which I shall take one of the ten groups of three elements as the example class. The system on this particular page shows Peirce returning to the basic triadic structure of semiosis first described in 1907: 'by "semiosis" I mean, on the contrary, an action, or influence, which is, or involves, a coöperation of *three* subjects, such as a sign, its object and its interpretant, this tri-relative influence not being in any way resolvable into actions between pairs' (CP: 5.484, 1907). It is clear that some sort of preparatory work for the ten classes set out on the post-scriptum diagram can be seen from the page in Figure 5.2. Here we find Peirce working through three stages in the derivation of a final set of ten classes of signs, in which the effects or subjects of the typology are not relational as in 1903 (the sign division excepted), but, instead, as in the hexadic system described in the letter of 23 December, the correlates themselves. This we can see from the instructions with which Peirce prefaces his method of identifying the classes of signs and in which we find a rule governing a hierarchical structure and a determination order similar to the ones in the letter (although there is no reference to a determination principle in the post-scriptum table):

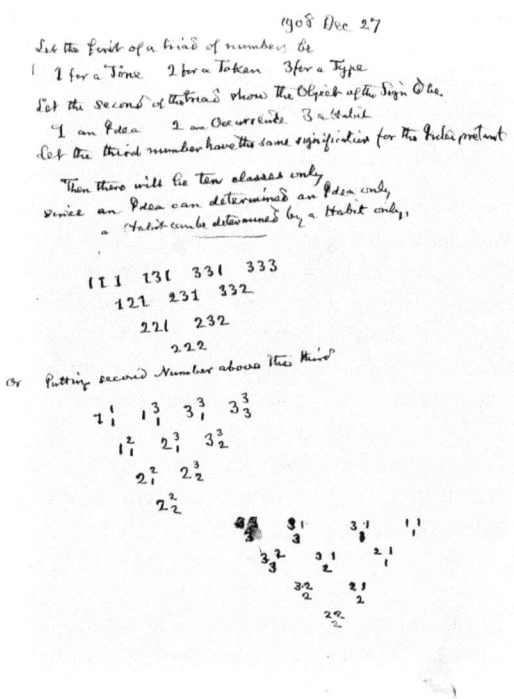

Figure 5.2 Possible preparatory workings for the post-scriptum diagram. R339: 339v, H636, 27 December 1908; MS Am 1632 (339), Houghton Library, Harvard University.

    Let the first of a triad of numbers be
        1 for a Tone   2 for a Token   3 for a Type
    Let the second of the triad show the Object of the Sign to be
        1 an Idea   2 an Occurrence   3 a Habit
    Let the third number have the same signification for the Interpretant
        Then there will be ten classes only
    since an Idea can determined [sic] an Idea only
    a Habit can be determined by a Habit only

The three schemata drawn down the page in Figure 5.2 clearly represent three different attempts to set up a valid typology.

The 'classes' analysed in Figures 5.3–5.6 are all extracted from the three schemata in Figure 5.2, and, to simplify, they all represent what, drawing on Peirce's summary instructions concerning tone, token and type, the values associated with each number and the order of appearance in the triangular scheme, would be identified as a collective gratific token (identified for convenience as O3 S2 I1), namely the class at the centre of each triangular set, the case where the object in the top left-hand corner is, according to Peirce's ordering instructions, a habit (3), while the sign in the lower vertex position is a token (2) and the interpretant top right is an 'idea' (1). As an aid to reading, in each case the representation given by Peirce for this class of signs is accompanied by the alphabetic key showing to which correlate each number corresponds: S for sign, O for object and I for interpretant.

In the first schema he places the items in the classes in linear, 'correlate' order (Figure 5.3). This was the order established initially in 1903 in his definition and descriptions of triadic relations (CP: 2.235–2.242), in which we find:

> A **Representamen** is the First Correlate of a triadic relation, the Second Correlate being termed its **Object,** and the possible Third Correlate being termed its **Interpretant,** by which triadic relation the possible Interpretant is determined to be the First Correlate of the same triadic relation to the same Object, and for some possible Interpretant. A **Sign** is a representamen of which some interpretant is a cognition of a mind. Signs are the only representamens that have been much studied.
>
> (CP: 2.242, 1903)

Hence the designation 'correlate' order. As we saw in Chapter 3, 'correlate' or, we might say, 'triadic relation' order is the order, too, of most of the six- and ten-division typologies Peirce established between 1905 and 1908: they typically begin with the sign division, followed by two or three divisions concerning the object, finishing with either the three or the six divisions concerning the interpretant.

In the case of the first attempt in Figure 5.3, correlate order is clearly problematic as far as the process of determination is concerned since the sign, a token, is followed by an object of higher order, a habit, a situation which runs counter to the rule stating that a habit can only be determined by a habit. For this reason, this order is incorrect, as is also the case with three further classes on the first schema in Figure 5.2 (**131, 121** and **232**).

In order to resolve this difficulty, his first solution in the second schema down the page is to place the second number directly above the third – 'Or Putting second Number above the third' – thereby placing the object above the interpretant, in other words. This has the effect of removing any form of linearity in the schema, particularly as the sign is singled out by its prominence. Peirce must have found this scheme unsuitable, too, as it still did not respect the hierarchical constraint set out in the instructions, and it also destroys the sense of linear dyadic determination which is integral to the structure of the classes of signs that he was seemingly trying to derive.

2 3 1 S O I

Figure 5.3 The three relata arranged in correlate order.

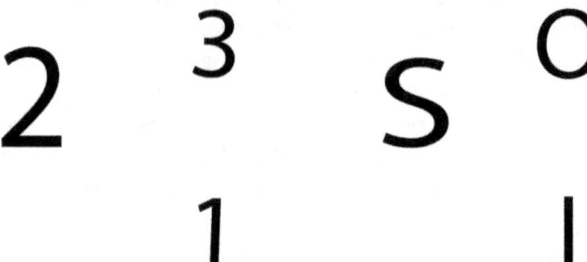

Figure 5.4 The three relata arranged non-linearly.

Finally, as the schema in the second attempt displayed in Figure 5.4 is still unable to accommodate the determination rules, Peirce elects to place the more complex correlate, namely the object, in top-left position. This is the order characteristic of the ten classes of signs he was to add as a post-scriptum the following day as shown in Figure 5.5: object followed by sign followed by interpretant.

At this point it is important to remember that semiosis was defined in 1907 as 'an action, or influence' involving three subjects, namely sign, object and interpretant. Now, in the letter to and the drafts intended for Lady Welby late in December 1908 he variously describes ten-division typologies, whereas in sequence 339v from the Logic Notebook between the 23 December letter and what appears to be the final draft dated 28 December 1908, he seems to have been experimenting with the sorts of classes that a very basic form of *semiosis* would produce. This was a strategy that he could have performed in 1903 since, as we see below, the basic, three-correlate semiosis as described in 1907 and realized in the post-scriptum table as examined above corresponds in all points to the numerous triadic definitions of the sign. These can be summarized, to simplify as: a sign is an entity which is so determined by its object that it determines an interpretant, in such a way that the interpretant is thereby mediately determined by the object. Such a definition corresponds, too, to the one given in the letter to Lady Welby of 23 December 1908, a definition which, although framed five years later, corresponds broadly to those of the Syllabus discussed in Chapter 2. In both cases, as seen earlier, the object determines the sign to provoke an effect or reaction in an interpreter, but as Peirce hastens to explain obliquely in the later 'sop to Cerberus' definition, not necessarily a human one (SS: 80–1, 1908).

Returning to the central class from Figure 5.1 again, the 3 2 1 class, we can conclude as follows: this and all the other classes on the lowest schema of ten on page 339v from the Logic Notebook (Figure 5.2) can be shown to correspond to an abridged version of Peirce's description of the hexadic signifying process – the 'determination sequence' – in the 23 December letter discussed in Chapter 4. For example, the final schema displayed in Figure 5.5 can be modified to include the determination process (Figure 5.6), and thus the 3 2 1 class used in the illustrations, like all the others in Figure 5.1, can reasonably be considered to equate class of sign with class of semiosis.

Figure 5.5 The three relata arranged in the order of semiosis.

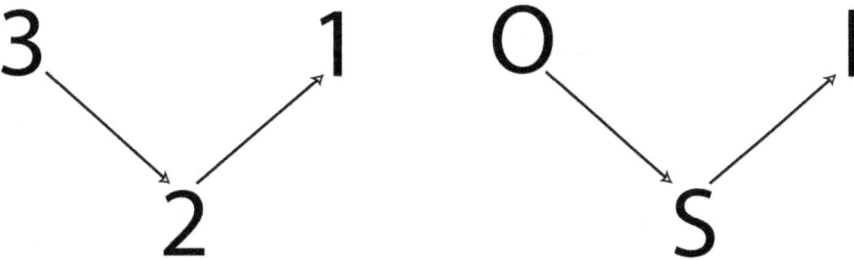

Figure 5.6 The class of collective gratific tokens as its corresponding class of semiosis.

In the case, then, of the post-scriptum system, the above analysis strongly suggests that classes of signs are inseparable from classes of semioses: in all cases, the leftmost element, the object, is always at least as complex as, or more complex than, the other two, while the sign is never less complex than the interpretant. Put differently, just what is it that these ten classes of signs can be said to represent? Certainly not an object, as in the case of the ten classes from 1903, given that the object is already present in the process. The answer is simple, and we return to the topic in the next chapter: these classes, as do the twenty-eight of the hexadic system examined in the previous chapter, can only represent the processes – semioses – that produced them: classes of signs correspond to classes of semioses. Such a hierarchical dependency manifested by the post-scriptum table corresponds to the set of classes of signs in Figure 5.1 and Table 5.2. In conclusion, on the post-scriptum table class of sign and class of semiosis can be shown to share the same modal structure, and that to each class of signs there corresponds a unique class of semiosis.

Figure 5.7 is the determination sequence obtained if the immediate object, immediate and dynamic interpretant divisions are removed from Figure 4.1 from the previous chapter, on which the correlates were set out in determination order. The determination structure displayed in Figure 5.7 corresponds in abridged form, too, to the one examined in Chapter 4, which was certainly not a definition of the sign, but, rather, a description of the determination process of semiosis, a process in which the sign occupies the central position.

Figure 5.7 Basic semiosis in which the object mediately determines the interpretant.

Table 5.1 The ten-class post-scriptum table

	Correlate		
	Od →	S →	If
Universe			
Necessitant	collective	type	to produce self-control
Existent	concretive	token	to produce action
Possible	abstractive	mark	gratific

Table 5.1, in which the designations for the various classes of signs have been drawn from Table 4.2 in Chapter 4, displays the post-scriptum table as it might have been developed if Peirce had had the time or the inclination; additionally, it indicates the determination process from object to interpretant via the sign mentioned by Peirce in the page from the Logic Notebook in Figure 5.2 and implicit in the scrap in Figure 5.1. The example class used to illustrate the development of the system in the Figures above is formed from a necessitant object (labelled 3 by Peirce), an existent sign (2) and a possible interpretant (1) yielding the class of collective gratific tokens.

The ten classes yielded by the post-scriptum typology, although obtained from distinctions offered by a carefully constructed ontological 'architecture', are not artificial in the way those of the 1903 typology are: they are active, since they function within natural processes. They are abridged versions of the hexadic process, which, corresponds to sign-processing by animate organisms. The ten classes are listed by name in Table 5.2, which displays them from most to least complex, with redundant information signalled by parentheses. The discriminating criteria here are the three universes (necessitant, existent, possible) while the respects are indicated as Object (O), the sign (S) and the interpretant (I) as given on the post-scriptum page.[4]

The question that we need to ask on inspecting such a table of 'signs divided into ten classes', according to Peirce's heading on the post-scriptum, was: what do they represent? The answer, again, is that they don't represent anything in the way those in Figure 2.4 do: to represent their objects they would need the S-O relational division as defined in the Syllabus and used as a respect in Figure 2.4. Moreover, the object itself is already in the table as 'leading' respect in each class: Table 5.2 and the post-scriptum

Table 5.2 The ten post-scriptum classes[5]

Criteria	Respect	Classes
	O S I	
Necessitant	3 3 3	(collective) self-control producing type
	3 3 2	(collective) action-producing type
	3 3 1	(collective) feeling-producing type
	3 2 2	collective action-producing token
	3 2 1	collective feeling-producing token
	3 1 1	collective mark
Existent	2 2 2	action-producing concretive (token)
	2 2 1	feeling-producing concretive (token)
	2 1 1	concretive mark/tone
Possible	1 1 1	abstractive

table it represents display classes of signs which are also processes. One serious consequence is that whereas the classes in Figure 2.4 do not require that we know the identity of object and interpretant, those in Table 5.2 cannot be fully analysed as signs without such knowledge. This, too, is the case with the hexad discussed in Chapter 4. However, the situation is not as difficult as it seems, and we return to it in the next chapter. In the meantime, we examine three examples of possible signs yielded by the post-scriptum typology.

We begin with class 333, the most complex, and formed by necessitant object, sign and interpretant. Such cases would involve intentionality or physical laws or institutions, etc., examples being the way general cultural conventions condition the behaviour of the inhabitants of a given community or country, or externally stimulated inferential processes determining a habit over time. Peirce seems already to have been thinking along these lines in the extract from the earlier Neglected Argument text: 'Such, too, is a living consciousness, and such the life, the power of growth, of a plant. Such is a living institution, – a daily newspaper, a great fortune, a social "movement"' (EP2: 437, 1908).

Class 331, formed from a necessitant object and sign and a possible interpretant, is a difficult class to illustrate. It is possibly a cognitive sequence followed by a feeling – a religious experience, an epiphany? Or identarian nostalgia, perhaps, as in Browning's 'Home Thoughts, from Abroad'. We tend to see nostalgia as the sign of sadness, but it can also be seen as the effect of some necessitant sign, transforming what is a sign in the early system into an interpretant in the later. Whatever instigates the sentiment is presumably communicated to the sufferer via some cognitive medium.

Finally, class 321, the example used throughout this section, is formed from a necessitant object, an existent sign and a 'possible' interpretant. One case might be a performance of a piano sonata pleasing or displeasing an audience: the musical principles determining the melodic line and harmonies are necessitant – a musical composition – while the performance executing the musical notation is existent and any feeling of pleasure is classified as a possible effect (but if the performance provokes applause or boos it becomes an action-producing collective token, class 322). Cf. this example of a gratific collective token from Peirce: 'Qualities of feeling may be meanings of signs. Thus, a piece of concerted music, since it mediates between the quality of the composer's succession of musical emotions and another in the breast of the auditor, is a sign' (R318: 665–7).

If the above conclusions are correct, then the ten classes displayed on the post-scriptum table can effectively be synthesized by the structure in Figure 5.6. I again conclude from this that the classes on the post-scriptum table constitute, at one and the same time, determination processes – semioses – and a typology. More significantly, Figure 5.6 is both a diagram of the determination flow of semiosis *and* of the basic three-relate structure of the various definitions of the sign given in 1903, when Peirce chose not to employ all three relates, but one relate division and two relational divisions in the establishment of his ten classes. The post-scriptum typology is what Peirce would have obtained in 1903 if he had made the three relates of the definition the effects of a typology instead of the single sign and the two relational trichotomies. It now remains to compare and contrast this ten-class system with the well-known ten-class typology from the Syllabus, a task which, for reasons of consistency, we hold over to Chapter 6.

Looking

At this point, we return to a problem raised in the concluding remarks of Chapter 1, namely, relevance. Peirce's final statements on the sign were consigned in various ways over a hundred years ago. This means inevitably that some parts of the theory will have been contested or considered superseded by more recent pronouncements, both within and without the field of semiotics. One such area that has been host to innovative developments concerns a central preoccupation of the entire Peircean edifice: the role and nature of observation in the sciences. A certain way of looking, in short; and this has brought to the surface a number of important binary distinctions. With it comes the relation between the observer and the object observed, and, more generally and as a theoretical consequence, the relation between the observing organism and the environment. Finally, there comes the question of mind – what it is, and, more importantly, where it is located – in all this, a topic much debated in the cognitive and neurosciences, and for which there is a Peircean approach.

In Peirce's classification of the sciences, it was axiomatic that 'All knowledge whatever comes from observation; but different sciences are observational in such radically different ways that the kind of information derived from the observation of one department of science (say natural history) could not possibly afford the information required of observation by another branch (say mathematics)' (CP: 1.238, 1902). Moreover, claimed Peirce, 'Observation is, in Agassiz's phrase, the "ways and means" of attaining the purpose of science' (ibid.). Now, Peirce was wont to assimilate the search for, and classification of, different types of signs to the tasks of the zoologist seeking to define the term 'fish': 'We are in the situation of a zoölogist who wants to know what ought to be the meaning of "fish" in order to make fishes one of the great classes of vertebrates' he wrote to Lady Welby in the letter dated 12 October 1904 (CP: 8.332); see, too, CP: 1.224, 1902,[6] and R318: 585, 1907.[7] For Peirce, then, in scientific endeavours, observation is key, hence his affection for the terminological division between the sciences of discovery into cenoscopic and idioscopic, the 'scopic' suffix deriving, as seen in Chapter 1, via Bentham, from the Greek infinitive, σκοπεῖν, to examine, to observe. Although there are many ways in which looking and observation can be approached, two are particularly pertinent to Peirce's position on the subject. For convenience in isolating the different topics, in the subsections to follow topics and authors will, most often, simply be signalled in the text by title.

The context

Lakoff and Johnson

Peirce's assimilation of the search for all possible signs to the tasks of the zoologist suggests a scientific modus operandi that conceives of entities in the world as objects to be observed and then compartmentalized, and presupposes a rigid separation between said objects and observers and a corresponding objectivist conception of our experience and knowledge of the world. Does this mean that Peirce's avowed realism it to be taken for objectivism or that this is not a charge that can be laid at Peirce's door? Certainly subsequent developments in the cognitive sciences, in the neurosciences and also in semiotics have proposed models of knowledge, experience and our relation to our environment with which Peirce's own conceptions have to be appraised if his continuing relevance to semiotic enquiry is to be maintained and genuine neo-Peircean approaches to signs are to be developed. One of the challenges to objectivism comes from various theories of embodiment. As a linguist, my first encounter with a nascent form of embodiment came with the discovery of Lakoff and Johnson's *Metaphors We Live By* (1980), from which I extract the two authors' programme for future research, which very explicitly introduces the problem of objectivism:[8]

> The heart of the objectivist tradition in philosophy comes directly out of the myth of objectivism: the world is made up of distinct objects, with inherent properties and fixed relations among them at any instant. We argue, on the basis of linguistic evidence (especially metaphor), that the objectivist philosophy fails to account for the way we understand our experience, our thoughts, and our language. An adequate account, we argue, requires
> —viewing objects only as entities relative to our interactions with the world and our projections on it
> —viewing properties is interactional rather than inherent
> —viewing categories as experiential gestalt's defined via prototype instead of viewing them as rigidly fixed and defined via set theory
>
> (1980: 210)

This comes towards the end of a study in which metaphorical conceptualization was linked to the human body and its place in the world, producing such 'orientational' metaphors as 'He's at the *peak* of health' and 'He *dropped* dead',[9] for example: 'These spatial orientations arise from the fact that we have bodies of the sort we have and that they function as they do in our physical environment' (1980: 14). Whether linguistics alone proves the failure of the objectivist hypothesis is questionable, but the authors offer a persuasive research programme concerning the observer and the observed and an interactional relation to the entities in the world.

Varela et al.

Lakoff and Johnson's visionary insights concerning embodiment in metaphorical expressions were followed by research in cognitive science of a more radical nature, one which rejects outright the sort of fixed and 'pregiven' world mentioned in Lakoff and Johnson's programme given above. Consider this remark from a complex study with the challenging title of *The Embodied Mind* (Varela, Thompson and Rosch 1993), in which the concept of embodiment is explicitly given a double sense, encompassing both the body as a lived, experiential structure and the body as the context or milieu of cognitive mechanisms: 'Such commonsense knowledge [successfully directed movement such as driving a car, for example] is difficult, perhaps impossible, to package into explicit, propositional knowledge—"knowledge *that*" in the philosopher's jargon—since it is largely a matter of readiness to hand or "knowledge *how*" based on the accumulation of experience in a vast number of cases' (1993: 148),[10] where the concept of common sense is defined as 'knowing how to negotiate our way through a world that is not fixed and pregiven but that is continually shaped by the types of actions in which we engage' (1993: 145). The statement prefigures subsequent research programmes that reject representationalism,[11] and investigate the cognitive status and its consequences of this dynamic relation between observer-participants and an environment which they modify as they engage with it. As in many cases in the investigation of what Clark (2011: 222) calls a 'coupled system',[12] research tends to target the relatively accessible fields of perception and visual phenomena. In Varela et al., colour is an important example of the enaction or creation of one such coupled system:

> Contrary to the objectivist view, color categories are experiential; contrary to the subjectivist view, color categories belong to our shared biological and cultural world. Thus color as a study case enables us to appreciate the obvious point that chicken and egg, world and perceiver, specify each other.
>
> It is precisely this emphasis on mutual specification that enables us to negotiate a middle path between the Scylla of cognition as the recovery of a pregiven outer world (realism) and the Charybdis of cognition as the projection of a pregiven inner world (idealism) .... Our intention is to bypass entirely this logical geography of inner versus outer by studying cognition not as recovery or projection but as embodied action.
>
> (1993: 172)

The authors thus reject the distinctions between mind and body, between 'inside and out' that are generally imputed to Descartes, and propose research into an enacted, creative conception of experience and cognition. More recently, such programmes have stimulated a particular line of research, four different but converging views of which are clearly presented in Legg (2021):[13]

> Intellectualism [i.e. the privileging by philosophers of 'knowledge *that*'] has been a powerful actor in modern philosophy from the time of Descartes' influential distinction of a 'mental act' from its (somehow encapsulated and commodified) 'content'.
> However, since Ryle (1946, 1949), intellectualist assumptions have been increasingly foregrounded and challenged in mainstream philosophy. A particularly widespread critique has been launched by a rapidly-growing philosophical movement advocating *embodied, embedded, extended* and *enactive* (so-called '4E') cognition. This movement rejects Descartes' traditional cleavages between mind and body, and mind and world, and the corresponding 'mentalization of knowledge'. Instead, theorists of *embodied* cognition view knowledge as located in both mind and body, and theorists of *embedded* and *extended* cognition view knowledge as located in both mind and world. These movements may be understood as 'querying the pure subjectivity of the knowing subject'. This naturally generates a correlative process of 'querying the pure objectivity of the known object' – which leads to the arguably most controversial arm of 4E cognition – 'the fourth e' – *enactivism*. Enactivism holds that the world is not antecedently given but 'enacted', through natural organisms' capacities for lived meaning-making.
>
> (2021: 2–3)

The theme of the replacement of a pregiven world to be observed from outside by one that is created actively by the organism and its environment is central to the posited complex interaction between organism and environment advanced by the radical enactivists. It is the latter view that is of most interest to the present discussion, one of its principal exponents being Alva Noë and his research into perception and mind.

Noë and enactivism

Herewith a radical enactivist's take on perception; '"Perception is not something that happens to us or in us, it is something we do" (Noë 2004: 1)', this from Alva Noë, quoted by Clark (2011: 170). In a later study, presented in a slightly bewildering 'fireside chat' style, Noë, still concerned with perception, is nevertheless more interested in proposing a depiction of the role and function of brain and mind that differs considerably from the traditional 'folk' conception of the brain as the central cognitive engine inside the body:

> We are, to use Merleau-Ponty's phrase again, empty heads turned to the world. The world is not a construction of the brain, nor is it a product of our own conscious efforts. It is there for us; we are here in it. The conscious mind is not inside us; it is, it would

be better to say, a kind of active attunement to the world, an achieved integration. It is the world itself, all around, that fixes the nature of conscious experience.

(2009: 142)

But it's not so much what characterizes Noë's version of the brain that is of interest with respect to Peirce, although, as we see later, Peirce's presentation of the brain-body relation to a certain extent anticipates Noë's 'model', as what Noë sees as the brain's role in the relation between an organism and its environment, and the manner in which visual perception, for example, contributes to this active engagement, or rather, interaction, with the world:

[T]he brain's job is, in effect, to coordinate our dealings with the environment. It is thus only in the context of an animal's embodied existence, situated in an environment, dynamically enacting with objects and situations, that the function of the brain can be understood.

This is a dramatic outcome of our investigation. For one thing, it means that the world itself can be described as belonging to the very machinery of our own consciousness. This isn't poetry; this is a well-supported empirical hypothesis. *Perceptual consciousness, at least, is a kind of skillful adjustment to objects (and the environment). Seeing is a style of skillful interaction with the things we see.* We couldn't do that if we had no brain, but we couldn't do it if there were no objects, either. The same point can be made about the body (that is, the rest of the body that is not our brain): the body gives structure and shape to the kinds of relations we can have to the world around us; the world shows up for us thanks to our bodily ability to coordinate our relation to it.

(2009: 65; emphasis added)

Note that like Lakoff and Johnson, and like Varela and his co-authors, Noë seems preoccupied by human interaction with the environment, and hardly extends his analyses to non-human organisms.

To summarize: Peirce's cenoscopy/idioscopy distinction, and with it the importance of observation in scientific practices, was introduced (reintroduced) at the beginning of the twentieth century, whereas by the end of the century a different conception of how we 'know the world' had already evolved and taken shape, promoting, in certain cases, a radical version of 'knowledge how' in opposition to the older objectivist, intellectualist 'knowledge that': one example being enactivism. This has come to posit a different type of relation between the analyst and the object, between the organism and its environment, for in place of a putatively unidirectional observation of the object by the analyst, enactivism posits one that promotes interaction between the two agencies. And we now have a distinction between a representational (Peirce) as opposed to a non-representational conception of knowledge (radical enactivism: see Legg 2021) and, concomitantly, between what is potentially a late nineteenth-century objectivism and a conception of the organism's relation to its environment that necessarily undermines such objectivism. In this way, by the end of the century, a different conception of how we 'know the world' had acquired academic status, and has come to posit a different type of relation between ourselves and the world, and, consequently, between two ways of looking at that world and what inhabits it.

It might be possible for certain Peirce scholars and commentators to dismiss the '4Es', enactivism or the research objectives of Varela, Thompson and Rosch, and other, similar types of scientific investigations, as extreme, unproved theories of mind specific to the fields of the cognitive and neurosciences; however, the semiotician can't. For, between the 1903 cenoscopic and idioscopic propositional 'knowledge that' and the extreme enactivists' non-representationalism, between, on the one hand, a potentially objectivist vision of the relation between analyst and analysand and, on the other, an interactive conception of the relation between organism and environment and a matching interactive relation holding between observer and observed object, there appeared one Thomas A. Sebeok, whose own position is somewhere midway between the scientific theories and practices described above and Peirce's own.

Sebeok

Although from very different origins and with major differences in outlook, the two conceptions of our relation to the world – enactivism and Sebeok's conception of semiotics – are in some ways comparable. Sebeok readily concedes that Peirce and von Uexküll were major influences on his theory of the sign – Peirce, though, more as a semiotician than as a logician – a judgement supported by many researchers in semiotics and biosemiotics stimulated by Sebeok's work. As he comes after Peirce and was able to draw on many more recent and more varied information, authorities and scientific sources – Morris, Jakobson, for example, and von Uexküll, of course – it is natural that there should be differences between his comprehensive and self-contained conception of the semiotics presented, for example, in Sebeok (2001) and the protean unfinished theory left by Peirce almost a century earlier. Which raises anew the problem of continuing relevance of a century-old theory of the sign. What follows is a comparison of certain key aspects of the two approaches to signs, not to award points or choose a winner, but to highlight significant differences between them. These pertain to aspects of the context introduced in the previous section, and are implicated in the problem of 'looking', thus bringing us back to the cenoscopy/idioscopy distinction discussed in Chapter 1 involving 'scopic' activity: namely, the relation holding between observer and object, and more broadly between organism and environment, topics inseparable from semiosis, representationalism and language.

Sebeok's departure from Peirce's conception of the sign can clearly be seen in several fields. One simple such case is the reduction to six the classes of signs that he defines. These are symptom, signal, icon, index, symbol and name, none of which is identified by reference to defining and discriminating criteria from, for example, phenomenology, although, judging by the order of the three that he takes from Peirce's three modes of representation – icon, index and symbol – they are organized in order of increasing complexity.

Furthermore, although Sebeok references the structure of the dicent sinsign in a discussion of types of models (2001: 147), there seems not to be any form of informational sign like Peirce's dicent symbol. As biosemiotics is by definition based upon a conception of the sign, as a theory it is representational in the sense dismissed by Varela and his co-authors, but it is not, like Peirce's, explicitly propositional. In Sebeok's case information is communicated by means of messages: 'Messages can be constructed on the basis of single signs or, more often than not, as combinations of them. The latter are known as *texts*. A *text* constitutes, in effect, a "weaving together" of signs in order to communicate something. The signs that go into the make-up of texts belong to specific *codes*' (2001: 7). The two theories also differ with respect to the scope of semiotics, as can be seen from Sebeok's assimilation of Jakobsonian linguistics and information theory: 'These six key factors – messages and code, source and destination, channel and context – separately and together make up the rich domain of semiotic' (2001: 32). What is commonly referred to as Peirce's semiotics is, by contrast and as emphasized forcefully in Chapter 1, an extended conception of the scope of logic, a logic of which applied, idioscopic versions were later incorporated into linguistics, varieties of descriptive semiotics and biosemiotics.

Observation

Consider these remarks from Sebeok (2001):

> One obvious implication of this postulated duality [between sign and object] is that semiosis requires at least two actants: the observer and the observed. Our intuition of reality is a consequence of a *mutual interaction* between the two
>
> (2001: 33, emphasis added)

> [W]hat a semiotic model depicts is not 'reality' as such, but nature as unveiled by our method of questioning. It is the *interplay* between 'the book of nature' and its human decipherer that is at issue.
>
> (2001: 26, emphasis added)

A polymath like Sebeok would no doubt have been aware of the research undertaken by contemporaries in the cognitive science field such as Varela, Thompson and Rosch, but it is common knowledge now that his conception of what Clark (2011) has called a 'coupled system' derived not from cognitive science but from his acquaintance with the biological theory of von Uexküll. For Varela and his co-workers this coupled relation was seen specifically from the point of view of the organism and its orientation through, and adjustment to, the constraints of the environment. This is the case, too, in Noë's work on enaction, where the emphasis again is on the organism's active construction of perception of and its engagement with its environment, whereas for Sebeok, the relation holding between observer and observed is clearly characterized by *mutual* interaction, by reciprocal interplay between what he refers to neutrally as the two 'actants' involved in the moment of observation. Moreover, the nature of this interaction is doubly dynamic: it involves this interplay, certainly, but in doing so each participant affects the other – in observing the object the observer 'perturbs' the latter's condition as Sebeok has it. In other words, observation – looking – is reactive in such cases:

> Any observer's version of his/her *Umwelt* will be one unique model of the world, which is a system of signs made up of genetic factors plus a cocktail of experiences,

including future expectations. *A complicating fact of life is that the bare act of observation entails a residual juncture that disturbs the system being observed* [emphasis added]. The essential ingredient, or nutriment, of mind may well be information, but to acquire information about anything requires, via a long and complex chain of steps, the transmission of signs from the object of interest to the observer's central nervous system. *Its attainment, moreover, takes place in such a manner that this influential action reacts back upon the object being observed so as to perturb its condition* [emphasis added].

(2001: 34)

This statement shows clearly the extent to which Sebeok breaks with the tenets of contemporary cognitive science. Not only is the relation between observer and object one of mutual interaction, but through the very act of observing the object the analyst is held to disturb or perturb that object in some way.

Semiosis

For the dictionaries, the concept of semiosis was defined by Peirce in 1907, and Sebeok indeed gives the quotation from the *Collected Papers* (45-6), but throughout the study offers definitions which derive from his research in biosemiotics. To wit, semiosis is conceived above all as an animate organism's capacity to engage with signs: '[Semiosis] can be defined simply as the instinctive capacity of all living organisms to produce and understand signs' (2001: 3), and '*Semiosis* is the biological capacity itself that underlies the production and comprehension of signs, from simple physiological signals to those that reveal a highly complex symbolism' (2001: 8). Semiosis, for the biosemioticians, thus constitutes the organism's capacity to 'model' or organize its '*Umwelt*', this being defined by Sebeok, following von Uexküll, as the 'domain that a species is capable of modelling (the external world of experience to which a species has access)' (2001: 157). Cobley (2018) explains this theoretical position simply and clearly:

> The human *Umwelt*, according to Sebeok, drawing upon von Uexküll, is a model; or, put another way, various acts of modelling on the side of the *Innenwelt* (the inner, subjective world of the animal) contribute to the constitution of the 'objective' or 'public' world of an animal species as *Umwelt*. Models are made up of signs: thus, semiotic systems are modelling systems.
>
> (2018: 34)

Language

Such modelling within Sebeok's conception of signs and their actions governs organisms' means of communication seen as the transmission of messages. Innovatively, Sebeok sees language as multimodal, composed initially of nonverbal communication followed later by verbal language. He posits nonverbal communication as basic and common to all animate organisms: 'One of the main targets of a biological study of semiosis is nonverbal communication. Indeed, it is the "default mode" of communication. Only the members of the species Homo sapiens are capable of communicating, simultaneously or in turn, by both nonverbal and verbal means' (2001: 11), such a capacity being uniquely available to animals by means of a variety of media or channels: 'Animals communicate through different channels or combinations of media. Any form of energy propagation can, in fact, be exploited for purposes of message transmission' (2001: 12). Any such exchange of information between humans, the species that uses the primary modelling system of language, is explained in terms of the encoding and decoding of messages, these being various types of text as mentioned above.

This ability to communicate verbally, he has suggested, was the development of a modelling system proper to communication between humans, and evolving over time through the process of exaption (Sebeok 2001: 147). Moreover, according to Sebeok, who was possibly influenced in this by Noam Chomsky's putative language acquisition device,[14] the later verbal expressive system (a 'modelling device') is innate: 'With a brain capacity of 600–800 cc, this ancestral creature [homo habilis] must have had a mute verbal modelling device lodged in its brain, but it could not encode it in articulate, linear speech' (Sebeok 2001: 146). See, too, this comment by Cannizzaro and Cobley: 'Semiotics is the study of comparative *Umwelten* and, as such, must be concerned with animal and plant communication whilst principally attending to the human Umwelt which is characterised by what Sebeok called "language" – not linguistic communication but the innate and phylogenetically developed "modelling" device mentioned above'[15] (2015: 210).

It would be unrealistic in this subsection to review Sebeok's comprehensive and innovative conception of biosemiotics in its entirety, but it can conveniently be summarized with respect to the enactivists as interactive but representational. Although representational it is but not propositional in the Peircean sense: messages communicated within and between organisms are defined as texts, not dicent signs.

Peirce

The reader is again reminded at this point that Peirce was a logician, not a semiotician in the modern sense, nor was he a biologist. As such, his principal, but not exclusive, theoretical interest was in the information-bearing symbol, although, as seen earlier, by the 1880s he had realized that a complete logic of the symbol required icons and indices as indispensable adjuncts. For him, the 'unit' of informational content was the concept or conception, the constituents of which, like the categories, enter the intellect and are made available for ratiocination through perception, hence the remarkable formula already mentioned in Chapter 3: 'The elements of every concept enter into logical thought at the gate of perception and make their exit at the gate of purposive action' (CP 5.212, 1903). The important point of the definition in the present context is that, for Peirce, these elements *enter* willy-nilly into logical thought, they are neither actively sought nor brought in: they impose themselves upon our perception.

Now, Peirce adopted Kant's contention that the purpose of conceptions was to reduce the multitude of external stimuli to the unity of a proposition, since he held the proposition, more generally the dicent symbol, to be the minimal complete unit of knowledge: propositional 'knowledge *that*'. Just how such symbolic content is derived via perception from sense data is a complex affair which involves at least two forms of reasoning, hence of logic. One of these Peirce considered acritical, as being beyond our conscious control; the other he held to be conscious and therefore open to control and correction. In the first case, the intellect directly receives the disparate mass of external stimuli in the form of sense data, over which, quite naturally, it has no control, since these are never known directly. The form of reasoning that *is* known, however, is the percept, that is, what Peirce calls the 'evidence of the senses', which the intellect records as a positive, fallible but incorrigible and irreversible perceptual fact (CP: 2.140–3, 1902): 'The perceptual facts are a very imperfect record of the percepts; but I cannot go behind that record. As for going back to the first impressions of sense, as some logicians recommend me to do, that would be the most chimerical of undertakings' (CP: 2.142).

Peirce dismisses as pointless any attempt to observe the original sense data, for he holds that in some unexplained way we experience the percept and that we experience it in the form of a positive proposition which we cannot help thinking to be true. The best that we can do is unconsciously test the evidence of our senses by means of inferences. Such inferences form the basis of our future actions and constitute a class of judicative inferences which Peirce terms 'perceptual judgments', since the process involves an abductive judgement concerning the nature of the percept. It is, in other words, the non-conscious framing of a hypothesis. Since perceptual judgements *are* such as they are: positive, incorrigible and irreversible, they are not open to the questions of truth and falsehood that are a feature of epistemological querying: 'It follows, then, that the perceptual judgments are the first premises of all our reasonings and that they cannot be called in question' (CP: 5.116, 1903). The process is well explained by Murray Murphey: 'Because it is beyond control and criticism, the percept must be accepted without question as being both real and the given of experience. And because perceptual judgments are indubitable, their testimony as to what the percept is must be accepted as authentic. Thus the perceptual judgement is the first premiss of voluntary inference' (1993: 32; cf., too, CP: 2.27, 1902). The only way to block the gate of perception would be to shut down the entire sensorium.

In the period when he was developing his categories, Peirce showed much interest in perception in the Harvard lectures on pragmatism of 1903, on which the material above is based, and the force of perception at that time had the character of Secondness. However, logical structure figures more prominently than phenomenology in the various attempts to prove his pragmaticism in manuscript R318 of 1907. In spite of this theoretical switch in his approach to pragmaticism, his conception of the 'passive', receptive nature of perception itself hadn't changed in any way, as we see from this extract from Ms R299 of 1906, in which Peirce is explaining what he means by 'experience' and the inevitable shock that characterizes it:[16]

> Low grades of this shock doubtless accompany all unexpected perceptions; and every perception is more or less unexpected. Its lower grades are, as I opine, not without experimental tests of the hypothesis, that sense of externality, of the presence of a *non-ego*, which accompanies perception generally and helps to distinguish it from dreaming ... But the important point [is], that the sense of externality in perception consists in a sense of powerlessness before the

overwhelming force of perception. Now the only way in which any force can be learned is by something like trying to oppose it. That we do something like this is shown by the shock we receive from any unexpected experience.

(LI: 346–7, 1906)

Perception is thus initiated by the sense data emanating from the object observed, a principle that accords completely with his definition of reality as being independent of what anyone thinks it to be. Since the origin of any perception is the real, we cannot engage with it before and until we have become aware of it. Thus activated by the sense data, perception brings with it the elements of logical thought. And it follows from this principle that we don't perceive signs as such via the senses. Signs – language signs included – are identified solely by inference:

> If ... someone had asked me to guess in how many unrelated ways a sign could first come to be recognized as such ... the right answer is, By one only ... namely, By inference. For decidedly, significance can neither be seen, nor heard, nor smelled, nor tasted, nor known by touch, nor otherwise be directly perceived; and that which cannot be directly perceived can only become known by inference ... I term those three elementary modes of inference, Induction ... Deduction and Retroduction.
>
> (R318: 345-347, 1907)

The paragraphs to follow examine how such a principle relates to the issues raised by the enactivists and the biosemioticians, the latter referencing Peirce as an early theoretical influence.

Observation

We begin with the problem of looking, first mentioned in Chapter 1. Both the theorists of embodied mind examined above and Thomas Sebeok consider that the relation holding between an observer and an observed object, like the one holding between an organism and its environment, is one of reciprocal influence. Moreover, it is a form of interplay or mutual interaction, as Sebeok has it, in which in the observation the object is in some way disturbed:

> A complicating fact of life is that the bare act of observation entails a residual juncture that disturbs the system being observed ... the transmission of signs from the object of interest to the observer's central nervous system. Its attainment, moreover, takes place in such a manner that this influential action reacts back upon the object being observed so as to perturb its condition.
>
> (2001: 34)

Such a position is clearly at odds with Peirce's conception of perception. In his case, it is the object which unilaterally and unidirectionally perturbs the observer: the object is the origin of the sense data entering the observing intellect via the gate of perception, to repeat Peirce's striking metaphor. This is also the direction of the 'flow of influence' in all of Peirce's definitions of the sign: the sign is determined by the object to determine an interpretant, that is, a reaction in an observer. Consider, within the Peircean perspective, the trope of the lab technician as an example. When he or she peers into a microscope to examine some object, a rock, for example, it is the object which perturbs the technician, not the technician the object. This is an elementary example of semiosis: the rock projects via the light medium a combination of frequencies (including some that are invisible to the human eye) that form a sign as a complex sense datum; this then produces a series of effects upon the technician terminating in a cry of 'Eureka!', for example, if the rock turns out to contain gold, or an expletive, perhaps, if it only contains iron pyrite. The final interpretant in such a case, the action produced by the sign, is verbal. As proposed in Chapter 4, Peircean semiosis is linear, unlike more recent models. Deely's Figure 1, for example, from Deely (2001: 28), not discussed in the text but referenced in Deely (2009b: 76, and 76 n6; 136) is an inferential spiral, leading from abduction to induction through deduction in a series of cycles, while Barnham's Figure 11 with the caption, 'Semiosis as the Interaction of Peirce's Three Categories and the Three Elements of the Sign' (Barnham 2022: 242), also displays semiosis as a spiral moving in cycles from icon to symbol.

Keeping in mind the definition of cenoscopy and its Greek origins: (σκοπέω), 'I see', 'I look', and what is common, (κοινός), we turn to the issue of looking. Now, the earlier, Peircean position, can best be seen in these two definitions of the entry for the verb 'look' in the OED:

> look, v. I.I To direct one's sight. 1.I.1 intr. To give a certain direction to one's sight; to apply one's power of vision; to direct one's eyes upon some object or towards some portion of space
> behold, v. [...] 7.I.7 trans. a To hold or keep in view, to watch ... arch. This has passed imperceptibly into the resulting passive sensation: b To receive the impression of (anything) through the eyes, to see: the ordinary current sense.

In the first definition the verb signifies an active process, in the second, a passive. The two types of observation discussed above respect this division. An enactivist like Noë clearly espouses the active sense of the verb, as we saw above from Clark's quoting him (2011: 170): 'Perception is not something that happens to us or in us, it is something we do'. Moreover, Sebeok and biosemioticians that he has influenced, would all see looking, observing, as active, too, since the very process disturbs the object analysed. The Peircean position, on the other hand, assimilates the second, 'behold', definition of looking: quite the opposite of that of Sebeok and the biosemioticians, for example. Consider in respect of active and passive looking this remark by Martin Heidegger:

> In the statement 'Science is the theory of the real,' what does the word 'theory' mean? The word 'theory' stems from the Greek verb *theorein*. The noun belonging to it is *theoria*. Peculiar to these words is a lofty and mysterious meaning. The verb *theorein* grew out of the coalescing of two root words, *thea* and *horao*. *Thea*

(cf. theater) is the outward look, the aspect, in which something shows itself, the outward appearance in which it offers itself.

(1982: 163)

Combined with Peirce's theory of perception, Peircean semiosis offers a different perspective on how we look: the object determines, through the sign, a reaction in the interpreter-analyst. The 'directionality' involved in the looking begins logically with the object, not the analyst: the latter 'beholds' the former. This differs completely both from the OED active, sight-directed definition and from any interactive relation between analyst and object. In observation in its Peircean perspective, the 'σκοπέω', 'I look' is, rather, à la Heidegger, 'I am determined/modified in my look'. It is the object as the unique triggering agency in Peircean semiosis that activates the observing process, and in looking, it is the object in what Heidegger refers to as 'the outward appearance in which it offers itself' which determines the observer. In the laboratory example, the technician's eye is struck by a certain distinctive pattern of light emitted by the object and he or she reacts to it.[17] To take a theatre example, we conventionally consider the audience at a play or in the cinema to be 'spectators', active lookers, but in fact semiosis works here exactly as in the laboratory case: aural and visual stimuli in a variety of forms are not sought but 'absorbed', taken in, by the audience, and then produce a reaction, that is, interpretants, in its members – actions such as laughter, clapping or internal qualities of feeling. This might be dismissed as a radical form of objectivism; but whatever, it is the way observation presents itself from a Peircean perspective, if the reasonings in the previous chapters are correct.

Language

How would this Peircean combination of perception and semiosis apply to language? Sebeok sees speech, as do Cannizzaro and Cobley, the later verbal language, as innate, suggesting an innate device serving this purpose: an 'innate and phylogenetically developed "modelling" device' as Cannizzaro and Cobley have it (2015: 210). Now, since the elements of every concept are deemed by Peirce to enter into logical thought at the gate of perception in the guise of perceptual judgements – abductive inferences – it follows that any further activity of the intellect can involve nothing but further inferences involving all three types of argument – abduction, deduction, induction – and any phylogenetically developed capacity for language in any form will have been constructed from inferences. In short, animate organisms, at their different levels and according to their experience, are inference machines, and it is through myriad sequences of such inferences that, humans for example, have acquired the capacity to communicate verbally, perception ultimately producing, *pace* Noam Chomsky, habits – more or less idiosyncratic habits of syntax, of pronunciation, of articulation.[18] From a Peircean perspective, there is no need for a device of any sort – from the day we are born we perform inferences from the stimuli imposed upon us by the world we live in: we learn to communicate successfully with our fellow humans, verbally or by means of many types of semioses, in addition to acquiring inferentially a multitude of other skills.

Moreover, according to Peirce, 'No communication of one person to another can be entirely definite, i.e., non vague .... But wherever degree or any other possibility of continuous variation subsists, absolute precision is impossible. Much else must be vague, because no man's interpretation of words is based on exactly the same experience as any other man's' (CP: 5.506, 1905). In conjunction with every individual's distinct inferential acquisition of language and communicating skills, such a state of affairs is likely to be the source of much language dysfunction, breakdown in communication, misunderstandings, etc., and, at the same time, must surely be one of the sources of language change and the possibility of grammatical reanalysis and grammaticalization. It is difficult to see how an innate device might malfunction phylogenetically in such cases. Finally, it would be more in line with Peircean logic and with theoretical consistency to replace the better-known terms 'encoding' and 'decoding' by 'mediatization' (to be defined and illustrated in the following chapter) and 'interpretation': these terms avoid the dyadic nature of the code.

Thus, reasoning from the Peircean conception of perception and semiosis as presented in these pages, since all our knowledge is acquired by inference, there is no reason for our knowledge of language to be acquired any differently, particularly, if as Sebeok suggests, verbal communication is a later, secondary development. One of the frequently touted arguments in favour of generative grammar was the notion that although capable of understanding infinitely many sentences, no human being has more than a finite period of time in which to learn them, hence the necessity of an innate acquisition device. On the contrary, speakers bring to the speech act their unique experience of the world and try as best they can to make sense of what the other is saying: the evolution of thought – and with it, language – is dialogic (LI: 326, 1906; R318 583, 1907). This suggests that language is an aggregate, not an inviolable, perfect system, even less an innate, pre-existent, universally shared whole that speakers carry around in their heads. From a Peircean perspective, then, the argument for an innate device is irrelevant, for a purely quantitative conception of exposure to experience underestimates the nature of the inferential capacities of the human being, and until we find convincing proof to the contrary, there is no reason to suppose that knowledge of language is ever complete or that the 'structure' of one's native tongue is not inferred like the other information derived from perception. If this is the case, then language – verbal and nonverbal – is, from a Peircean point of view, an open-ended system, not a closed, pre-established one whose putatively determinate structure diligent linguists seek to uncover.

Mind

What of the brain and mind? Alva Noë's claim is that we are not our brains (2009). His thesis is that our awareness of our environment, our consciousness, does not reside in the brain, but is constructed, enacted by the sort of dynamic interplay or interaction with the environment in a manner consonant with the coupled systems as advanced by Sebeok and other biosemioticians, although for Sebeok the relation between organism and environment is less a question of enaction than of signification:

In brief, the brain, or mind, which is itself a system of signs, is linked to the putative world of objects, not simply by perceptual selection, but by such a far-off remove from physical inputs – sensible stimuli – that we can safely assert that the only cognizance any animal can possess, 'through a glass, darkly,' as it were, is that of signs.

(2001: 34)

What form would a Peircean view of this problem take? Consider, in this respect, these two extracts, the first from the Prolegomena paper of 1906, the second from MS R318 of 1907

Thought is not necessarily connected with a brain. It appears in the work of bees, of crystals, and throughout the purely physical world; and one can no more deny that it is really there, than that the colors, the shapes, etc., of objects are really there.

(LI: 326, 1906)

The action of a sign generally takes place between two parties, the *utterer* and the *interpreter*. They need not be persons; for a chameleon and many kinds of insects and even plants make their livings by uttering signs, and lying signs, at that. Who is the utterer of signs of the weather, which are not remarkably veracious, always?

(R318: 419, 1907)[19]

No doubt Peirce, whose time spent with Agassiz the zoologist wasn't entirely taken up with the rules of classification, would agree with Noë that mind and consciousness, awareness of the environment, were not the prerogative of the brain, for he holds even more radically that thought and semiosis are to be found not only in animate organisms such as humans and bees, but also in what Deely refers to as physiosemiosis,[20] namely sign activity in the inorganic realm, here crystals and 'throughout the purely physical world'. In manuscript R318, Peirce is even more emphatic on the capacity for semiosis of non-human animate organisms: many kinds of insects and plants survive by producing signs – 'lying signs, at that' – by camouflaging themselves, that is, formed by habit to pretend to be what they are not, either for protection or to attract prey. But in Peirce's case this is not zoology or ethology, but logic: 'In its broader sense, [logic] is the science of the necessary laws of thought […] which […] coincides with the study of the necessary conditions of the transmission of meaning by signs from mind to mind, and from one state of mind to another' (CP 1.444, 1896?). To which, we have the beginnings of a response from Thomas Sebeok:

No one, at present, knows how afferent neuronal activity acquires meaning, beyond the strong suspicion that what is commonly called the ' external world,' including the objects and events postulated as being contained in it, is the brain's formal structure (logos). For all practical purposes, we are ignorant about how the central nervous system preserves any structure and assigns a meaning to it, how this process relates to perception in general, and how it induces a response. Implicit in this set of queries is a plainly linear model: for example, that fear or joy 'causes' increased heart rate. Not only does such a model seem to me far too simplistic, but there is not even a shred of evidence that it exists at all.

(2001: 80)

The broader sense of logic in Peirce's text quoted above is, of course, his logic as semeiotic, not the traditional Critic as described in the Syllabus (EP2: 256, 1903). What he was saying, over a hundred years ago, is that the transmission of meaning is not from brain to brain as might be thought in some folk theory of psychology, the sort Sebeok is implicitly rejecting, but from mind to mind, which, in his broader conception of logic, is described in the following remarkable manner and is, in effect, a linear model: 'signs specially function between two minds, the one being the sign's *utterer*, (not necessarily a vocal utterer, but putting forth the sign in any way) the other the sign's *interpreter*. Indeed, a *mind* may, with advantage, be roughly defined as *a sign-creatory in connection with a reaction-machine*' (R318: 425, 1907). Note that Peirce is careful to avoid any psychological implications in this definition as the reaction-machine, which could, alternatively, be designated an interpretant-machine or interpreting machine is connected not to a creator, but to a creatory. This definition of mind, purely mechanical, stripped of any possible association with any particular animate organism, is pure logic, and is typical of the difference between the 'perception-semiosis' conception of observation, language, mind and the brain presented as Peircean in these pages and those of the alternative systems described above.

Summary and discussion

In itself the post-scriptum table must remain a mystery: Peirce gave no additional information as to its purpose or use, and one wonders what Lady Welby would have made of it if she had ever received it. Nevertheless, developing it through the first part of the chapter has resulted in three important conclusions. First, analysis and reconstruction have strongly suggested its status as both a typology and a potential process. Second, the endeavour has shown the table's organic relation to the definitions of the sign proposed in 1903: the table is likely to be what Peirce would have found if he had derived a correlate typology in 1903 instead of the extant relational version. Third, with the table shown to be an abridged version of the determination sequence in Chapter 4, such a finding adds further support from within to the idea that the determination sequence analysed in Chapter 4 is indeed both a process and a typology.

The second part of the chapter returned to the problem of Peirce's continuing relevance introduced in Chapter 1, and with it the comparison of a theory of the sign over a hundred years old with contemporary developments in the cognitive sciences and a more modern, alternative theory of sign and semiotics. The central issue here was observation, 'looking', a notion fundamental to a conceptualization of the sciences that promotes the scopic. Now, in view of the importance of the dicisign, amongst other channels of information, as the unit of propositional information and the transmission of knowledge, the Peircean 'point of view' might be dismissed as a radical form of objectivism. Wrong. First, as seen in Chapter 1, it is logic, the cenoscopic science that Peirce held in 1903 to be the philosophy of representation (R465: 25, 1903). Second, Peirce was a realist of an extreme stripe, and reality for him is such as it is independently of what anyone, semioticians included, think it to be.

Summary presentations of theories of embodied mind and enactivism revealed the rejection of one conception of 'looking', in which the analyst observes the object in an 'active' one-way relation: from analyst to object, corresponding to a naïve view of how an audience directs its sight to the stage in a theatre. To this was opposed an interactive conception of the observer-observed relation, characterized by one commentator as a 'coupled system'. Furthermore, one strain of enactivism was shown to conceive perception itself as an active collaboration between organism and its environment, a relation to be constructed with the environment.

Similar, but not identical, positions were found to be shared by biosemioticians, most notably by Thomas Sebeok, who drew on the theories of Jakob von Uexküll concerning animal behaviour and the organism's relation to its environment. As Sebeok also claimed Peirce as a source of his personal account of signs and semiosis, Peirce's approach to these problems was compared with Sebeok's. Comparison revealed that Peirce's conception of the compulsive nature of perception was such that it conditioned all cognitive activity to be the construction of inferences from inescapable incoming perceptual data. In this way, in complete contrast to the positions attributed to the enactivists and to Sebeok and other biosemioticians, 'looking' and the relation holding between observer and the observed object were demonstrated to be unidirectional, specifically from object of perception to observer: a passive process of beholding as opposed to the observer-directed interactive position of a specific theory of biosemiotics. Similarly, the nature of perception thus conceived was shown to correspond to Peircean semiosis as posited in this study, in which the object of observation mediately determines an effect upon an observer-interpreter. This conception of perception also revealed differences between Sebeok's account of the innate device-based workings of verbal language and an abductive description of how a Peircean theory of language might be modelled as an 'open' inference-based developmental process. Such differences are not to be unexpected, given that one conception of the sign is defined and employed in a contemporary semio-biological context, the other in an earlier much amplified theory of logic.

And what of relevance? What the comparisons conducted above were intended to show was that the more recent theory of the sign seemingly adopted by biosemioticians claiming Peirce as a forerunner was neither better nor less powerful than the Peircean theory presented in this study, but simply that it was different. The comparisons brought to light some very stark differences between the two, which shows them to be parallel theories of the sign. In this respect, the relevance of Peircean semiotics, old as it is, and as many practitioners 'out there' are continuing to prove, is in no way threatened by developments in comparable disciplines. The chapter to follow also seeks to illustrate this enduring relevance.

6

Perspectives

Having devoted the previous chapters to showing how different the systems of 1903 and 1908 are, the principal aim of this chapter is to explain and exemplify how they can nevertheless be combined in a hybrid form of semiotic analysis – one version of neo-Peircean semiotics.[1] The chapter begins by exploring the theoretical limits of the post-scriptum typology described in the previous chapter and here identified as a typology formed from the 1903 definitions of the sign. These limits appear when the two ten-class typologies are briefly compared. The analyses that follow adopt the principle that the sign can be considered as any sort of medium, according to Peirce's definition given in Chapter 3. Finally, this hybrid analysis of a series of signs associates the initial stages of semiosis with the hypoicon system introduced in Chapter 2. This system is represented by an introductory series of typical examples of the three hypoicons followed by three case studies illustrating their potential for the qualitative analysis of pictorial representation.

At the same time, the chapter also demonstrates in little how semiosis models complex anthroposemiotic activity as formulated famously in Edward Bernay's 1947 apology for 'scientific' persuasion, a theory to which he referred as the 'engineering of consent'. Bernays was a public relations 'counsellor' and published his views most notably in a paper entitled 'The engineering of consent' (Bernays 1947). We find this reasoning resonating in our present age in nudge theory (Thaler and Sunstein 2008), with the lobbyists and fixers plaguing parliaments, the 'influencers' on social media platforms, and, more worryingly, in the opaque and sinister workings of what Zuboff (2019) calls 'surveillance capitalism' and in the seemingly unfettered instrumentarian power wielded by the barons of Silicon Valley. Given this context, the engineering of consent is of interest to Peircean semiotic analysis in its being a scheme for purposive, deliberate manipulation programmed in a rational series of stages: 'Just as the civil engineer must analyze every element of the situation before he builds a bridge, so the engineer of consent, in order to achieve a worthwhile social objective, must operate from a foundation of soundly planned action' (Bernays 1947: 116). Additionally, we must add, in order to achieve any worthwhile objective, this objective has to be made public. From a semiotic point of view, such soundly planned action is an example of semiosis, of which the initial stages assure the implementation of mediatization, the making-public of the agency of said planned action. The argument begins with the comparison of the ten-class typologies of 1903 and 1908.

Comparing two ten-class typologies

It is tempting to try to determine in what possible way the post-scriptum classes, assuming perhaps optimistically that they are what Peirce might have had in mind, might correspond to the Syllabus table in Figure 2.4 and the examples examined in Chapter 5. In comparison with the Syllabus typology, class 333, the control-producing type in Table 5.2, might tentatively be assimilated to the argument class of 1903, but in fact it is much broader, hosting cognitive and ampliative inferential *processes* more complex than those displayed by the syllogisms of traditional logic; and in any case, the argument is a subdivision of a relational trichotomy. Classes 332 and 331 in Table 5.2 would have no equivalents in the Syllabus typology, either. While, again, it might be tempting to consider the first two respects or subjects in Table 5.2, namely O (object) and S (sign), as somehow related to symbolic legisigns, this would be to confuse legisigns, 'static' signs which are laws, like the statute book or the Highway Code, with complete processes which are initiated or engineered by some agency. We know, too, that there is no icon-index-symbol division in the 1908 three- and six-division typologies. Clearly, the 'values' of the final interpretant divisions in classes 332 and 331 in Table 5.2 bear no resemblance to the earlier dicisign and rheme, two relational subdivisions in 1903. This seems to be the general problem with any an attempt at a comparison: the status of the sign is the only division that might be comparable – it stands as a correlate division in both systems, and as such is a determination of the dynamic object and in either it can be general, particular or abstract.

However, even this can be misleading as one system's sign can be the other system's interpretant, as the example of nostalgia mentioned in Chapter 5 suggests: we see it in others as the sign of a form of unhappiness – homesickness – but the indications of disquiet can also be seen as the result or effect of some event or other. In this respect Jappy (2019c: 106–7) offered the example of trees flagging under the force of the wind on cliffs near Brighton, England. This visible bending-action is an indication of the direction and strength of the prevailing winds or even a landmark, and is thus an index in the typology of 1903. But for the trees, the entities enduring the unrelenting strength and direction of the winds, the flagging is an interpretant: it is the continuing consequence of a general systematic meteorological process, of a variety of semiosis, therefore. In the system outlined in Chapter 5, observed on a *single* occasion, this class would be 322, a *particular* occurrence of the class of collective habit-forming types (class 333), since the specificities of the prevailing winds are the form 'communicated' to the trees from more general, regular and, therefore, necessitant, meteorological conditions. These conditions are the complex necessitant dynamic object, the winds themselves constitute the medium, and the flagging is the final effect, that is, the interpretant, a condition appropriately referred to technically as their 'habit' acquired over time. As in the case of nostalgia, the flagging is a sign in the first case and an interpretant in the second. And what of loneliness? This, too, is the sign of something, but can also be seen as that something's effect ...

To appreciate more completely how the post-scriptum table differs from the original ten classes, we draw on class 321, the class discussed throughout section 'Deriving the post-scriptum diagram' of Chapter 5, and examine, to begin with, Peirce's example of the piece of music for piano played at a public concert: one or more of Mendelssohn's *Songs without words*, say. Note that, as with the hexadic typology, in order to classify signs within this system knowledge of both object and interpretant is required, as both are respects participating in the typology. This is how Peirce describes such a sign in 1907:

> Now the problem of what the 'meaning' of an intellectual concept is can only be solved by the study of the interpretants, or proper significate effects, of signs. These we find to be of three general classes with some important subdivisions. The first proper significate effect of a sign is a feeling produced by it. There is almost always a feeling which we come to interpret as evidence that we comprehend the proper effect of the sign, although the foundation of truth in this is frequently very slight. This 'emotional interpretant,' as I call it, may amount to much more than that feeling of recognition; and in some cases, it is the only proper significate effect that the sign produces. *Thus, the performance of a piece of concerted music is a sign. It conveys, and is intended to convey, the composer's musical ideas; but these usually consist merely in a series of feelings.* If a sign produces any further proper significate effect, it will do so through the mediation of the emotional interpretant, and such further effect will always involve an effort.
>
> (R318: 63–5, 1907; emphasis added)

Peirce here offers a simple explanation: the sign is the performance of the music conveying to the audience the composer's musical ideas. Such a performance would be classified in the later semiosis-structured, ten-class typology quite precisely. Within this typology, the sign is obviously collective, since at the dynamic object stage the musical ideas that the composer is seeking to communicate have to be related to key, rhythm and the dynamic potential of the piano and then consigned to a musical score, which is, by definition, a type; these are stages conditioned by the intentions of the composer. The performance itself is necessarily existent, but the quality of feeling experienced by members of the audience is simply a *possible* effect of the sign. Such a performance exemplifies the class in Figures 5.4–5.7 from Chapter 5, the collective, gratific token. Remember that if the performance produces what Peirce refers to as 'any further significate effect', such as clapping or noisy disapproval – existent interpretants – the sign would then constitute an example of a collective action-producing token (322). More interestingly, this class is also the class of the *semioses* producing such a sign: the dynamic nature of the communication of musical ideas from composer to audience via the accomplishments of the pianist is an example of semiosis. Consider, now, how Peirce conceived this same musical performance in the phenomenological background of 1904:

> In respect to their relations to their dynamic objects, I divide signs into Icons, Indices, and Symbols (a division I gave in 1867). I define an Icon as a sign which is determined by its dynamic object by virtue of its own internal nature. *Such is any qualisign, like a vision, —or the sentiment excited by a piece of music considered as representing what the composer intended.*
>
> (CP: 8.335, 1904; emphasis added)

With respect to the 1903 typology, the performance itself is irrelevant here: what is classified as a sign is the sentiment excited by the music, a 'quality of feeling'. The performance would be the object of a separate classification, and its origin (the composer's musical project) would be inaccessible, as the object, here the intention to produce a positive reaction in an audience, is only indirectly related to the classification as the second of the two 'poles' of the sign-to-object relational division. In the 1903 typology, such a sign would be the quality of feeling experienced by the listener, a qualisign. Consider anew, Peirce's 'Ground arms!' example discussed in Chapter 3. Within the 1903 typology the command is the replica of a dicent symbol. But, then, all the sentences in the quoted text are undifferentiated dicisigns, irrespective of differences of syntax, rhetorical intent, tone of voice, force of delivery, etc. However, although the terminology employed is not that of the systems of 1908, Peirce himself explains how the command functions in this sequence, illustrating class 322 in Table 5.2, in which the interpretant grounded musket butts are mediately determined by the officer's will:

Officer's will → command → musket butts grounded

We know, moreover, that if the order is followed by the (highly unlikely) remark 'Well done, chaps!', although yet another dicisign, the semiotic structure of the remark is entirely different; the officer's attitude is different, as would be the reaction of the squad of soldiers. Assuming that after the officer's compliment the soldiers felt a glow of pride, the two utterances would be classified respectively as instances of a collective action-producing token (322) and a collective gratific token (321), though classification is less important than determining the nature of object and interpretant in such cases.

On the other hand, where the 1903 typology has analytical superiority over its 1908 successors is in the possibility it offers of identifying precisely the 'imitative' potential of indexical or symbolic signs. Of the three typologies under consideration (the 1903 ten-class, the later twenty-eight-class and post-scriptum typologies), only the 1903 typology can offer such information. Consider, for example, another musical sign proposed by Peirce, an air played on a guitar (R318: 283, 1907). The traditional folksong, *Skewbald*[2] as sung by the British folk-singer, Martin Carthy, narrates a legendary winning run by a racehorse in Ireland, and would presumably, since composed not only of a characteristic musical sound-structure but also of rule-governed verbal signs, qualify as a legisign: its combinations of English words and phrases would make it symbolic in the Peircean sense, and, as the informative narration of a sequence of events, a dicisign. However, Carthy, an accomplished guitarist, plays the rhythm of the song like a series of hoof beats, such that the music imitates the galloping horse iconically, a feature of the sign not explicitly available in the two later typologies, for neither provides any way of identifying a mode of representation, that is, the way the sign represents it object. One problem is that what is actually classified in such a sign is moot. Is it the score? Is it a single moment in the performance of the folk song? Peirce sometimes cites the change in wind direction and the changing height in barometers, and identifies weathercocks and barometers as indexical. Is the sound of the guitar playing similarly indexical? In the extract from R318, Peirce is discussing what he called the emotional interpretant at the time: he was exploring the idea of associating specific effects or reactions with types of signs and, as seen in Chapter 3, was developing a broader view of what constitutes a sign:

> A 'sign,' I say, shall be understood as anything which represents itself to convey an influence from an Object, so that this may intelligently convey a 'meaning,' or interpretant. According to this, a performance of a piece of instrumental music is an event, and, at the same time, a sign of the piece of music itself (this latter not being an event, but a complex musical idea, itself a sign of a complex series of musical feelings in the composer's real or feigned breast).
>
> (R318: 383, 1907)

The three- and six-division typologies discussed in this and the previous two chapters can classify the entire performance of the song as, perhaps, a gratific collective token, but are incapable of capturing the iconicity of the guitar-playing, while the 1903 typology can only classify, for example, the score, or a moment in the singing, or the effect it produces on the listener, if identifiable.

There is one obvious problem with this type of analysis. Whereas the object in a typology like the post-scriptum may empirically be identifiable, the interpretant, by definition an 'event' to come, is more difficult to include in any attempt to classify a sign, and yet it must be included otherwise the sign supposedly determining it cannot be said to be a sign. In other words, how can we surmount the problem of the conceivable non-identification of the interpretants in semiosis? And is it possible to account for iconic form, for example, in the later typologies? Such questions require that we broaden the scope of the analysis and reintroduce the hexad from Chapter 4.

There is yet a more fundamental issue which is brought to light with the realization that the three correlates in the definitions of the sign correspond precisely to those forming the post-scriptum table. This issue concerns the logical status of the *relation* holding between the object and the sign. Theoretically, this relation cannot be immediate, and yet this is how the 1903 (and other) definitions of the sign and the post-scriptum table present the triadic relation: sign determined by object to mediately determine interpretant. This is problematic in the case of the post-scriptum system as it is surely logically and empirically impossible in any semiosis for a sign to be directly, that is, immediately, determined by its dynamic object. For example, can a painting be an immediate realization of an artist's or a sponsor's intention, or are there intermediary stages from conception to realization (e.g. what Peirce refers to as 'masses of accidental and hardly relevant semioses', R318: 123, 1907)?

This question of immediacy also pertains to the concept of semiosis in that the 'coöperation' mentioned in Peirce's definition cannot in actual occurrences of the *process* be limited to three correlates, any more than can the determination of the sign by the dynamic object as stated, for example, in the 'sop to Cerberus' definition: 'I define a Sign as anything which is so determined by something else, called its Object, and so determines an effect upon a person, which effect I call its Interpretant, that the latter is thereby mediately determined by the former' (SS: 80–1, 1908). The definition states that the interpretant is mediately determined by the object, which might imply that the sign is *immediately* determined by the object. But this, too, is empirically and logically impossible. Inconveniently for triadicity, as seen already, Peirce defines the term 'immediate' as 'to say that A is immediate to B means that it is present in B' (R339: 243Av, 1905). Consequently, any agency or object, human or otherwise, triggering the process of semiosis cannot possibly have the sign 'present in' it; were this the case, the interpreter would not perceive it, and the sign could not function as a sign. It is the sign that must have something of the triggering object or agency 'present in' it – in the form of the immediate object. As seen in Chapter 4, the process of signification, therefore, requires more than three correlates, a process explicitly described by Peirce in the letter to Lady Welby of 23 December 1908 as the series of the five determination 'stages' (Figure 4.1).

Peirce was presumably already aware of this problem when in 1904 he introduced his first hexadic typology, described in Chapter 3, as it coincided with his growing interest in the action of the sign. Moreover, he was subsequently led to drop from his typologies the two relational trichotomies involving the sign and immediate object and sign and immediate interpretant, since he later defined both immediate correlates as being 'in' the sign. His work on classifications was leading to a more specific conception of the role of the sign as medium, and the immediate object and interpretant were to become distinct 'stages' in the action of the sign. This 'immediacy' problem in no way affected the highly influential relational typology of 1903 since there was no organic relation between the trichotomies; they were simply set out in 'correlate' order, itself a determination of the categories. Nor did it, obviously, compromise the definitions of the sign: the three correlates are necessary and sufficient to define both the sign and, in 1907, semiosis. On the other hand, the same three are totally inadequate as far as any description of the *action* of the sign is concerned. Peirce's awareness of this is evident in the 1906 definition of the sign as a medium for the communication of a form, as he included the two objects in the definition as well as the highly instructive description of the three interpretants. The problem was finally resolved with his renewed interest in semiosis in the years 1907–8, although he was clearly working towards the solution in the period I have named as a 'transition'. It devolves from the purposive nature of communication: such purpose as is involved requires that it be made public, and the public, perceivable 'version' cannot possibly be identical to the object determining it.

Mediatization

It was seen in Chapter 3 that in his symbol-centred pragmatism Peirce defines and describes a restricted scope of meaning, but that he declares, too, that meaning is communicated from mind to mind by signs. In this study, the actual *making* of meaning is effected elsewhere, namely in semiosis conceived for simplicity as a six-stage 'mediatization-interpretation' process. Any initial intentionality – the engineering of consent by some sort of guru, for example – in order to be effective, has to be made manifest, that is, it has to be mediatized in a special sense of the term. The intentionality, to be rendered 'public', has to be inscribed in some way in a perceivable medium: in the case of the soldiers in the 'Ground arms!' example, this is an audible sign made public through the air. Such an organization of means – a soundly planned action, a military command – can be modelled by the linear structure of semiosis as the five-stage determination sequence described by Peirce in 1908. Furthermore, for such a command to be understood and obeyed, it has not only to be perceivable, but must also make sense. This, it is argued below, is the function of the immediate object, which Peirce in a letter to Lady Welby qualifies as the 'hint', or the substance of this hint, of the dynamic object presented by the sign (SS: 83, 1908). The focus of this section, therefore, is not on demolishing the dubious aspects of Bernays' and others' social projects but in investigating the material representation of intentionality, which is the dynamic object in the majority of cases of anthroposemiosis.

Having examined the nature of semiosis in Chapter 4, we are now in a position to account for every stage in the process, and in doing so will examine in particular the nature of the relation and its possible realizations holding between signs and their immediate objects. This will make it possible to examine in greater detail than in Chapter 4 the stages in semiosis from the dynamic object to the sign via the immediate object in selected examples, since it is axiomatic that the communication or sharing of any persuasive or influential activity requires the formal organization of its public manifestation. To this end, the following paragraphs present one possible explanation of the conditions enabling 'utterers' in Peirce's general sense – fauna *and* flora[3] – to determine the initial stages in the way in which purposive action is to be implemented. Such a project is, of course, speculative and necessarily abductive. It requires, initially, that the logical status of the sign itself be reviewed.

The sign as medium

I quote anew part of Peirce's definition from 1906, in which the problem of the object-sign relation is explicitly broached: 'I use the word "*Sign*" in the widest sense for any medium for the communication or extension of a Form (or feature). Being medium, it is determined by something, called its Object, and determines something, called its Interpretant or Interpretand' (SS: 196, 1906). For a full discussion of this important passage see the section on the sign as medium in Chapter 3. Herewith a summary of some of the points made there with a bearing on the topic of the present section. First, the concept of the medium occurred in several of Peirce's text in that period; the 1906 draft insists upon the fact that the sign is a medium for the communication of a 'form'; and the form communicated by the dynamic object to the sign via the immediate object is qualitative, quality being the only category of being that can simultaneously be 'the same form' embodied in sign, objects and interpretants and can therefore be communicated from the object to the interpretant via the sign. The sign being defined as the medium through which form is communicated, such a position requires that the forms that media thus adopt be accounted for. It is to that task that the rest of the section is devoted.

Diamesia, semiosis and the immediate object

From Aristotle to Saussure, writing has been considered by authorities as secondary to speech, itself composed in some way of symbols of 'affections of the soul'.[4] In 1983, in a sociolinguistic study of the vernacular of the Italian working classes, the Italian linguist Alberto Mioni introduced an additional language dimension (Mioni 1983), namely diamesic variation, to the four established by Eugenio Coseriu.[5] Mioni's was a dimension of language variation according to the specificities of oral and written discourse, considered as two distinct media for communication, the polar opposites of a continuum, no longer ordered hierarchically but enjoying parallel theoretical status. For, what has not always been explicitly questioned by many linguists as immediate, namely the relation between the 'affections of the soul' and their physical manifestation in language, in fact requires the association of a third element, a medium.[6] Mioni's distinction offers an interesting slant on the problem under discussion in this section: how could the same thought or idea possibly be expressed immediately and yet differently in speech and writing? In other words, could the inscription of some 'affection of the soul' in the medium which makes it manifest be immediate? And if it is not immediate, through what stage or stages is it mediated? The important point in this discussion is that Mioni has removed the problem from a simple but not entirely outdated 'dispute' about speech and writing, and replaced it, some years after Peirce, note, by the introduction of the notion of the medium: he has added medium to the long-debated theoretical mix; and the Aristotelian trio of 'affection of the soul–words spoken–words written' can be rethought as a necessitant object inscribing form in some medium.[7]

By making the problem semiotic as opposed to linguistic, Peircean semiotics offers an innovative perspective. Peirce originally defined logic as the philosophy of representation, but his conception of the action of the sign evolved significantly over the following years. As stated earlier, no idea, thought, desire or purpose, no type of 'affection of the soul' in other words, can be communicated without being represented or externalized in some medium, and this is as true of verbal communication as it is of other forms of social process such as publicity campaigns or the drawing-up of legislative documents. Such mediatization is a stage in the process of semiosis, and the section seeks to show how, within semiosis, the sign's immediate object functions as a relay in the process of the transfer of thought, etc., to the medium, spoken or written, through which it is communicated.

One way to determine the nature of the immediate object and to show how it communicates to the sign form from the dynamic object is by adopting the definition from 1906 and treating the sign *strictly* as a medium – airwaves, a page in a book, a piece of canvas or an oak panel, a computer or cinema screen, bone, even human skin ... This is the strategy adopted here: *any sign determining its series of interpretants is the fusion of the form-communicating immediate object and a medium.* Consider anew this definition: 'The Mediate Object is the Object outside of the Sign; I call it the *Dynamoid* Object. The Sign must indicate it by a hint; and this hint, or its substance, is the *Immediate* Object' (SS: 83, 1908). The semiotic nature of this 'hint or its substance' constituting the immediate object can be exemplified in (1), the written version of a spoken utterance and (2), its broad phonemic transcription and the corresponding sound spectrogram (Figure 6.1).

1) What are those blue remembered hills
2) /ˈwɒtəˈðəʊzˈbluːrɪˈmɛmbədˈhɪlz/

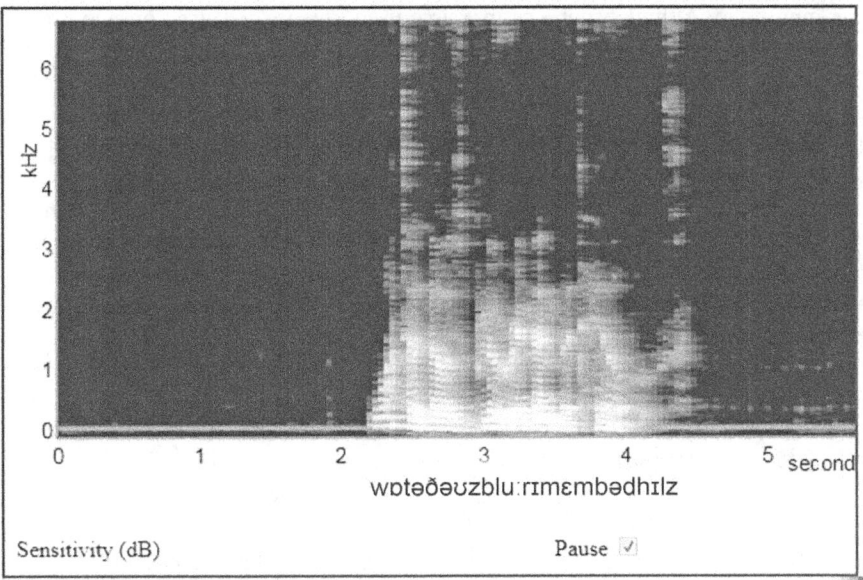

Figure 6.1 A sound spectrogram of spoken utterance (2).

Utterances (1) and (2) constitute a simple case of diamesic variation: the same assertion expressed potentially simultaneously in two different media. In the case of the written utterance, it is the paper and the series of ink marks on it forming the written page that constitute the medium. In the second case, it is the air which transmits its particular form as the two and a half second sequence of troughs and peaks of the airwaves conveying the message, crudely represented by the diagrammatic structure in Figure 6.1 obtained from an on-line sound spectrograph. This displays the voiced components of the utterance (vowels and certain voiced consonants), the characteristic frequencies of the phonemes composing the utterance, the falling intonation of the WH-question and evidence that the speaker is running out of breath. It is a 'photograph' of the air medium being disturbed by patterns of waves organized by the sign's immediate object, and when the line is read aloud, what we hear is a flow of displaced air with a specific structure imposed by the immediate object. However, the utterance could just as easily be communicated in other media, the particular distribution of the marks contributing to such media being, here too, the determining form of the immediate object. In each case, the intentionality of the dynamic object is the same, but the two distinct media in the examples will have been informed by equally distinct medium-adapting immediate objects.

For Mioni, diamesic variation was principally a sociolinguistic concept – language variation between social classes determined by the media to which they were exposed and in which discourse was communicated. What we have in utterances (1) and (2) becomes a specifically semiotic problem when seen as the relation between the immediate object and the medium through which the initial intentionality is to be communicated. Although not a term Peirce used, this is mediatization, the process by which the object intentionality is rendered perceivable in some medium. In the 1903 phenomenology-based system, both variants would be classified as replicas of a dicent symbol. The ten classes of this period are a-temporal, and intentionality is not only untraceable in them but also theoretically irrelevant, since the dynamic object, although a necessary correlate in the definition of the sign, does not participate as an independent division in the derived typology. The hexad of 1908, on the other hand, specifically involves both a dynamic and an immediate object, the latter communicating to the sign – in this case, a line of English poetry – form inherited from the dynamic, a property which makes Peircean semiosis a model of purposive, intention-based representation.

However before continuing, it is important to see how Peirce himself viewed the trichotomy of signs classified with respect to their immediate object to be seen in Table 6.1, and the exemplification he proposed in a draft to Lady Welby dated 25 December 1908:

Adopting this enumeration as a basis of a division of Signs, I obtain:

A. *Descriptives*, which determine their Objects by stating the characters of the latter.
B. *Designatives* (or *Denotatives*), or *Indicatives*, *Denominatives*, which like a Demonstrative pronoun, or a pointing finger, brutely direct the mental eyeballs of the interpreter to the object in question, which in this case cannot be given by independent reasoning.
C. *Copulants*, which neither describe nor denote their Objects, but merely express universally the logical sequence of these latter upon something otherwise referred to. Such, among linguistic signs, as 'If _____ then _____,' '_____ is _____,' '_____ causes _____,' '_____ would be _____,' '_____ is relative to _____ for _____,' 'Whatever,' etc. ... So with 'It rains and hails,' 'It rains concurrently with hailing,' 'It rains concurrently with the concurrence of hailing,' and so forth. I call all such signs Continuants. They are all Copulants and are the only *pure* Copulants. *These signs cannot be explicated*: they must convey Familiar universal elementary relations of logic. We do not derive these notions from observation, nor by any sense of being opposed, but from our own reason.

(CP: 8.350–8.352, 1908)

Like the other examples proposed by Peirce in the drafts and elsewhere, these are all verbal, which is not surprising in view of Peirce's quest to enrich his logic with as many possible signs and semioses as possible. They are the choice of a logician but are not necessarily appropriate for the semiotician investigating the language of advertising or advising a company on brand management, or for the case studies to come in this chapter. Consequently, the complex copulant signs (i.e. signs classified according to the universe status of their immediate object), to be analysed later won't necessarily be as 'pure' as they had to be for Peirce the logician, nor will they be logical sequences of the 'if ... then' type.

The argument that follows thus assumes three principles. First, the sign is taken in the process of semiosis to be a medium informed in successive stages by the objects of which it is a determination. Second, as art historians have known for centuries, traces of the creative impulse determining the sign can be identified in the *form* that the sign takes, in its composition, which logically precedes any interpretation. Finally, the influence of the intentionality determining the action of the sign in the six-stage sequence as described in the letter to Lady Welby cannot be immediate as is implicit in the 1903 definition of the sign and necessarily the case with the post-scriptum table. It follows, then, that in order to function, any intentionality initiating semiosis, in other words the purpose of the agency responsible for the process, has to be in some way perceivable in some medium, and that to achieve the purpose of the agency it emanates from, this intentionality has to be composed and mediatized. The following sections hypothesize the way this mediatization is achieved and how this may accommodate iconicity. This hypothesizes, obviously, the function of the immediate object, the object 'present in' the sign and the nature of the interpretants that it produces.

The hexadic system again

Having shown, like Farias and Queiroz, that the post-scriptum typology was an abridged version of the twenty-eight-class typology described in the 23 December letter to Lady Welby, from now on, analysis will involve the latter, as it offers a greater heuristic potential. Before moving to a new section we examine two example signs, the structure of which can be traced through the arrow sequence in Table 6.1.[8]

We begin with the analysis of another of the classes identified by the post-scriptum typology, namely class 332, which is formed by a necessitant object and sign and an existent interpretant. With a necessitant and therefore unperceivable sign, this is a difficult class to illustrate: possibly a cognitive 'thought sequence' followed by an action of some sort – a spiritual experience, perhaps, leading to prostration or prayer. To take a more prosaic example, a publicity campaign observed to result in the actual purchase of commodities would be classified under 322 in Table 5.2, as a (collective) action-producing token, characterized by a necessitant object and an existent sign and interpretant. However, if we refer the same class to the typology of Table 6.1,[9] which includes the immediate object and instances or occurrences of types, in such cases the hexadic system described in Chapter 4 is better equipped to deal with the design aspect of an advertising campaign, namely the inscription in some form or other of the aims of the project in some medium for it to make a perceivable impact. In a given campaign, the necessitant object would be the detailed contract between client and publicist outlining objectives and methodology, the immediate object would be the complex necessitant form that the campaign is to take, while the sign as medium is the support adopted: TV, social media, cinema, newspapers, magazines, etc. Clearly, the role of the immediate object – absent from the post-scriptum table and the three-correlate definition of the sign if taken as an embryonic model of the *action* of the sign – is of considerable semiotic interest in such cases. However, the interpretant series

Table 6.1 The table yielding twenty-eight classes of signs

	Respect					
(semiosis)	Od →	Oi →	S →	Ii →	Id →	If
Universe						
Necessitant	collective	copulant	type	relative	usual	to produce self-control
Existent	concretive	designative	token	categorical	percussive	to produce action
Possible	abstractive	descriptive	mark	hypothetical	sympathetic	gratific

also requires to be identified, and ways to resolve this problem are advanced in the following analyses.

There are at least two possible analytical procedures by means of which to overcome the potential inaccessibility of any interpretant in the examination of semioses: one by a form of retrospection, the other by anticipation. In the first case, given a discernibly complete process – semiosis being, in this study at least and as displayed in Table 6.1, a structured linear process – we can trace the reaction produced back to the initial intention or object. The sequence below, an extract from a detective novel, is exemplary since it is possible to identify all six correlates in the process. A private detective is quizzing a young woman about a handkerchief with initials like hers found in the bed of a murdered man. The final two sentences have been italicized.

> 'Miss Fromsett just never keeps her hankies under a man's pillow. Therefore this has absolutely nothing to do with Miss Fromsett. It's just an optical delusion.'
> 'Oh, shut up,' she said. I grinned.
> 'What kind of girl do you think I am?' she snapped.
> *'I came in too late to tell you.'*
> *She flushed, but delicately and all over her face this time.*
>
> (Chandler [1943] 2001: 116)

Both italicized utterances – indeed, all the sentences in the extract – would be classified within the 1903 ten-class system as dicisigns, for they all are replicas of dicent symbols, irrespective of their very different syntax and lexical content. And yet this relational classification tells us nothing of their communicative purpose, which we nevertheless understand clearly as we read the story to be an oblique and unexpected complimentary remark provoking an embarrassed nonverbal reaction from the addressee. In such a case, the post-scriptum table provides us with an overall view of the sequence: intention of declaring an impossible love interest, its overt verbal realization and the reaction from the addressee. However, the more complex hexadic 1908 system provides us with a more appropriate analytical approach to the semioses represented here, namely a retrospective analysis of the interpretant sequence, which enables us to explain within a logical framework why the two sentences were uttered and the effect that they produced.

We infer from the narrative context that the first italicized utterance is a cryptic declaration that, were the circumstances different, the speaker would declare a genuine love interest in the addressee. We understand the speaker to have been questioning her aggressively, but then he unexpectedly destabilizes her with a flattering remark: this destabilization is the intentionality, the dynamic object. The wave-forms through the air of the spoken medium are conditioned by configurations of the speaker's vocal cords, and it is these configurations which determine how the air is displaced. We read the italicized utterances in the narrative as two individual signs, but behind the narrative context, as it were, what we have is a series of displacements of air producing the provocative response of the speaker. In the neo-Peircean approach proposed in the study, any sign determining its series of interpretants is the fusion of the form-communicating immediate object and a medium: the sign in itself is a medium. In the case of the italicized utterance – indeed of all the *utterances* – it is the air that is the medium, while the precise forms displacing the air are determined by the immediate object. In short, the speaker's obliquely complimentary remark has been mediatized as a specific configuration of airwaves. Any semiosis must respect this linear order in which the dynamic object is mediatized by means of the conditioning by the immediate object of some medium; the immediate object is the intentionality's 'structure' that is present 'in' the sign; in other words, 'present in' the medium.

The second italicized utterance describes a reaction from which we as readers infer that the unexpected declaration of romantic interest of the preceding utterance has been understood by the interpreter. At this point the immediate interpretant enters the picture, since it represents the meaning of the utterance and its tone of delivery. The dynamic interpretant is an existent reaction, conditioning the final. This is a nonverbal 'action' and, with respect to the three universes, it is existent, otherwise it would be invisible; here it is realized delicately as the full-featured blushing sign of emotion. Such an analysis thus involves following an observed sequence of actual reactions or effects – interpretants, in other words – as they are determined by a given sign.

The utterances are a sequence of replicas within the 1903 three-division system, and as instances of action-producing, categorial, collective types within the hexad of 1908. Since we are dealing with spoken instances of types, as indicated in Table 6.1, the dynamic and immediate objects must also be necessitant: the immediate would be the complex syntax and intonation characterizing each communicated form – syntactic structures, not the logical structures offered as examples given by Peirce – while in the case of the final sentence the dynamic object is the inferred complimentary intention of the speaker. However, what is of interest here is not so much a complete classification of these utterances as signs as the use of the hexad system as an exploratory scheme.

Returning briefly to the controversy of interpretant order discussed more fully in Chapter 4, one view of Peirce's order in the typology was that in the sequence 'the Sign itself which determines the Destinate interpretant, which determines the Effective interpretant, which determines the Explicit interpretant', the interpretants were ordered as final interpretant followed by dynamic followed by immediate. If this were the case it would mean, returning to the extract from the detective story, that the blushing somehow, illogically, precedes the addressee's *immediate* realization that the speaker was paying an unexpected compliment. Nonsense. The immediate interpretant is defined as the sign's inherent interpretability, in other words, its meaning. This being the case, the final interpretant couldn't possibly determine its own interpretability. From a logical perspective, the sign's meaning represented by the immediate interpretant is also defined as being 'present in' the sign, in the airwaves in the case in point, and must precede and determine the reaction of the dynamic interpretant – the actual reaction in an individual proving that, rightly or wrongly, the meaning has been understood – which in turn determines the final interpretant, the logical status of which is defined as 'the ultimate effect of the sign' (R339: 289r, H542, 1906).

A multimodal example of the second, anticipatory or prospective, interpretative strategy is a poster taped to a bus shelter in a French village. The poster is composed of photograph and text requesting information concerning a kitten that has gone astray (Figure 6.2), although what the observer, like the reader, actually perceives is a structured assemblage of forms and colours and *infers* from experience that it is a request for information.

Figure 6.2 An appeal for information concerning a lost kitten.

Within the 1903 ten-class system displayed above in Table 6.1 this multimodal sign integrating an image of the missing kitten called 'Rousquille' (a *rousquille* is a variety of Catalan biscuit), and a message in French asking people to check for its presence in their sheds, garages and gardens, would, like the utterances from the extract discussed above, be classified as a dicisign. Being multimodal, Figure 6.2 represents a complex replica of a dicent symbol. But this is all we could say about it, as we can only establish its object by some form of collateral reasoning. On the other hand, with what we know of Peirce's late conceptions of the two objects and the three interpretants, we can analyse and classify the poster very differently by means of the system set out in Table 6.1. We recognize it as an appeal for information, which means that we have understood the interpretants 'targeted' to be the hoped-for resultant information. The dynamic object is not, contrary to what we might think working within the 1903 system, the missing kitten on the poster, but, rather, the universe defined by the owners' wish – necessitant volition – to receive information leading to the discovery of the kitten's whereabouts. This volition is realized, made manifest in the poster, by means of the immediate object in the form of the specific blend of text and image of the appeal: the request for information cannot be immediate as the volition can't produce the specific organization of the poster by willpower alone. At the Od and Oi stages in Table 6.1, then, the sign is respectively, collective and copulant. The sign itself, the medium communicating the owners' wish to prospective interpreters, is the existential paper and coloured inks support attached to the protective partition of a bus stop with sticky tape: it is a token – it has to be, otherwise no one would perceive it. As far as the targeted interpretants are concerned, the immediate would be some member of the public's seeing the poster and understanding its meaning and import, while the dynamic would be their psychic or physical reaction, as the sign is intended to be, in a neutral sense, percussive or 'shocking', that is, a sign producing an existent dynamic interpretant (EP2 490, 1908). Now such an existential dynamic interpretant is the precondition for the final interpretant to be an action, and so hopefully this final reaction would be a phone call or even the return of the missing animal. The sign in Figure 6.2 would be classified as an action-producing, collective copulant token, but the really useful aspect of the analysis is our ability to identify the stages in the process involving the poster.

This has important implications for semiotic analysis. It is notable in Peirce's logic that the hexad determining the typology in Table 6.1 approximates our normal interpretive processes as, for example, we follow films by identifying the patterns of colour, light and shade on cinema or TV screens as human beings or moving objects, etc., patterns in which we recognize politicians, famous semioticians and stars of stage and screen. These are manifestations of the forms communicated to different media – cinema screen, printed paper and the LED displays on the TV screen – by their immediate objects, determined precedently by dynamic objects which are of necessity different, by existing in a greater number of dimensions or by not always being in evidence in the sign or by possibly belonging to a different universe of experience. This leads to important considerations with respect to the mediatization of the dynamic object, to the scope of intentionality in signification, and to its semiotic analysis, and, more pertinently, to the complex process of the making and interpretation of meaning. Since the dynamic object is – logically – the origin of semiosis, and since such necessitant entities as 'a living consciousness [...] the life, the power of growth, of a plant [...] a living institution, – a daily newspaper, a great fortune, a social "movement"' are all potential objects of signs, and, as Table 6.1 clearly shows, if both dynamic and immediate objects are necessitant and general but determine an existent sign, it follows that such entities can be sources of an intentionality that is not immediately perceivable: the foot determining a foot-print in the sand and the wind responsible for the change of direction of a weather-vane are existent, perceivable dynamic objects, but the intentions behind campaigns for a political party, a charity appeal for donations or orders given on a parade ground are less so.

Hybridization

In the analyses to follow, the first point to bear in mind is that all signs are preceded by their objects not only in Peirce's logical order, but also empirically in a *chronological* order, in an order of determination: we would hardly expect the interpretant effects of some sign to precede the intentionality targeting them. Second, to take the example of a portrait such as the *Mona Lisa*, the actual production of the painting as a (captionless) iconic sinsign is necessarily historical: it didn't suddenly appear out of the blue, and Leonardo wasn't the only agent involved in its being brought into existence. Thus the analyses perforce present what can be considered as 'macrosemioses' as the semioses described are a general framework within which there are obviously multiple other – generally relevant, in such cases – actions of signs. Finally, in order to simplify the argument to follow and to avoid an excess of schemata, the reader is referred back to the discussion of the hypoicons introduced in Chapter 2. These are illustrated summarily below and identified in their 1903 terminology.

Hypoiconicity, historicity and the immediate object

All signs have histories: one semiotic, the other, 'secular', the secular, irrespective of chronology, being structured logically by the semiotic. In the first case, as the determinations of two successive objects – the dynamic and the immediate – they are the product of a complex semiotic process, communicating in turn meaning thus inherited to a series of interpretants, and this is as true of paintings as of any other sign. Furthermore, the stages in this semiotic process were not only untraceable but above all the process itself was 'unthinkable', inconceivable, within the theoretical framework of the 1903 system of signs and sign action. The process is, of course, semiosis, which has since become an indispensable operational concept in a wide range of disciplines from musicology, literary theory and sociology to, most spectacularly, biosemiotics. The following paragraphs examine its contribution to the analysis of pictorial representation and the way it integrates the structures of hypoiconicity as presented in 1903 but redefined in 1905.

Second, the process involves, inevitably, linear development, and with it, a necessary 'external' historicity in the determination process, and this is as true of paintings as of any other sign, and the hexadic sequence of correlates introduced by Peirce in 1908 exhibits the dynamism and historicity of the process quite explicitly. Now, Baxandall (1972: 1) notes in the case of a particular generation of painters 'A fifteenth-century painting is the deposit of a social relationship', and this is typically the case with the pictorial representations to be examined below. For example, within the 1903 theory of hypoiconicity, the portrait of Mona Lisa is an image in the Peircean technical sense. But other than to identify the painting with its caption as a replica of a dicent indexical legisign and to identify its hypoiconic structure, this is about all that the 1903 system of ten classes can contribute to our understanding of the painting: any other information concerning it, that it is a commissioned portrait, for example, or the way in which it has become the deposit of a social relationship, in which, of course, we find persuasion and the expression of purpose, is a consequence of semiosis.

The three hypoicons illustrated

Before examining the case studies, the reader is reminded, within this necessarily personal neo-Peircean perspective, of the principles of hypoiconicity presented in the final section of Chapter 2. The figures representing their formal structures are reproduced and illustrated below for convenience, bearing in mind that by 1905, Peirce had redefined the three subclasses of the icon as likeness, analogue and diagram. The standard 1903 definition of the hypoicons was given in Chapters 2 and 3 as the terse definition from the Syllabus to be found in EP2: 274.

Within the category-derived theory of hypoiconicity, Figure 6.3 is a representation of some of the qualities (here, patterns of sounds) presumed to be inhering in the represented object. Since the qualities – First Firstnesses in Peirce's category-based terminology – thus represented are phenomenologically less complex than the Secondness of the existential medium, namely the airwaves in oral discourse, for example, the intended representation of the qualities in the object is in no way inhibited by potential differences in complexity between the medium and its two correlates. In other words, the existent medium is complex enough phenomenologically – and empirically-to convey the qualities of the intended representation. Onomatopoeia, like the deliberate rhythm of the folk song described above, provides an interesting verbal example of this type of resemblance, as in the following well-known line from the *Æneid* with its dactyl-like meter in which the rhythm informing the spoken sequence of verbal elements composing the verse is intended to suggest the sound of horses galloping over a plain (long syllables in bold):

(3) **quadru**pedante **pu**trem sonitu quatit **un**gula **cam**pum (Virgil, *Æneid* VIII, 596)[10]

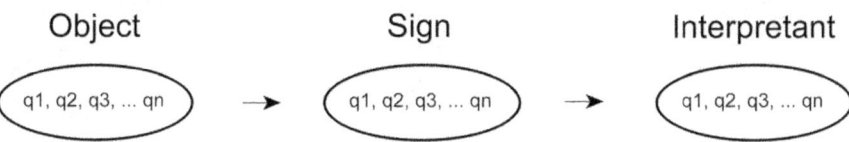

Figure 6.3 The formal structure of a sign with image hypoiconicity.

Figure 6.4 represents the structure of a very basic diagram, an icon composed essentially of the Second Firstnesses implicit in the definition, namely one or more dyadic relations shared by object and sign, but represented in Figure 6.4 as the single relation **a—b** holding between the two partial objects **a** and **b** in the entity, fact or event represented by the sign.

Such relations were defined to be a step up the phenomenological scale from the simpler Firstnesses composing the image: the latter are interpreted to conform to an object, the portrait-painter's model, for example, or the sound of horses galloping over a battlefield, but there is no necessary correspondence between the image and the model. The diagram, by contrast, is the icon composed of relations between elements corresponding to relations between elements in the object. A simple verbal example is provided by the two parts of this 'contrary' from William Blake's *Proverbs from Hell*:

(4) *Sooner murder an infant in its cradle than nurse unacted desires.*

Here the contrasting predicative expressions 'murder an infant in its cradle' and 'nurse unacted desires' correspond respectively to the participants, **a** and **b**, in the schema in Figure 6.4, while the compound linking expression 'sooner ... than' corresponds to the ' – ' relation associating them, also commonly expressed as 'It is better to …. than'. Such a structure, with its point-to-point correspondence between the elements of the utterance and those of the schema, is clearly a step up the phenomenological scale from the onomatopoeia in utterance (3). Moreover, the sentence presents other analogical conflicting associations on the semantic level between *infant + cradle* and *unacted desires*, and the relation contrasting the verbs *murder* and *nurse*. From a purely formal point of view, the contrary is a complex set of diagrams. Within the phenomenological framework of 1903, the diagrammatic complexity informing the sign is compatible with the necessarily existent medium, which is why the representation of the structure 'inherited' from the object is, as in the case of the image, in no way inhibited by the medium through which it is communicated.

Finally, as indicated in Figure 2.8 from Chapter 2, metaphor is the hypoiconic structure presenting an implicit Third Firstness, a phenomenological complexity which requires the experience of the interpreter in the interpreting process for the construal of the nature of the association or comparison concerning the two (or more) generally disparate domains of experience being communicated. According to Peirce's concise and innovative definition, the metaphor subclass informs a sign whose object – the 'something else' of the definition – is structured by a two-tiered parallelism and

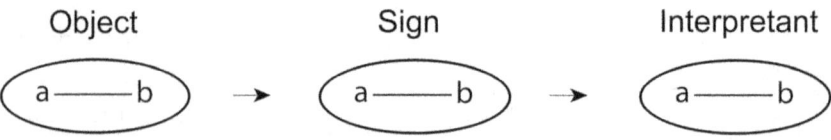

Figure 6.4 The formal structure of a sign with diagram hypoiconicity.

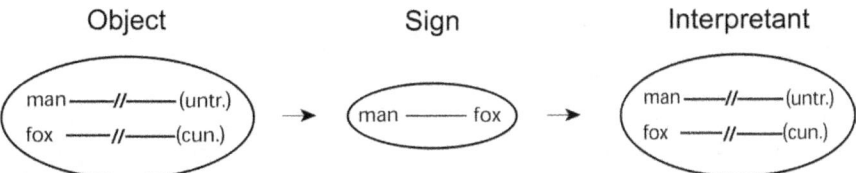

Figure 6.5 The metaphor structure of *This man is a fox*.

is thus significantly more complex than the unidimensional medium representing it. Figure 2.8 represented this third grade of resemblance in Chapter 2.

Figure 6.5 exhibits the metaphorical structure of an early example provided by Peirce himself, a verbal sign blending elements from the two facts forming the basis of the metaphor *This man is a fox* (CP: 7.590, ?1867). The utterance is an attempt to pass judgement on the behaviour of a certain human being, and the parallelism informing the object and 'synthesized' in the sign is composed of entities represented in two distinct facts.

The schema of the sign correlate in Figure 6.4 contains a single 'diagrammatic', that is, dyadic, relation which is the formal structure, too, of some simple fact such as *This man is untrustworthy*, where **a** and **b** are, respectively, *This man* and the property *untrustworthy*. Metaphor, on the other hand, as defined by Peirce, presents at least two such relations in parallel in the object, as in Figure 6.5. Here we find counterpart mappings between elements in the relation (**man** – // – (**untr.**)), *This man is untrustworthy*, which constitutes the state of affairs that is being evaluated, and elements from the putative well-known fact (**fox** – // – (**cun.**)), *A fox is a cunning animal*, providing the evaluation. The two parallel relations can be identified, following the conceptual metaphor tradition, as the 'target' and 'base' domains, respectively. The elements in the target domain are somehow controversial or contentious or not yet accepted, while the fact considered to be the basis of the judgement and hopefully self-evident to the addressee or interpreter is the idea that foxes are cunning, a culturally accepted and widely exploited negative judgement, even if anthropomorphic and therefore of dubious validity. In the very simple case in Figure 6.5, **man** maps to its counterpart in the base domain, **fox,** while the mapping from (**untr.**) to its counterpart in the base domain, (**cun.**) (*untrustworthy* and *cunning animal* respectively on the schema), is absent from the sign. Owing to its vectorial, existential character, within Peirce's phenomenological framework the spoken sign *This man is a fox* is necessarily constrained in the amount of information that it can represent in the existential medium of air or a sheet of paper, and, like Figure 2.8, Figure 6.5 shows how certain participants in the original parallelism (displayed in parentheses) are bracketed by the unavoidable quantitative restriction caused by the sign's being an existent perceivable medium.

The structure of metaphor proposed in Figures 2.8 and 6.4 calls for three remarks. First, it should be noted that the repetition of the parallel structure of the object in the structure of the interpretant is a useful graphic convention for showing that the intended meaning of the sign has been understood; in other words, it is a way of showing that the metaphor has been fully interpreted. As Peirce defined them, all three hypoicons are subclasses of a subdivision contributing to the establishment of the ten classes of signs of 1903. By definition, a 'Sign is a Representamen with a mental Interpretant' (EP2: 273); these ten classes being classes of *signs*, not simply representamens, they therefore necessarily determine a mental interpretant, hence the additional interest, in the case of metaphor, of including the structure of the interpretant in the schema. Should a child hear an adult remark 'Careful! This man is a fox!' the child might object and say 'But that's silly, a man can't be a fox, a fox is an animal'. In such a case the structure of the interpretant has not recovered the structure of the intended parallelism, and the import of the utterance has been misunderstood. Any interpretation of metaphor is fully dependent, therefore, upon the experience of the interpreter, experience being, remember, that 'cognitive resultant of our past lives' (CP: 2.84, 1902); in necessitating the experience of the interpreter for its full interpretation, metaphor is like the symbol, and is similarly triadic.

Second, although Peirce never used such schemata, what Figures 2.8 and 6.4 are intended to show, too, is that while the necessarily perceivable medium – the airwaves in a spoken utterance, any page on which the utterance is written or the canvas and paint marks in the case of a painting – partakes necessarily of Secondness within Peirce's theory of hypoiconicity, the parallelism in the structure of the object constitutes a Third Firstness and its two-tier structure is therefore phenomenologically more complex than the audible, written or pictorial sign representing it. In this highly abstract theory of form, that of metaphor is more complex than the medium by which it has to be communicated, the medium thereby forming the aforementioned phenomenological bottleneck obstructing communication of the full complex form of the object. This is why the elements represented in parentheses in the object and interpretant ellipses in Figures 2.8 and 6.4 stand for participants that do not feature – or have not been selected to feature – in the sign. Note, too, that domains, counterparts and mappings are not Peircean concepts, as Peirce seemingly never took the 1903 conception of metaphor any further, and never developed a specific terminology for it.

Finally, we see that in this conception of metaphor in 1903 – if the present analysis is accepted, and there are, of course, many others – the representation of the full structure of the object is condensed, with the consequence that when viewed from a Peircean perspective all metaphorically informed signs are both *underspecified* – not all the elements of the original parallelism in the object find their way into the sign – and characteristically *incongruous*, as such signs represent elements drawn from distinct and generally dissimilar domains reflecting to varying degrees the intensity of the judgements or commentary directed at elements in the target domain. However, developments in Peirce's conception of signs and the process in which they function led to the radical modification of the theoretical status of the subclasses of icons, and with them the hypoicons, examined in Chapter 3. In the following paragraphs we nevertheless continue with the original three formal configurations to exploit their potential for the qualitative analysis of pictorial signs.

✳✳✳

Figures 6.2–6.4 were basic illustrations of hypoiconicity. Taking into account the relaxation in 1905 of the original strict definition of the three subclasses of the icon, we now turn to the exposition of a hybrid approach to signs that associates those same formal configurations with the sign's semiotic history, more precisely, with its mediatization by means of the immediate object, this being the initial stages in the semiosis or semioses that produced it. For obvious reasons, the interpretants are barely discussed in the analyses, although they are not difficult to imagine in all three cases. The three verbal cases discussed above were offered as illustrations of the basic qualitative, formal principles of hypoiconicity, but the following pictorial examples have the advantage of their origin and the motivation behind their production and mediatization being more clearly established. Consider, then, in the light of the foregoing examples, Figure 6.6, Leonardo da Vinci's painting of Lisa Gherardini, the Mona Lisa hanging in the Louvre in Paris. This, one of the most famous paintings in the world, is composed of oil pigments on a wood panel arranged in such a way that we recognize a woman with an enigmatic smile playing about her lips and seated against a distant landscape. This arrangement, from a semiotic point of view, is assumed by observers to correspond to features of the model.

The painting in Figure 6.6 is a famous representation of some of the qualities, presumed to be inhering in the model, which determine corresponding qualities in

Figure 6.6 Mona Lisa. Photo © RMN-Grand Palais (Musée du Louvre)/Stéphane Maréchalle.

the painting, this being an iconic sinsign but also an image or likeness from a strictly qualitative point of view. The general definition of the hypoicons given earlier, 'any material image, as a painting, is largely conventional in its mode of representation; but in itself, without legend or label it may be called a hypoicon', describes this state of affairs. The qualities represented – lines, shapes, shades of colour, etc. – are thus defined to be less complex phenomenologically than the existential medium, namely the wood panel and oils 'hosting' them. Consequently, the intended representation of the qualities in the model is in no way inhibited by potential differences in complexity between the sign and the structure of the object as projected. Note that although we know from Vasari ([1568] 1991: 294) that the model existed and, indeed, who she was, the painting itself offers no proof of this: an image in this Peircean technical sense represents an object whether it exists or not, a fact to which numerous animated cartoons for children bear witness.

The mediatization sequence of the *Mona Lisa* is an example of Baxandall's 'deposit of a social relationship', a negotiation between patron and artist. Although the painting is renowned for the artistry displayed by Leonardo in the portrait, from the point of view of semiosis and the history of the painting as a sign from inception to production, the artist was not the agency that produced the painting but was, principally, the executor of pictorial skill – of 'brush' as Baxandall has it (1972: 14–17). The primary agency in this case was, rather, Francesco del Giocondo's desire – an intentionality – to have his wife Lisa immortalized in a portrait, although art historians might find this a scandalous suggestion. This is a case of macrosemiosis, as there were obviously innumerable intermediary stages – including the contribution of Leonardo's artistic genius – leading to the final realization of the portrait, but Francesco's intention was what set the process in motion. The medium was the combination of white wood panel and oils, while the particular arrangement of these oils on the panel is the realization of the form communicated to the medium by the immediate object, in other words, the 'hint' or its 'substance' inherited in this particular famous form from the dynamic object. Obviously, the composed brush strokes producing the painting are a far cry from the 'pure' verbocentric immediate objects that Peirce was interested in.

Now, as seen in Chapter 3, for Peirce the photograph was an example of the class of signs – a dicent indexical sinsign – which *did* offer proof of the existence of its object. The photograph was considered there as a type of proposition in which, since there is an existential relation between the model and the photographic plate or film, the section of rays constitutes the quasi-subject of the photograph's propositional structure while the print itself is its quasi-predicate (EP2: 282, 1903). As a subclass of icon, the form presented by the photograph is one degree more complex than the Mona Lisa: the existential status of the relation associating model and photograph is phenomenologically and ontologically more complex than the simple, monadic possibility of the relation between Lisa Gherardini and the complexus of qualities on the painting representing her. For example, while there is no proof that the space between the eyes of the woman depicted on the Mona Lisa painting corresponds exactly to the space between the eyes of Lisa Gherardini herself, we understand that the space between the left and right eyes of a person in an unmanipulated photograph must correspond point by point to those of the model represented, irrespective of

Figure 6.7 Margaret Cameron's portrait of Beatrice Cenci, 1866. Courtesy the Science Museum Group.

scale, camera angle and the nature of the pose. Margaret Cameron's study of Beatrice Cenci, Figure 6.7, is a fine example.

Figure 6.8 represents the structure of a very basic diagram or analogue, a formal arrangement in an object composed essentially of at least one dyadic relation between its parts, and illustrated here for convenience as the single relation **le—re** between the two partial objects in the domain of experience represented by the sign, namely the left and right eyes and the space between them on the face on Cameron's albumen print. Multiple other relations exist, of course – the distance between lips and chin, size of forehead, length of neck, etc. In all such cases, the diagrammatic complexity of the sinsign is such that the representation of the structure of the object is, as in the case of the image, in no way inhibited by the unavoidable existential status of the print medium by means of which it is communicated.

The history of the photograph in Figure 6.7 is a complex blend of Roman history and artistic intention. This was a study for a series of portraits by the early photographic artist, Margaret Cameron, celebrating Beatrice Cenci. Beatrice was the daughter of a Roman aristocrat who repeatedly raped her and abused his wife and sons. Beatrice

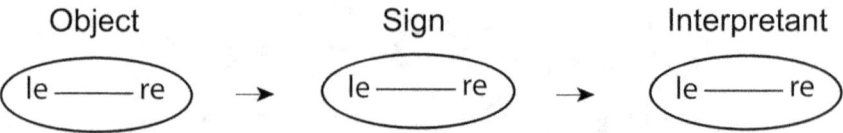

Figure 6.8 One example of the diagram structures composing the Beatrice Cenci photograph.

participated in the murder of her father, was tried, found guilty and publicly executed by beheading in 1599, but became a symbol of resistance to the depravity and moral unaccountability of the Roman nobility. Cameron's series of images were intended to capture the suffering Beatrice was forced to endure, whence, via the immediate object, the angled pose exposing the neck and the model's pensive expression. In the sign-system of 1903, the model in a photograph would constitute the sign's object (not yet designated the dynamic object at the time): the photographic print is indexical. However, analysis within the structure of semiosis requires us to individualize the function of the various stages in which the intentionality of the object is mediatized, made manifest, and in this case it is the intentionality of Cameron's desire to capture the spirit of Beatrice's martyrdom that has determined the poignant composition of light and dark lines and shapes – the form of the immediate object – on the 'passive' print medium.

Finally, as illustrated by Figure 6.9, metaphor is the structure of resemblance presenting a phenomenological complexity compatible with mediation, synthesis and representation – a degree of complexity, like the symbol's, which requires the experience of the interpreter in the interpreting process in order for us to construe the nature of the association or comparison being communicated. According to Peirce's original definition, metaphor hypoiconicity informs a sign whose object is structurally more complex than the sign itself, while in 1905 he saw such complexity as informing signs which 'partake of a symbolic flavor': they were redefined as icons being 'made for the purpose'. They now became, in other words, the determinations of some intentionality. The two conceptions of the subclass are not incompatible.

With this in mind, we examine a metaphor-informed photographic montage composing a politically motivated poster, Barbara Kruger's *Untitled (Your Body Is a Battleground)*. At the time, the Bush administration was seeking to overturn the 1973 Roe v. Wade Supreme Court decision guaranteeing women's reproductive rights. In view of the current mood in the United States, the poster is, sadly, as appropriate today as it was all those years ago.[11] The poster itself (Figure 6.9), which Kruger conceived, produced and helped to distribute, incongruously features a partially exposed photograph of a woman's face appropriated from the 50s, overlaid by a militant slogan and short informative statements (in colour in the original).[12] Whereas Cameron posed and photographed a model in a certain manner in order to represent an individual young woman's martyrdom, by reproducing the photograph of an anonymous woman's face from another era Barbara Kruger has creatively exposed

Figure 6.9 Barbara Kruger, *Untitled (Your Body Is a Battleground)*, 1989, Poster for March on Washington in support of legal abortion, birth control and women's rights. Courtesy the artist and Sprüth Magers.

the plight not of an individual but that of 'everywoman'. Now, in Kruger's case both manipulated photograph and text have metaphor structure as Peirce defined it in 1903.

Referring back to Figure 6.4, and bearing in mind that in the west we naturally scan verbal structures and imagery spatially from left to right and temporally from present to future, the base domain of the pictorial metaphor is composed of the positively exposed half of the face on the left, **a**, signifying that at present women enjoy 'full' autonomous status, **b**, while, juxtaposed as the ' – ' relation, the target is composed of the negative exposure of the face on the right, **a'**, implying that woman's social status and political influence would be reduced to a simple potentiality, **b'**, if the original Supreme Court decision were to be overturned. Both (**b**) and (**b'**) are characteristically absent from the pictorial metaphor, Kruger thereby dramatically picturing the abstract concept of the threat of woman's potential loss of social status and empowerment by means of a strikingly incongruous manipulated pictorial sign. Figure 6.10 represents the truncated parallelism in the structure of the facial metaphor.

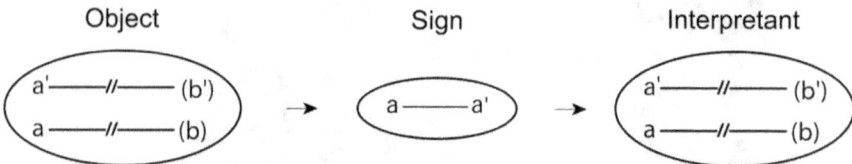

Figure 6.10 The metaphor structure of the pictorial element of Kruger's poster.

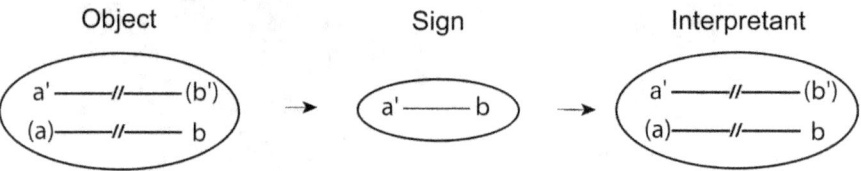

Figure 6.11 The metaphor structure of the verbal element of Your body is a battleground.

Analysis of the verbal metaphor (Figure 6.11), which represents explicitly Kruger's general thesis, reveals a similarly truncated parallelism, in this case based on military strategy. The target is women's control of their bodies to be defended in the political and ideological arena in the United States at the time, while the base component of the metaphor establishes the relation between some important strategic position to be defended on a battlefield. The violence explicit in the verbal metaphor is reinforced visually by the information tags in Figure 6.9 streaked in red and white over the woman's face like war paint (on the original poster). Schematically, the deliberately underspecified and incongruous metaphorical structure of the slogan can be summarized as follows, where, as seen in the earlier examples of metaphor, the elements in brackets – in this verbal example (**a**) and (**b'**) – are not reproduced in the sign:

> Target: women's control of their bodies = **a'**, to be defended in (the political and Ideological arena = **b'**).
> Base: (strategic position to defend = **a**) on a battlefield = **b.**

If the metaphor were rewritten as a simile – similes have analogue structure – all the elements involved in the threatened status of women would be mentioned: *Defending women's control of their bodies in the political and ideological arena is like the defence of a strategic position on a battleground*: here the parallelism is complete, and simile constitutes the only way it can be. This far less striking assimilation is displayed in the simple abstract structure in Figure 6.12. This represents the proportion **a is to b as a' is to b'**, which is communicated in identical structure from the dynamic object via the immediate object to the medium and on to the interpretant. In the case of the metaphor in Figure 6.9, this parallel structure has been manipulated, truncated

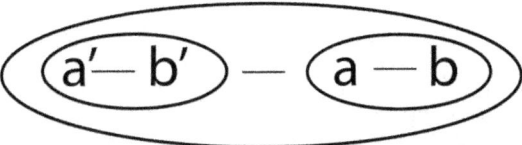

Figure 6.12 The diagram structure of a typical simile.

on purpose to render the message more dramatic and hopefully more effective. To simplify, only the structure of the sign is shown in Figure 6.12.

Finally, consider the text beneath the vertically divided image on the original poster:

> On April 26 the Supreme Court will hear a case which the Bush administration hopes will overturn the Roe vs. Wade decision, which established basic abortion rights. Join thousands of women and men in Washington D.C. on April 9. We will show that the majority of Americans support the woman's right to choose. In Washington: assemble at the Ellipse between the Washington Monument and the White House at 10 am; rally at the Capitol at 1:30 pm.

With respect to the poster's socio-political history, it was produced to support the Woman's March on Washington, a protest march against the Bush administration's attempt to overturn the Wade v. Roe decision in 1989. While qualitative analysis of the poster showed how metaphor informed both text and pictorial representation, the poster thus has a social, political and ideological significance that neither hypoiconicity nor, indeed, any of the ten classes of the three division, a-historical system of 1903 can account for. This is a militant sign, as the predella-like text on the poster clearly states: it was determined by one woman's desire to rally American citizens in defence of women's basic rights threatened by an all-male government, and this intense desire is the sign's dynamic object within Peirce's 1908 sign-system.

The (necessarily partial, interpretant-less) semiotic history of the poster begins, on the other hand, with the desire to rally the citizens through the process of conceiving the actual design that we see on the poster (Figure 6.9) and culminates with the production of the poster, one of the most powerful and hauntingly beautiful militant images of the era. As a hypoicon it displays the characteristic truncated parallel structure implied by Peirce's original structural definition of metaphor; as an example of the later description of the subclasses of the icon, it was most certainly a sign 'made for the purpose'. The medium is the duplicated ink and paper poster that was plastered on walls and telephone poles, while the form – the complex hypoiconic form analysed above – is the dramatic, tabloid-style expression, via the immediate object, of this desire. From an aesthetic point of view, the poster is typical of Kruger's photographic artistic preferences at that time, and her characteristic mediatization of social criticism by combination of red, white and black inks was probably a throwback to her professional background as a fashion designer and pictorial editor.

***

Irrespective of whether Peirce's category-based theory of hypoiconicity was valid or not after 1905, the formal distinctions it provides clearly function, and make it possible to hypothesize and explain differences in structure in a variety of different types of imagery, while the mediatization process can also be established in each case. But it should be remembered that the three increasingly complex configurations are purely formal. Adopting for simplicity the terminology of Charles Morris and certain currents of contemporary linguistics, the several configurations described above do not – cannot – provide semantic or pragmatic information: they have no meaning content. Peirce's speculative grammar, which was the basis of the 1903 Lowell Lectures on logic, simply established the purely formal criteria concerning what might constitute a class of signs or any one of its subdivisions, with no provision at all for a logical or linguistic semantics. However, structure is not the only aspect of pictorial representation that Peircean semiotics enables us to understand.

As was seen in each of the three cases, the embodiment of the form emanating from the dynamic object and communicated via the immediate object to the sign is treated as a specific stage in the semiotic history of signs, and this mediatization stage in the process of semiosis is summarized in Table 6.2. According to the 23 December 1908 letter to Lady Welby, the dynamic object is the origin of the determination sequence, the object outside the sign and the potential locus of intentionality; the sign is the medium or support in which the intentionality of the dynamic object is made manifest, that is, mediatized, inscribed in a medium. Since no purpose can be manifested immediately in a sign, the immediate object constitutes the particular form this intentionality takes with respect to the medium: it is Peirce's 'hint', in other words. For obvious reason, it is not possible to include the interpretant stages in Table 6.2 without information concerning the interpretants themselves; and in any case, they do not participate in the mediatization of intentionality – on the contrary, they are mediately triggered by it. The neo-Peircean hypothesis developed here, then, is that the inscription of intentionality in the medium, that is, the mediatization of intentionality, is the transformative function of the immediate object.

Note that in the determination process the immediate object must somehow contribute to the choice and materiality of the medium. But it does not cause the medium to be what it is – in the examples, a wooden panel and oils, paper covered with egg-white and salt and a sheet of paper and coloured inks. That is not what the Figures above were intended to show, for such a determination depends upon a variety of factors. The immediate object is what Peirce refers to as the object present in the sign. The analyses were intended to show that this immediate object has a distinct role to play in semiosis, and that the medium is only operational as a sign by displaying the form communicated when the immediate object functions as a relay of the influence of the object 'outside' the sign.

Table 6.2 shows that while the sign with its diagrammatic structure – Figures 6.9 and 6.10 are in fact diagrams, analogues of metaphorical form – is unavoidably existent in order to be perceived by potential or targeted interpreters, the two objects can both

Table 6.2 The stages participating in the materialization of intentionality

		Subject		
(*semiosis*)	Od →	Oi →	S →	
Universe				
Necessitant	**collective**	**copulant**	type	
Existent	concretive	designative	**token**	
Possible	abstractive	descriptive	mark	

be necessitant: that is, both can be more complex than the sign representing them. If the schemata system is valid, this is the most probable arrangement for complex mediatizations such as the sort displayed by Barbara Kruger's poster. The greater complexity of both dynamic and immediate objects exempts them from the existential constraints inhibiting the sign, necessarily a token, thereby allowing the immediate object to communicate the purposely truncated structure of the parallelism of metaphor. This parallelism also constitutes a 'Form (or feature)' extended to the medium in the 1906 definition of the sign, independently of any intended underspecification to follow in the sign, as on Barbara Kruger's poster, where some of the original elements of the parallelism are excised by artistic manipulation of the constraints of a perceivable medium. In short, it is the structure of the parallelism that counts, not the labels 'hypoicon' and 'metaphor', and there is no reason not to consider the parallelism as a diagram partaking of a 'symbolic flavor' or an abstract iconic structure 'made for the purpose'. This implies that Peirce's conception of metaphor in 1903 is not in any way invalidated by the redefinition of the icon's subclasses in 1905. Moreover, the fact that the determination sequence of semiosis is composed solely of correlate divisions, thereby excluding the sign-object division of 1903, does not render the three formal configurations, or iconicity in general, irrelevant and inoperative. On the contrary, the phenomenological distinctions defined in the 1903 version of the semiotics can be clearly seen to inform the incomplete parallel structure of the signs in Figures 6.9 and 6.10, while the immediate object in the dynamic process of semiosis, which is necessarily inscribed in time, constitutes the informing agency of such structure in actual communicative processes.

Summary and discussion

The following points were raised in the chapter. It was shown in the previous chapter and in the present one that the post-scriptum table was equivalent to the 1903 definition of sign, and that was in fact in fact an abridged version of the hexadic process of semiosis. Comparing it with the triadic definitions of the sign was a useful exercise as it brought to light the fact that each was problematic in two ways: first, identifying the interpretant in particular was impossible without appeal to retrospective or projective analytical techniques; but more importantly, composed simply of the three 'basic' relates, both implied, controversially, that the object determined the sign, and the sign the interpretant, *immediately*. The relates function perfectly as the many definitions of the signs listed by Robert Marty and John Deely testify, but they can only provide a condensed, inoperative version of the action of the sign. This was deemed to explain why Peirce in 1904 was led to introduce two objects and three interpretants in his first hexad. Furthermore, discussion in Chapter 3 had established that intentionality can be the triggering element of semiosis. In this chapter it was now established that any intentionality, in order to be realized, needs to be made manifest, needs to be made perceivable; and it was shown how this could be accomplished. It was shown in the chapter, too, that it was possible to consider, as Peirce did in 1906, the sign to be a medium, and that the perceivable realization of any triggering agency in semiosis was implemented by the immediate object in the stages of mediatization. Unlike alternative discussions of the hypoicons, this study considers the sign *is* the medium, and that what we conventionally call a sign such as the *Mona Lisa* hanging in the Louvre is, in these pages at least, the fusion of the organizing composition of the immediate object and the wood panels and oils medium on which it is realized. Now, what is true of the series of verbal and pictorial cases of semiosis analysed above is true of semiosis in any other semiotic field: anthroposemiotics is a personal specialism but there is no logical reason why the workings of semiosis as described in this chapter and the previous should not be universal.

The chapter has adopted the principle that the dynamic object as a logical agency is the source of intention and has shown how certain distinguishing properties – its form – are communicated to the sign as the structure of the immediate object and thence to the three interpretants. But Tables 6.1 and 6.2 showed how both the dynamic and immediate objects can be necessitant, general and therefore unperceivable, whereas the sign, if it is to 'engineer consent', for example, has to be existent. This being the case, identifying the dynamic object – that is, correctly interpreting such signs – requires caution. For the naïve observer or reader, the lifeless, two-dimensional, on-screen depictions in the case of TV and film and the unidimensional stream of, say, a newspaper report, manifestly represent three-dimensional living film stars and politicians, and these are easily taken to be the objects of said film, TV or newspaper report. However, the real dynamic object is constituted predominantly by the editorial decisions of the TV stations or the newspaper, or, in less open, more opaque circumstances, by the political views of their proprietors: meaning made by an unperceived and unsuspected source – a meaning which, given Peirce's interpretive differential discussed in Chapter 3, may or may not be interpreted correctly.

Conclusion

How would we feel if art historians suddenly decreed that Picasso's interest as a painter stopped after the so-called blue period, thereby banishing to obscurity *Les demoiselles d'Avignon, Guernica* and his collaboration with Braque, not to mention the later 'periods' of his artistic development? What would have been true of Picasso is likely to be the case with Peirce if we don't continue to develop his legacy – it is so easy to be content to exploit the logic of 1903. However, taking the legacy further is not an easy task, owing to the dearth of information concerning his later statements on logic, and it has been hampered, too, by the thematic organization of the *Collected Papers*: for nearly half a century these, the sole source of workable texts in print, have inevitably obscured the chronology, and with it, the development of Peirce's thought.

The present study has sought to reveal aspects of this development and thus to contribute to the continuing relevance of the legacy. Some of these, which constitute a neo-Peircean approach to the problem, are as follows. One is the clear distinction established between Peirce's logic and a version of the 'practical science' of semiotics appropriate for the principled scrutiny of the world around us. By adopting a chronological approach to the available data the study has shown, too, how Peirce's thinking on signs significantly evolved in the period following the Syllabus. In the 1905–7 period, for instance, he was seen to have developed a more dynamic model of the sign, to have redefined the subclasses of the icon, qualifying metaphor, the formally most complex subclass, as purpose-made, to have established an abstract dialogic context for communication and hence for the action of the sign by the introduction of quasi-minds, and, finally, to have produced the first definition of semiosis. Indeed, the changing definitions of the subclasses of the icon have served as a leitmotiv of Peirce's developing thought. To these must be added the exploitation of the 1908 letter sent to Lady Welby which has enabled a (contested) interpretation of the determination sequence of semiosis and the exposition of significant differences to be found between Peirce's theory of perception and semiosis and those of more recent theories of sign, language and mind. Finally, exploitation of the later stages of Pierce's logic has made it possible to demonstrate why any form of intentionality requires mediatization, namely the specific contribution to semiosis of the immediate object if the intentionality is to be made manifest. And at all times, the study has sought to respect, project and develop what were considered to be Peirce's original statements.

Why should that be important? As I conclude this study, our world of information is taking on an end-of-the-age appearance. We have propagandists on social media defending the bombing and shelling of defenceless civilians. We have populations in thrall to military, religious and ideological oppressors who control, suppress, reformulate and ration information to stay their power. We have, in the most powerful country in the world, educated politicians who wittingly endorse fake news for political advancement. In civilized countries, attesting to the signal failure of their education systems, millions are addicted to a journalism which promotes entertainment and opinion over information, at the behest of proprietors and their political affiliations. We have the subterranean strategies of Internet services covertly harvesting and distributing for profit the personal information of the individuals who use them. And unless we learn to live with it – and we really have no choice, however we define intelligence – we have potentially the greatest threat to future generations already at the door: generative AI, while capable of performing surgery more precisely, more efficiently than the human surgeon, can also, when appropriately seeded, produce counterfeit discourse, and imagery in the styles of the great masters that unguarded experts can barely distinguish from the original. Such a situation surely renders the continuing development of a theoretically grounded semiotics both a scientific and ethical necessity.

One response is a militant semiotics. The semioticians, the scrutineers of signs, have the means to establish the facts and set the record straight. However, in reality they have two sets of facts to engage with, one the facts of our world of information, the other the facts of their own discipline. In order to complete successfully the investigation and interpretation of the first they have to make sure that the second are in order. The reader coming to this book expecting to find readily exploitable methods and examples for a neo-Peircean approach to signs – a sort of toolkit for anthroposemiotics – would be disappointed, for it is to the second task, an attempt to establish the facts of the discipline, of a contemporary semiotics in its Peircean strain, that the book is addressed.

Notes

Introduction

1   The colloquium, '*Sémiotique peircienne: États des lieux*/Peircean Semiotics: The State of the Art' was organized at Canet-Plage by my colleague at the University of Perpignan, Joëlle Réthoré, with myself and Michel Balat in attendance.
2   For a very different alternative conception, see Wilson and Price (2018).

Chapter 1

1   In the Introduction to the *Bloomsbury Companion to Contemporary Peircean Semiotics*, I suggested that the audience paid to follow Peirce's Lowell lectures (Jappy 2019a: 17). This was a mistake: public lectures at the Lowell Institute were free.
2   See Fisch (1986: 270) and Parker (1998, Chapter Two), for more complete charts of Peirce's 1903 classifications. The purpose of Figure 1.1 is simply to show the differences between Peirce's cenoscopic disciplines and the idioscopic status of most contemporary semiotic research. See Kent (1987), Vehkavaara (2003), and Ambrosio (2016) for additional material and details of earlier systems.
3   The title of Bentham's text, *Chrestomathia derives from the Greek khrestos*, 'useful' and *mathein*, 'learning': it was intended as an exhaustive guide to instruction. This is how Bentham describes the two sciences under discussion, claiming that 'metaphysics' is used by some as another word for the coenoscopic, a suggestion that Peirce would have found repugnant: '*Coenoscopic* and *Idioscopic*, by successively attaching to the subject *Ontology* these two adjuncts, the field of art and science may thus be divided, the whole of it, into two portions; in one of which, viz. the *coenoscopic*, shall be contained the appalling and repulsive branch of science, to which the no less formidable, and to many a man intensely odious, appellation of *metaphysics*, is sometimes also applied; while to the other, viz. the *idioscopic*, all the other branches of art and science, may, without distinction, be consigned' (1816 Annex IV: 'Essay on nomenclature and classification', 76). Note that the nominals 'cenoscopy' and 'idioscopy' are Peirce's creation, as Bentham only referenced the adjectival terms 'coenoscopic' and 'idioscopic'.
4   Consider, too, this passage from the Carnegie application (emphasis added): 'Methodeutic … can have no direct and primary concern with anything but arguments, notwithstanding *the great part that definition and division have always played in this branch of logic*' (L75: 242–4, 1902). Definition and division are the basic instruments of classification, hence their importance to Peirce.
5   CP: 8.202, 1985.
6   'It thus appears that all knowledge comes to us by observation. A part is forced upon us from without and seems to result from Nature's mind; a part comes from the

depths of the mind as seen from within, which by an egotistical anacoluthon we call our mind' (EP2: 24).

7   'A common mode of estimating the amount of matter in a MS or printed book is to count the number of words. There will ordinarily be about twenty *thes* on a page, and of course they count as twenty words. In another sense of the word "word," however, there is but one word "the" in the English language; and it is impossible that this word should lie visibly on a page or be heard in any voice, for the reason that it is not a Single thing or Single event. It does not exist; it only determines things that do exist. Such a definitely significant Form, I propose to term a *Type*. A Single event which happens once and whose identity is limited to that one happening or a Single object or thing which is in some single place at any one instant of time, such event or thing being significant only as occurring just when and where it does, such as this or that word on a single line of a single page of a single copy of a book, I will venture to call a *Token*. An indefinite significant character such as a tone of voice can neither be called a Type nor a Token. I propose to call such a Sign a *Tone*. In order that a Type may be used, it has to be embodied in a Token which shall be a sign of the Type, and thereby of the object the Type signifies. I propose to call such a Token of a Type an *Instance* of the Type. Thus, there may be twenty Instances of the Type "the" on a page' (LI 315, 1906).

8   See Champagne (2018: 22–7) for an interesting discussion of the absence of the third element, the tone, from contemporary usage of the type-token distinction.

9   The OED entry for 'semiosis' gives this reference to Aldous Huxley: '1938 A. Huxley Let. 18 Nov. (1969) 438 "It interests me a lot and has set me reading along a number of interesting lines – Carnap, Neurath, Morris and Korzybski on the problems of semiosis"'. These authorities had obviously taken the concept seriously before Sebeok made it more widely known.

10 See this from Max Fisch: 'It is important to note, however, that though logic is now (1903?) wholly semeiotic, it is still not the whole of semeiotic. It is semeiotic variously qualified as cenoscopic (MS 499), formal (NEM 4: 20f.), general (1.444), normative (2.111), speculative (MS 693). It is "General Semeiotic, the a priori theory of signs" (MS 634); "the quasi-necessary, or formal doctrine of signs" (2.227); "the pure theory of signs, in general" (MS L 107). In addition to cenoscopic semeiotic, there are, or may be, idioscopic studies of signs as various as the idioscopic sciences themselves – physical, chemical, biological, geological, anthropological, psychological, medical, musical, economic, political, and so on. None of these is any part of logic, though the reasonings they employ may be made matter for logical study. Take psychology for example. "Of course, psychologists ought to make, as in point of fact they are making, their own invaluable studies of the sign-making and sign-using functions, – invaluable, I call them, in spite of the fact that they cannot possibly come to their final conclusions, until other more elementary studies have come to their first harvest" (MS 675). (1986: 339–40)'.

11 See, too, this early definition in which (traditional) logic is already identified as a classificatory science: 'And so you will find out that it is a universal rule that to have a testing art we need no other knowledge than a classifying science. And, accordingly, if we wish to be able to test arguments, what we have to do, is to take all the arguments we can find, scrutinize them and put those which are alike in a class by themselves and then examine these different kinds and learn their properties. Now the classificatory science of reasons so produced is the science of Logic' (W1: 359, 1866).

12 In the penultimate chapter of the *Critique of Pure Reason*, Kant writes: 'By the term *Architectonic* I mean the art of constructing a system. Without systematic unity, our knowledge cannot become a science; it will be an aggregate, not a system .... Reason cannot permit our knowledge to remain in an unconnected and rhapsodistic state, but requires that the sum of our cognitions should constitute a system. It is thus alone that they can advance the ends of reason. By a system I mean the unity of various knowledge under one idea. This idea is the concept – given by reason – of the form of a whole, in so far as the concept determines *a priori* not only the limits of its content, but the place which each of its parts is to occupy' (A831/B859, 1787).

13 See this remark from the drafts intended for Lady Welby dated 24–28 December 1908: 'In my paper of 1867 May 14 (*Proc. Am. Acad. of Arts & Sci.*, Vol. VII, p. 295) I said, "We come to this, that logic treats of the reference of symbols in general to their objects. In this view it is one of a trivium of conceivable sciences. The first would treat of the formal conditions of symbols having meaning, that is of the reference of symbols in general to their grounds, or imputed characters; and this might be called Formal Grammar [the *grammatica speculativa* of Duns]. The second, logic, would treat of the formal conditions of the truth of symbols. The third would treat of the formal conditions of the force symbols, or their power of appealing to a mind, that is, of their reference in general to interpretants, and this might be called formal rhetoric." I should still opine that in the future there probably will be three such sciences. But I have learned that the only natural lines of demarcation between nearly related sciences are the divisions between the social groups of devotees of those sciences; and for the present the cenoscopic studies (i.e., those studies which do not depend upon new special observations) of all signs remain one undivided science, – a conclusion I had come to before I made your acquaintance, but which the warm interest that you and I have in each other's researches in spite of the difference in their lines, decidedly confirms' (EP2: 481–2, 1908).

14 This is how Peirce introduces the human parameter in logical analysis: 'As a second order, we have psychotaxy, not a very good name for classificatory psychognosy or the study of kinds of mental manifestation. This order falls into two suborders, the one embracing studies of mental performances and products, the other of incarnations, or ensoulments of mind. To the latter suborder I would refer all studies of the minds of insects and (when there are any) of octopuses, of sexual characteristics, of the seven ages of human life, of professional and racial types, of temperaments and characters. To the former suborder, I would refer the vast and splendidly developed science of linguistics, of customs of all kinds, of Brinton's ethnology generally' (CP: 1.271, 1902).

15 However, John Deely found the term in the alternative spelling – semeiosis – in an early eighteenth-century dictionary (2004: n5).

16 A position shared by Short and, apparently Cheryl Misak. See Deely (2009a: 58–9).

17 https://plato.stanford.edu/entries/peirce-semiotics/.

18 Jakobson's work was, of course, predated by, most notoriously, Plato's *Cratylus*, but also by John Wallis in England, and others. See Genette (1976) for an exhaustively researched review of the history of investigations into sound–meaning correlations since the *Cratylus*.

19 See Jappy (1999), from which some of the material in this section draws, for a critical review of the first twenty years of the linguistic iconicity movement.

20 In Jakobson (1971), pages 345–59.

Chapter 2

1. 'But as far as I have studied it, [logic] is simply the science of what must be or ought to be true representation, so far as representation can be known without any gathering of special facts beyond our ordinary daily life' (R465: 25, 1903).
2. 'My classification of signs, however, is intended to be a classification of possible signs and therefore observation of existing signs is only of use in suggesting and reminding one of varieties that one might otherwise overlook' (EP2: 500, 1909).
3. In Deely's case this is probably through his reading of Jean Poinsot, amongst others: 'In Poinsot's time (1632), it was definitely established that the sign strictly speaking consists not in anything sensible or particular, but rather in a relation essentially and irreducibly triadic' (2004: 5). This attribution appears to be common to biosemioticians: 'For Deely, following Poinsot, signs are a matter of "relation" – not, as the representational perspective would have it, some entity standing in for some other entity from which it is different. For Poinsot and, later, for Peirce, the sign needs to be understood as the entire relation of its constituents' (Cannizzaro and Cobley 2015: 216). As it happens, far from following Poinsot in defining the sign as a relation, as Deely and others have asserted, Peirce in fact *broke* with this tradition, if tradition it was, by defining the sign, as demonstrated in the text, as a *member* or *correlate* of the triadic relation and not as the relation itself. It is notable that Thomas Sebeok, more circumspect, did not adhere to such a view: 'semiosis involves an irreducibly triadic relation among a sign, its object, and its interpretant' (2001: 27).
4. Deely (2014), on the other hand, seems to present a more orthodox position: 'A representamen whose interpretant is mental is a *sign* in the common or ordinary sense. The significate of the sign on this common or "ordinary" sense, i.e., the significate of a representamen with a mental interpretant, is an *object*' (2014: 1).
5. To quote but three: 'Peirce called the triad – the basic relational element in logic – quite simply a sign' Hoffmeyer (1996: 18); 'and Peirce also referred to this triadic relation itself as a sign', Gare (2019: 42); 'Inspired by Duns Scotus' stance on the Trinity, Peirce realized that, since all signs involve a triadic relation among a sign-vehicle, an object, and an interpretation, we can adopt three different perspectives on any meaningful phenomena' Champagne (2018: 4).
6. What Peirce meant by 'determination' and its dyadic structure as displayed in Figure 2.1 (and other figures later) is discussed fully in the section entitled 'Semiosis and the 23 December 1908 Typology' in Chapter 4.
7. The determination sequence is sometimes represented by commentators as a three-pronged figure with the three prongs meeting at the centre. Although Peirce does employ such 'triadic' diagrams, e.g., CP: 1.275, 1902, EP2: 364 1905, and RL463: 94, 1904, to the best of my knowledge, they are never used to represent the determination relation involving object, sign and interpretant: the relation of determination, as we see later, is dyadic, not triadic.
8. 'The interpretant relates to and mediates between the representamen and the semiotic object in such a way as to bring about an interrelation between them at the same time and in the same way that it brings itself into interrelation *with* them' (Merrell 2001: 28).
9. 'This is the mistake of assuming that the three elements of Peirce's triadic sign – the representamen, the object, and the interpretant – map onto structures familiar in 'secondary dualism'. These erroneous construals involve an object (behind the sign), a sense impression (which is transmitted from the object to the mind) and

an interpretation (which is the intellect's understanding of the sense impression). If this conventional structure is imposed on Peircean semiotics, signs are reduced to little more than a special class of sense data and his sign theory would be little more than another incarnation of 'secondary dualism'. But fortunately this is not the case; Peirce, following Hegel, views the sign as involving a mediating entity – the object within the sign. As a result, this chapter will suggest that the structure of the Peircean sign reflects Hegel's triadic model of Being, Essence and Notion' (Barnham 2022: 133–4).

10   Cf. too, 'A sign stands *for* something *to* the idea which it produces or modifies. Or, it is a vehicle conveying into the mind something from without. That for which it stands is called its *object*; that which it conveys, its *meaning*; and the idea to which it gives rise, its *interpretant*. The object of representation can be nothing but a representation of which the first representation is the interpretant. But an endless series of representations, each representing the one behind it, may be conceived to have an absolute object at its limit. The meaning of a representation can be nothing but a representation. In fact, it is nothing but the representation itself conceived as stripped of irrelevant clothing. But this clothing never can be completely stripped off; it is only changed for something more diaphanous. So there is an infinite regression here. Finally, the interpretant is nothing but another representation to which the torch of truth is handed along; and as representation, it has its interpretant again. Lo, another infinite series' (CP: 1.339, n.d.).

11   Conveniently borrowed from Jappy (2013: 20).

12   The first mention of the term seems to have been the French *interprétant* in an entry in his Logic Notebook dated March 1866 (W1: 347–8, although the acute accent on the second 'e' is not visible on the digitized Houghton manuscript (R339: 10v, H36)), presumably because the French term is active, meaning 'something which interprets', while the English *interpretand* would have a passive value, with the sense of 'to be interpreted' as in, for example, *multiplicand*, which is a number to be multiplied by another. See, too, 'The object is the sign's *determinant*; the interpretant is the *determinand* of the sign' (R499: 43, 1906–1907?). However, Peirce does use the term *interpretand* in a draft to Lady Welby of March 1906 in the definition of the sign given there: 'I use the word "*Sign*" in the widest sense for any medium for the communication or extension of a Form (or feature). Being medium, it is determined by something, called its Object, and determines something, called its Interpretant or Interpretand' (SS: 196, 1906).

13   'The fourth Trichotomy is the one which I most frequently use: Icon, Index, Symbol' (CP: 8.368, 1908).

14   'The categories show that signs are themselves of three kinds. For a sign may have as its sign-flavor, or significant character, merely the flavor, or quality, which belongs to it just as anything has a flavor or quality; and in this case it will stand for whatever its thing-flavor adapts it to standing for. Such is an icon, or image, which represents any object just so far as it resembles that object. Or, secondly, a sign may have as its significant character the fact that it stands in real relation to its object. It will then serve as a sign of that object to any interpretant that represents it as so reacting with that object. This is an index. Or, finally, a sign may have as its significant character its being represented to be a sign. That is a symbol. All merely conventional signs are symbols; and so are all signs which become such because they are naturally taken to be such, as ideas. Logic might, perhaps, properly be restricted to symbols. I have not paid sufficient attention, perhaps, to the formal laws of indices and icons to see that

the study of them ought to be separated from that of symbols. My not very decided opinion is that they should all be studied together' (MS L75, Draft D: 237–44, 1902).

15 'The representamen, for example, divides by trichotomy into the general sign, or *symbol*, the *index*, and the *icon*' (EP2: 163, 1903).

16 An important reference to Hamilton's presentation of Reid is to be found in section '1904' in Chapter 3.

17 However, the way he relates them to the subdivisions of the earlier division suggests that he hadn't completely worked them out to his satisfaction: 'Although the immediate Interpretant of an Index must be an Index, yet since its Object may be the Object of a Singular Symbol, the Index may have such a Symbol for its indirect Interpretant. Even a genuine Symbol may be an imperfect Interpretant of it. So an Icon may have a degenerate Index, or an Abstract Symbol, for an indirect Interpretant, and a genuine Index or Symbol for an imperfect Interpretant' (EP2: 275, 1903).

18 Peirce's term 'image' is unfortunate, as the same term is a general and easily used substitute for pictorial representations. Whenever there is a possible confusion, the text will have 'pictorial representation'.

19 'An *Icon* is a Representamen whose Representative Quality is a Firstness of it as a First. That is, a quality that it has *qua* thing renders it fit to be a representamen' (CP: 2.276, 1903).

20 Jappy (2013) represented this process as an inverted triangle, a schema based on the inverted triangles Peirce was working with late in December 1908 (see Chapter 5). This was common practice in our IRSCE seminars in Perpignan, and such schemata were no doubt introduced by either of the two mathematicians of the group, Robert Marty or Michel Balat, for they, like Peirce, were able to think in diagrams. Indeed, probably the earliest schematization of the hypoicons is to be found in Marty (1979). His representation of metaphor in particular, in which he inserted an intermediary object (*objet intermédiaire*) between object and sign, was highly innovative (1979: 9). As it happens, the presentation of the hypoicons in Jappy (2013), which the present section develops, was subjected to an unremittingly hostile, damaging and, surprisingly for such a reputable journal, unethical, review in *Semiotica* by Nöth and Jungk (2015). The authors removed from a section clearly entitled 'The structure of semiosis and the medium' my Figure 1.1 (which had the caption *The determination 'flow' in semiosis*), replaced the caption by *The Peircean model of the sign as Jappy (2013: 6) sees it* (2015: 666), and claimed that the study was more Saussurean than Peircean. The fact that they saw my Figure 1.1 as a model of the sign betrays the erroneous conception of the sign as a triad composed of the three correlates, thus revealing them again as unwitting proponents of the sign=triadic relation fallacy. Unfortunately, *Semiotica* didn't offer reviewed authors the opportunity to reply to criticism as other journals do. Strangely enough, Barnham (2022: 139) reproduces the same triangular figure with an almost identical caption: *Figure 5: Jappy's Version of the Peircean Sign*, which suggests greater familiarity with the review than with the study. The triangular representations in question were replaced by the 'bottleneck' schemas in Figures 5.8 and 5.18 introduced in a later chapter of the same Jappy (2013), namely the linear sequence of ellipses representing object, sign and interpretant employed in this study, as these are better able to represent the communication of form via a medium.

21 Note that Peirce makes no reference to a medium in his discussions of the hypoicons, but as we see later, the medium acquires considerable theoretical importance, and it can at this stage usefully, if prematurely, be associated with the hypoicons in representations of the action of the sign.

Chapter 3

1. See Peirce's response 'to the anticipated suspicion that he attaches a superstitious or fanciful importance to the number three, and forces divisions to a Procrustean bed of trichotomy' (CP 1.568, 1910).
2. See section 'Semiosis' in Chapter 1.
3. 'But all logicians distinguished two objects of a sign; the one, the Immediate object or object as the sign represents it, (and without this a sign would not be a sign); the other Real object, or object as it is independent of any particular idea representing it' (R318: 373, 1907).
4. There is another typology in the Logic Notebook with the 'standard' order: (S), Oi, S-Od, Ii, Id, Isignified (R339: 240r, H451, 1904).
5. Note, too, that two divisions in Table 3.1, the relational respects S-Oi and S-Ii, were subsequently abandoned completely, with the immediate object and interpretant henceforth occupying independent positions in all the typologies to follow. Since both immediate object and immediate interpretant were defined to be 'present in' the sign, these two relational divisions were redundant.
6. See Peirce's remark in a letter to William James: 'In the Second Part of my Essay on Pragmatism, in the *Popular Science* of November 1877 and January 1878, I made three grades of Clearness of Interpretation. The first was such Familiarity as gave a person familiarity with a sign and readiness in using it or interpreting it. In his consciousness he seemed to himself to be quite *at home* with the sign. In short, it is Interpretation *in Feeling*. The second was Logical Analysis = Lady Welby's *Sense*. The third was Pragmatistic Analysis, would seem to be a Dynamical Analysis, but [is] identified with the Final Interpretant' (CP: 8.185, 1909).
7. This, in the *Monist* paper of 1905, was an obligation he was to impose upon himself. At one point, seeking to distinguish his personal, experimentalist conception of pragmatism from the type presented by William James and Ferdinand Schiller, for example, he famously introduced the term 'pragmaticism', a name, he declared, which is 'ugly enough to be safe from kidnappers' (EP2: 335).
8. 'Moreover, since pragmatism, in my view, relates to intellectual concepts exclusively, and since these are all general, the mental element we seek must be general' (R318 373, 1907).
9. 'In its broader sense, [logic] is the science of the necessary laws of thought … also of the laws of the evolution of thought, which … coincides with the study of the necessary conditions of the transmission of meaning by signs from mind to mind, and from one state of mind to another' (CP: 1.444, *c.* 1896).
10. For the term 'example', *Oxford Languages* gives 'a thing characteristic of its kind or illustrating a general rule' and 'a person or thing regarded in terms of their fitness to be imitated'. It was presumably this general property that Peirce had in mind when composing the definition.
11. In the Logic Notebook on 7 July that year Peirce began a ten-division typology with this simpler definition of the sign: 'A Sign is a Priman (what?) which is Secundan (how) to an Object (what) and is Tertian in determining (how) an Interpretant (what) into Secundanity (what sort) to that Object', where the items in parentheses were written beneath the terms preceding them in this formulation (R339: 247r, H467, 1905).
12. The reference to an 'interpretand' in this context is surprising. See the discussion in note 12 of Chapter 2.

13 See, too, this from 1906 'As a *medium*, the Sign is essentially in a triadic relation, to its Object which determines it and to its Interpretant which it determines. In its relation to the Object, the Sign is *passive*; that is to say, its correspondence to the Object is brought about by an effect upon the sign, the Object remaining unaffected, … On the other hand, in its relation to the interpretant the Sign is *active*, determining the interpretant without being itself thereby affected' (R793: 1–2, 1906).
14 EP2: 544 n22.
15 'A sign stands *for* something *to* the idea which it produces, or modifies. Or, it is a vehicle conveying into the mind something from without. That for which it stands is called its *object*; that which it conveys, its *meaning*; and the idea to which it gives rise, its *interpretant*' (CP: 1.339; not dated but probably earlier than 1905).
16 'A medium of communication is something, *A*, which being acted upon by something else, *N*, in its turn acts upon something, *I*, in a manner involving its determination by *N*, so that I shall thereby, through *A* and only through *A*, be acted upon by *N*. We may purposely select a somewhat imperfect example. Namely, one animal, say a mosquito, is acted upon by the entity of a zymotic disease, and in its turn acts upon another animal, to which it communicates the fever. The reason that this example is not perfect is that the active medium is in some measure of the nature of a *vehicle*, which differs from a medium of communication in acting upon the transported object and determining it to a changed location, where, without further interposition of the vehicle, it acts upon, or is acted upon by, the object to which it is conveyed. A sign, on the other hand, just in so far as it fulfills the function of a sign, and none other, perfectly conforms to the definition of a medium of communication' (EP2: 391, 1905).
17 Meyer Schapiro, in a classic of semiotics, describes media as varieties of grounds, and offers interesting examples in his first chapter (1994: 1–32).
18 Note that by the term 'utter', Peirce intended a far more general meaning than a linguist would. By 'utter' he meant 'produce a sign': 'To signify that a person puts forth a sign whether vocal, ocular, or by touch, – and conventional signs mostly are of one or other of these three kinds or by taste, smell, and a sense of temperature which are the media of many natural *tests* and *symptoms*, – I like the word *utter*' (R793: 14, 1906).
19 Jappy (2018).
20 He informed Lady Welby that 'From the summer of 1905 to the same time in 1906, I devoted much study to my ten trichotomies of signs' (CP: 8.363, 1908).
21 The several cases of interpretants are preceded by a capital I on the table: *Intended*, for example, stands for Intended Interpretant.
22 This multiplication of logical interpretants complicates Peirce's search for possible semioses: 'Moreover, the great majority of instances in which formations of logical interpretants do take place are very unsuitable to serve as illustrations of the process, because in them the essentials of this semiosis are buried in masses of accidental and hardly relevant semioses that are mixed with the former' (R318: 123, 1907).

Chapter 4

1 Note that the three modalities of being were not new to 1908. Peirce had already introduced the notion in a defence of realism against nominalism in one of the Lowell lectures of 1903 (CP: 1.15–1.26, 1903), in which he writes; 'My view is that

there are three modes of being. I hold that we can directly observe them in elements of whatever is at any time before the mind in any way. They are the being of positive qualitative possibility, the being of actual fact, and the being of law that will govern facts in the future' (CP: 1.23). In 1908, as we see from the letter, the three modes or modalities of being are more logical in nature, whereas in 1903 he was describing them in phenomenological terms: he continues from CP: 1.23 to introduce Secondness, then Firstness and Thirdness.

2   Savan (1988: 31), discussing the immediate object division of the 1908 system, is one of the first to place the theoretical background in phenomenology. He was followed in this by many others, as mentioned in Jappy (2016: 78–80). This is not the place to name names, as such an exercise is futile, but it should be mentioned Freadman, whose work was discussed in Chapter 1, is particularly damning of the late system described in the present chapter. Consider: 'I shall suggest that the ever more elaborate classifications represent attempts to override these problems in a rationale deriving from the most general account of the three categories, that sometimes does, and sometimes does not, forget the lessons of "things and events"' (2004: 138). And here: 'The whole theory starts with the definition of the sign, and moves directly to the "three universes" (the categories) in order to give the rationale of any trichotomy. ... The classifications are potentially endless variations on the very familiar theme: there are triads everywhere, all displaying the distinctions among quality or possibility, fact or actuality, and law or continuity. But these classifications signally failed to do what the invention of the first trichotomy brought off so brilliantly: they do not arise as the response to a theoretical "surprise" and hence cannot represent the solution to a real problem' (2004: 161–2).

3   And Peirce offers further examples of possible 'members' of such universes a little later in the text: 'Let us begin with the question of Universes. It is rather a question of an advisable point of view than of the truth of a doctrine. A logical universe is, no doubt, a collection of logical subjects, but not necessarily of metaphysical Subjects, or "substances"; for it may be composed of characters, of elementary facts, etc.' (CP: 4.546, 1906).

4   Note that 1908 was not the earliest mention of such universes. In the Logic Notebook, manuscript R339, in April 1906, Peirce was working on a new set of trichotomies, which he called 'triplets', and has this to say of the third triplet, the division concerning the 'Dynamical or Genuine Object': 'The second class of this triplet is that of signs of *actual* objects. This is the familiar class of *concrete* signs... Take the existence of a chair or table. By saying that it exists we mean that it is in the one universe of existence' (R339: 281r, H527, 1906).

5   'The universe of discourse is the aggregate of the individual objects which "exist," that is are independently side by side in the collection of experiences to which the deliverer and interpreter of a set of symbols have agreed to refer and to consider' (R493: 3, n.d.).

6   See this introductory statement from Max Fisch; 'In 1865, the first year of the first founding, Theodor Gomperz published an edition of the Herculaneum papyrus remains of a Greek treatise on inductive logic by the Epicurean philosopher Philodemus. The papyrus lacked the title, but the one most often given it is the Latin *de Signis* ("On Signs"). Peirce seems not to have made the acquaintance of this work immediately, but at the Johns Hopkins University he had a student named Allan Marquand, with whom he made an intensive study of it in 1879–80. To meet the thesis requirement for his Ph.D. degree, Marquand translated the treatise under

the title "On Inductive Signs and Inferences" and wrote an introduction to it. The introduction, or an abridgment of it, was published under the title "The Logic of the Epicureans" as the first essay in a volume of *Studies in Logic* edited by Peirce in 1883. One of the most striking features of the treatise is the frequency of the term *semeiosis*. The Greek suffix – *sis* means the act, action, activity, or process of. Peirce was prepared to understand semeiosis in either of two ways: (1) from the side of the sign, as sign-action, the functioning of a sign, or (2) from the side of the interpretant, as sign-interpreting or inferring from signs. Philodemus used it primarily in the latter sense, and even more narrowly as drawing inductive inferences from inductive signs. But for Peirce sign-action and sign-interpretation were not two different kinds of semeiosis but one and the same semeiosis considered from two points of view. To act as a sign is to determine an interpretant' (1986: 329).

7   At this point Hardwick, in his footnotes, reminds the reader that Peirce's usual term for tone, token and type is qualisign, sinsign and legisign, continuing a tradition of not adhering to Peirce's chosen terminology in this typology. See, too, Savan (1988: 19–20), who describes the first trichotomy as concerning the 'ground' of the sign, and after recognizing that Peirce had moved from the original qualisign, sinsign, legisign terms to tone, token and type, nevertheless elects to employ the 'original' triad of names, *Qualisign, Sinsign,* and *Legisign*'. The fact that this new typology might be an important new development in Peirce's thinking on signs seems to have occurred neither to Hardwick nor to Savan.

8   Cf. 'My three grades of Interpretant were worked out by reasoning from the definition of a Sign what sort of thing *ought* to be noticeable and *then* searching for its appearance. My Immediate Interpretant is implied in the fact that each Sign must have its peculiar Interpretability before it gets any Interpreter. My Dynamical Interpretant is that which is experienced in each act of Interpretation and is different in each from that of any other; and the Final Interpretant is the one interpretive result to which every Interpreter is destined to come if the Sign is sufficiently considered' (SS: 111, 1909).

9   Another problem is that he appears to contradict himself when he names signs identified by their having possible, existent and necessitant immediate objects at the end of the passage, after having remarked earlier that the immediate object might not be capable of all three modalities of being.

10 '(N: Peirce sometimes used "Explicit Interpretant" as an alternative name for the Immediate Interpretant, as in the Welby Correspondence (PW: 84 [= SS: 84]). Weiss and Burks, and Lieb, mistakenly identify the Explicit Interpretant with the Final Interpretant) (Savan 1988: 52)'.

11 Buchler ([1940] 2011).

12 'The rise of the mercury in an ordinary thermometer or the bending of the double strip of metal in a metallic thermometer is an indication, or, to use the technical term, is an index, of an increase of atmospheric temperature, which, nevertheless, acts upon it in a purely brute and dyadic way. In these cases, however, a mental representation of the index is produced, which mental representation is called the *immediate* object of the sign; and this object does triadically produce the intended, or proper, effect of the sign strictly by means of another mental sign; and that this triadic character of the action is regarded as essential is shown by the fact that if the thermometer is dynamically connected with the heating and cooling apparatus, so as to check either effect, we do not, in ordinary parlance speak of there being any semeiosy, or action of a sign, but, on the contrary, say that there is an "automatic regulation," an idea opposed, in our minds, to that of semeiosy' (CP: 5.473).

13 Thus Atkin: 'Indeed, Peirce treats the immediate interpretant as "all that is explicit in the sign apart from its context and circumstances of utterance"' (2008: 68).
14 'In regard to the Interpretant we have equally to distinguish, in the first place, the Immediate Interpretant, which is the interpretant as it is revealed in the right understanding of the Sign itself, and is ordinarily called the *meaning* of the sign; while in the second place, we have to take note of the Dynamical Interpretant which is the actual effect which the Sign, as a Sign, really determines. Finally, there is what I provisionally term the Final Interpretant, which refers to the manner in which the Sign tends to represent itself to be related to its Object. I confess that my own conception of this third interpretant is not yet quite free from mist' (LI: 314–15, 1906).
15 'Habits differ from dispositions in having been acquired as consequences of the principle, virtually well-known even to those whose powers of reflexion are insufficient to its formulation, that multiple reiterated behaviour of the same kind, under similar combinations of percepts and fancies, produces a tendency – the *habit* – actually to behave in a similar way under similar circumstances in the future. Moreover – *here is the point* – every man exercises more or less control over himself by means of modifying his own habits; and the way in which he goes to work to bring this effect about in those cases in which circumstances will not permit him to practice reiterations of the desired kind of conduct in the outer world shows that he is virtually well-acquainted with the important principle that *reiterations in the inner world – fancied reiterations – if well-intensified by direct effort*, produce habits, just as do reiterations in the outer world; *and these habits will have power to influence actual behaviour in the outer world*; especially, if each reiteration be accompanied by a peculiar strong effort that is usually likened to issuing a command to one's future self' (CP: 5.487, 1907).
16 But see this definition of the sign: 'However, this much is clear; that a sign has essentially two correlates, its Object and its possible Interpretant sign. Of these three, Sign, Object, Interpretant, the Sign as being the very thing under consideration is Monadic, the Object is Dyadic, and the Interpretant is Triadic. We therefore look to see, whether there be not two Objects and three Interpretants. There obviously are two Objects, the object as it is in itself (the Monadic Object), and the object as the sign represents it to be (the Dyadic Object). There are also three Interpretants; namely, 1st, the Interpretant considered as an independent sign of the Object, 2nd, the Interpretant as it is as a fact determined by the Sign to be, and 3rd the Interpretant as it is intended by, or is represented in, the Sign to be' (R939: 43–4, 1905).
17 In 1868, in the *Journal of Speculative Philosophy*, Peirce offers an explanation of the meaning of the German expression *bestimmt* and its bearing on the concept of determination: 'Possibly, the original signification of bestimmt was "settled by vote"; or it may have been "pitched to a key." Thus its origin was quite different from that of "determined"; yet I believe that as philosophical terms their equivalence is exact. In general, they mean "fixed to be *this* (or *thus*), in contradistinction to being this, that, or the other (or in some way or other)." – When it is a concept or term, such as is expressed by a concrete noun or adjective which is said to be more determinate than another, the sense sometimes is that the logical extension of the former concept or term is a part and only a part of that of the latter; but more usually the sense is, that the logical comprehension of the latter is a part and only a part of that of the former' (W2: 239, 1868).
18 The structure of Figure 4.1 and the determination sequence in Peirce's letter are sufficient reason for repudiating the sign=triadic relation fallacy mentioned

earlier. Just how its advocates envisage inserting a representamen, an object and an interpretant into the mid-process sign stage defies understanding. One possible explanation is that for them, Peircean semiotics ended in 1903.

19   See: 'Now the essential nature of a sign is that it mediates between its Object, which is supposed to determine it and to be, in some sense, the cause of it, and its Meaning, or, as I prefer to say, in order to avoid certain ambiguities, its *Interpretant*, which is determined by the sign, and is, in a sense, the effect of it, and which the sign represents to flow as an influence, from the Object' (R318: 373, 1907).

20   'Three studies are needlessly and very unhappily confounded: Phaneroscopy (as I call it, or Phenomenology), Logic, and Psychology Proper. One of the three is a Science, though youthful and immature; that is Psychology Proper. One is an Embrio-science, so I note Logic, because it lacks that considerable body of well-drilled workers pursuing methods acknowledged by all… The third, Phaneroscopy, is, still in the condition of a science-egg' (R645: 1, 1909).

21   But see the discussion of the officer's 'will' and the extract from R299 in Chapter 3.

22   The difference being that a purpose is 'merely that form of final cause which is most familiar to our experience' (EP2: 120). Cf., too, 'I shoot at an eagle on the wing; and since my purpose – a special sort of final, or ideal, cause – is to hit the bird, I do not shoot directly at it, but a little ahead of it, making allowance for the change of place by the time the bullet gets to that distance. So far, it is an affair of final causation. But after the bullet leaves the rifle, the affair is turned over to the stupid efficient causation, and should the eagle make a swoop in another direction, the bullet does not swerve in the least, efficient causation having no regard whatsoever for results, but simply obeying orders blindly. It is true that the force of the bullet conforms to a law; and the law is something general. But for that very reason the law is not a force. For force is compulsion; and compulsion is hic et nunc. It is either that or it is no compulsion. Law, without force to carry it out, would be a court without a sheriff; and all its dicta would be vaporings. Thus, the relation of law, as a cause, to the action of force, as its effect, is final, or ideal, causation, not efficient causation' (CP: 1.212, 1902).

23   Note that two days later, on 27 December, he returns to the tone, token and type terminology in the Logic Notebook (R339: 339v, H636, 1908).

24   'Qualities of feeling may be meanings of signs. Thus, a piece of concerted music, since it mediates between the quality of the composer's succession of musical emotions and another in the breast of the auditor, is a sign.'

Chapter 5

1   This section was drawn almost verbatim from Jappy (2021). I should like to reiterate my thanks to the editorial board of the Chinese semiotics journal, *Language and Semiotic Studies*, for permission to use their copyright material.

2   'At the end of the letter, Peirce apologises for sending "such a dissertation" but immediately adds a postscript in which he lists the "ten principal classes of signs." These are close, but do not correspond precisely, to the ten classes outlined in the Syllabus; they appear to be derived from the rule of degeneracy, not from the combinatory. In the second classification, each class of sign is constituted by the combination of one element from each of the three trichotomies. Under this rule, no constituent element – for example, a "qualisign" – corresponds to a class of sign.

In the postscript list, by contrast, this rule is broken, so that both qualisigns and arguments appear as classes, not as constituent elements. Moreover, several classes in the postscript list are formed from two, not three, elements from the trichotomic table' (Freadman 2004: 141).

3   There is another version from 1908, namely the loose sheet RL463: 6 (H153), in which Peirce sets out an alternative description of the universe hierarchy to prove that the sequence of triangular classes resolves to only ten classes of signs.

4   Sanders (1970: 12–14) was possibly the earliest attempt to organize the 'scrap', as he calls it, into classes of signs involving the dynamic object, the sign and the dynamic interpretant. He doesn't explain why the interpretant should be the dynamic and not the final.

5   Interestingly, Peirce's reverse numerical category orderings for the ten classes of 1903, to be found on page 3 of manuscript R799, *c*.1903, corresponds to Table 5.2, which names the 1908 classes in order of decreasing 'universal' complexity.

6   'Possibly a zoölogist or a botanist may have so definite a conception of what a species is that single type-specimen may enable him to say whether a form of which he finds a specimen belongs to the same species or not. But it will be much safer to have a large number of individual specimens before him, from which he may get an idea of the amount and kind of individual or geographical variation to which the given species is subject'.

7   'Now how would you define a *sign*, Reader? I do not ask how the word is ordinarily used. I want such a definition as a zoologist would give of a fish, or a chemist of a fatty body, or of an aromatic body, – an analysis of the essential nature of a sign, if the word is to be used as applicable to everything which the most general science of sēmeï̈otic must regard as its business to study'.

8   For a more complete review of embodiment in the cognitive sciences and literary studies, see Samuelson and Wohlwend (2015).

9   The conceptual frame in these cases is: 'health and life are up; sickness and death are down' (e.g. 1980: 15).

10 Cf., too, 'Philosophers have traditionally distinguished knowing *that*, conceived as knowledge which can be shared in propositional form (e.g. "Snow is white"), from knowing *how*, conceived as bodily skills (e.g. riding a bicycle)' (Legg 2021: 2).

11 'If, however, our lived world does not have predefined boundaries, then it seems unrealistic to expect to capture commonsense understanding in the form of a representation–where *representation* is understood in its strong sense as the re-presentation of a pregiven world. Indeed, if we wish to recover common sense, then we must invert the representationist attitude by treating context-dependent know-how not as a residual artifact that can be progressively eliminated by the discovery of more sophisticated rules but as, in fact, the very essence of *creative* cognition' (Varela, Thompson and Rosch 1993: 148).

12 'In these cases [active externalism], the human organism is linked with an external entity in a two-way interaction, creating a *coupled system* that can be seen as a cognitive system in its own right. All the components in the system play an active causal role, and they jointly govern behavior in the same sort of way that cognition usually does' (2011: 222). Clearly, it is difficult to escape binarism in the enactivism Clark is critiquing.

13 Pagination follows the online version: https://www.researchgate.net/publication/355193693_Discursive_Habits_A_Representationalist_Re-Reading_of_Teleosemiotics (accessed October 2022).

14 'Accordingly, languages – consisting of a set of features that promotes fitness – can best be thought of as having been built by selection for the cognitive function of modelling, and, as the philosopher Popper and the linguist Chomsky have likewise insisted, not at all for the message-swapping function of communication. The latter was routinely carried on by nonverbal means, as in all animals, as it continues to be in the context of most human interactions today' (Sebeok 2001: 147).

15 'Early humans' possession of a mute verbal modelling device featuring a basic capacity for syntax allowed humans to assemble standardized tools but circumstances had not yet arisen whereby it was expeditious or hominids were in agreement to encode communication in articulate linear speech' (Cannizzaro and Cobley 2015: 209).

16 See, too, this passage from the Prolegomena, in which perception is explicitly associated with signification: 'The Immediate Object of all knowledge and all thought is, in the last analysis, the Percept. This doctrine in no wise conflicts with Pragmaticism, which holds that the Immediate Interpretant of all thought proper is Conduct. Nothing is more indispensable to a sound epistemology than a crystal-clear discrimination between the Object and the Interpretant of knowledge; very much as nothing is more indispensable to sound notions of geography than a crystal-clear discrimination between north latitude and south latitude; and the one discrimination is not more rudimentary than the other. That we are conscious of our Percepts is a theory that seems to me to be beyond dispute; but it is not a fact of Immediate Perception. A fact of Immediate Perception is not a Percept, nor any part of a Percept; a Percept is a Seme, while a fact of Immediate Perception or rather the Perceptual Judgment of which such fact is the Immediate Interpretant, is a Pheme that is the direct Dynamical Interpretant of the Percept, and of which the Percept is the Dynamical Object, and is with some considerable difficulty (as the history of psychology shows), distinguished from the Immediate Object, though the distinction is highly significant. But not to interrupt our train of thought, let us go on to note that while the Immediate Object of a Percept is excessively vague, yet natural thought makes up for that lack (as it almost amounts to), as follows. A late Dynamical Interpretant of the whole complex of Percepts is the Seme of a Perceptual Universe that is represented in instinctive thought as determining the original Immediate Object of every Percept. Of course, I must be understood as talking not psychology, but the logic of mental operations' (LI: 316, 1906).

17 Cf. this remark in the draft letter to Lady Welby discussed in Chapter 3: 'By the way, the dynamical object does not mean something out of the mind. It means something forced upon the mind in perception, but including more than perception reveals. It is an object of actual *Experience*' (SS: 197, 1906).

18 'Habits differ from dispositions in having been acquired as a consequence of the principle, virtually well-known even to those whose powers of reflexion are insufficient to its formulation, that multiply reiterated behaviour of some kind, under similar combinations of percepts and fancies produces a tendency, – the *habit*, – actually to behave in a similar way under similar circumstances in the future' (R318: 113, 1907).

19 As mentioned in Chapter 3, for Peirce, 'to utter' simply means to produce a sign verbally or otherwise: 'To signify that a person puts forth a sign whether vocal, ocular, or by touch, – and conventional signs mostly are of one or other of these three kinds or by taste, smell, and a sense of temperature which are the media of many natural *tests* and *symptoms*, – I like the word *utter*' (R793: 14, 1906).

20 'Besides the three main levels of semiosis that have been briefly described above and are firmly established regions of sign activity, there is reason to think that sign activity has also been at work in an anticipatory way even at inorganic levels before the advent of life in nature, as is suggested by the formula established by Poinsot: "it suffices to be a sign virtually in order to signify in act". … Sign activity in the inorganic realm would, according to this formula, occur less visibly and in the background, then, but virtually and as a matter of fact throughout the material realm' (Deely 1990: 30).

Chapter 6

1 Part of section 'Mediatization' draws on Jappy (2022), for which I thank once more the editors of the *Revue roumaine de philosophie*. Section 'Hybridization' uses material originally published in Jappy (2019c), for which I thank the editors of *Language and semiotic studies*.
2 Martin Carthy, 'Skewbald', from the album *Sweet Wivelsfield*, 1974. This presents a musical iconism similar to the onomatopoeic representation of hoof beats analysed in the line from the *Aeneid* in Chapter 2. https://www.youtube.com/watch?v=xiW4fa-fUQ0 (accessed September 2022).
3 'The action of the sign general takes place between two parties, the *utterer* and the *interpreter*. They need not be persons, for a chamelion and many kinds of insects and even plants make their livings by uttering signs' (R318: 419, 1907).
4 Aristotle"Εστι μὲν οὖν τὰ ἐν τῇ φωνῇ τῶν ἐν τῇ ψυχῇ παθημάτων σύμβολα, καὶ τὰ γραφόμενα τῶν ἐν τῇ φωνῇ. *De Interpretatione*, 6a 4–5 (Words spoken are symbols or signs of affections or impressions of the soul; written words are the signs of words spoken (Loeb)).
5 Namely, diachronic, diatopic, diastratic and diaphasic variation in Coseriu (1981).
6 It is certainly not necessarily the case (as Derrida and others have argued) that writing is the immediate sign of words spoken. This would imply *ad absurdum* that Joyce, Dickens, Tolstoy, writers of theses, students writing finals papers in exam halls, and writers of learned tomes on semiotics all shout out the words of the work before committing them to paper, etc. The positing of diamesic variation is an elegant if contentious way of explaining that problem away.
7 Note that for Mioni there are only two media for language – speech and writing, which has long held to be a representation of speech (a Saussurean concept famously discussed by Jacques Derrida). However, there is a third medium for communication, namely the human body providing various paralinguistic features. The so-called body language, e.g. facial expressions, gestures, etc., exploits the body as medium for nonverbal communication.
8 See, too, Figure 4.1 from Chapter 4.
9 Table 4.3 from Chapter 4 is reproduced here for convenience as Table 6.1.
10 This translates roughly as 'the four-hoofed sound (of the horses) shakes the dusty plain'.
11 See Barbara Kruger's recent comment in *The Guardian* of 7 July 2022 https://www.theguardian.com/artanddesign/2022/jul/07/barbara-kruger-artist-roe-v-wade-abortion-art (accessed December 2022).
12 To be seen by scrolling down this site: https://www.dannywithlove.com/blog/about-barbara-krugers-untitled-your-body-is-a-battleground (accessed January 2023).

References

Abu Arqoub, O., B. Ozad and A. Elega, (2019), 'The Engineering of Consent: A State-of-the-art Review', *Public Relations Review*, 45 (5), (n.p.) https://doi.org/10.1016/j.pubrev.2019.101830 (Accessed January 2022).

Ambrosio, C., (2016), 'The Historicity of Peirce's Classification of the Sciences', *European Journal of Pragmatism and American Philosophy* [Online], VIII-2 | 2016, Online since 17 January 2017, http://journals.openedition.org/ejpap/625; DOI: https://doi.org/10.4000/ejpap.625 (Accessed September 2021).

Atkin, A., (2008), 'Peirce's Final Account of Signs and the Philosophy of Language', *Transactions of the Charles S. Peirce Society*, 44 (1), 63–85.

Atkin, A., (2013), 'Peirce's Theory of Signs', in Edward N. Zalta, ed., *The Stanford Encyclopedia of Philosophy*, https://plato.stanford.edu/archives/sum2013/entries/peirce-semiotics/ (Accessed February 2022).

Bar-Hillel, Y., (1954), 'Indexical Expressions', *Mind*, 63, 359–79.

Barnham, C., (2022), *The Natural History of the Sign; Peirce, Vygotsky and the Hegelian Model of Concept Formation*, Berlin: Walter de Gruyter.

Barrena, S. and J. Nubiola, (2019), 'Abduction: The Logic of Creativity', in T. Jappy, ed., *The Bloomsbury Companion to Contemporary Peircean Semiotics*, London: Bloomsbury, 185–204.

Baxandall, M., (1972), *Painting and Experience in Fifteenth Century Italy*, London: Oxford University Press.

Bellucci, F., (2016), 'Inference from Signs: Peirce and the Recovery of the σημεῖον', *Transactions of the Charles S. Peirce Society*, 52 (2), 259–84.

Bellucci, F., (2017), *Peirce's Speculative Grammar: Logic as Semiotics*, London: Routledge.

Bellucci, F., (2020), *Charles S. Peirce: Selected Writings on Semiotics 1892–1912*, Berlin: de Gruyter.

Benedict, G. A., (1985), 'What Are Representamens?', *Transactions of the Charles S. Peirce Society*, 21 (2), 241–70.

Bentham, J., (1816), *Chrestomathia*, in *The Works of Jeremy Bentham*, John Bowring, ed., Edinburgh: William Tait, 1838–1843.

Bernays, E. L., (1947), 'The Engineering of Consent', *Annals of the American Academy of Political and Social Science*, 250, 113–20.

Bierman, A. K., (1962), 'That There Are No Iconic Signs', *Philosophy and Phenomenological Research*, 23 (2), 243–9.

Borges, P., (2010), 'A Visual Model of Peirce's 66 Classes of Signs Unravels His Late Proposal of Enlarging Semiotic Theory', in L. Magnani, W. Carnielli and C. Pizzi, eds, *Model-Based Reasoning in Science and Technology: Abduction, Logic, and Computational Discovery*, Berlin: Springer, 221–37.

Borges, P., (2016), 'A System of 21 Classes of Signs as an Instrument of Inquiry', *American Journal of Semiotics*, 31 (3–4), 245–76.

Borges, P and R. Gambarato, (2019), 'The Role of Beliefs and Behavior on Facebook: A Semiotic Approach to Algorithms, Fake News, and Transmedia Journalism', *International Journal of Communication* 13, 603–18.

Brier, S., (2010), 'Cybersemiotics: An Evolutionary World View Going Beyond Entropy and Information into the Question of Meaning', *Entropy*, 12, 1902–20.
Buchler, J., ed., ([1940] 2011), *Philosophical Writings of Peirce*, New York: Dover.
Burks, A., (1949), 'Icon, Index and Symbol', *Philosophy and Phenomenological Research*, IX, 673–89.
Cannizzaro, S. and P. Cobley, (2015), 'Biosemiotics, Politics and Th. A. Sebeok's move from Linguistics to Semiotics', in E. Velmezova, K. Kull and S. J. Cowley, eds, *Biosemiotic Perspectives on Language and Linguistics*, Dordrecht: Springer, 207–22.
Champagne, M., (2018), *Consciousness and the Philosophy of Signs: How Peircean Semiotics Combines Phenomenal Qualia and Practical Effects*, Dordrecht: Springer International Publishing.
Chandler, R., ([1943] 2001), *The Lady in the Lake and Other Novels*, Eastbourne: Gardners Books.
Clark, A., (2011), *Supersizing the Mind Embodiment, Action, and Cognitive Extension*, Oxford: Oxford University Press.
Cobley, P., (2018), 'Observership, Knowing, and Semiosis', *Cybernetics & Human Knowing*, 25 (1), 23–47.
Collinson, W. E., (1937), *Indication: A Study of Demonstratives, Articles and Other 'Indicaters'*, The Linguistic Society of America, Baltimore: Waverley Press.
Coseriu, E., (1981), 'Los conceptos de 'dialecto', 'nivel' y 'estilo de lengua' y el sentido propio de la dialectologia', *Lingüística española actual*, 3, 1–32.
Deely, J., (1990), *Basics of Semiotics*, Bloomington: Indiana University Press.
Deely, J., (2001), 'Physiosemiosis in the Semiotic Spiral: A Play of Musement', *Sign Systems Studies* 29 (1), 27–46.
Deely, J., (2004), *Why Semiotics?*, Toronto: LEGAS. [Cf. http://www.legaspublishing.com]
Deely, J., (2009a), '"To Find Our Way in These Dark Woods" Versus Coming up Short', *Recherches sémiotiques/Semiotic Inquiry*, 26 (2/3), 57–126.
Deely, J., (2009b), *Purely Objective Reality*, Berlin: Mouton de Gruyter.
Deely, J., (2014), 'The Terms "Sign" and "Representamen" in Peirce', (Paper delivered at the Charles S. Peirce International Centennial Congress, July 16–19, 2014, Lowell, MA: University of Massachusetts).
Deely, J., (2015), 'Objective Reality and the Physical World: Relation as Key to Understanding Semiosis', *Green Letters*, 19 (3), 267–79, DOI: 10.1080/14688417.2015.1063239.
Deledalle, G., (2000), *Charles S. Peirce's Philosophy of Signs: Essays in Comparative Semiotics*, Bloomington: Indiana University Press.
Diversey, A., (2014), 'The Correct Order of Peirce's Ten Trichotomies', (Paper delivered at the Charles S. Peirce International Centennial Congress, July 16–19, 2014, Lowell, MA: University of Massachusetts).
Eco, U., (1976), *A Theory of Semiotics*, Bloomington: Indiana University Press.
Eco, U., (1984), *Semiotics and the Philosophy of Language*, Bloomington: Indiana University Press.
Farias, P. and J. Queiroz, (2014a), 'On Peirce's Diagrammatic Models for Ten Classes of Signs', *Semiotica*, 202, 657–71.
Farias, P. and J. Queiroz, (2014b), 'On Peirce's Visualization of the Classifications of Signs', in T. Thellefsen and B. Sorensen, eds, *Charles Sanders Peirce in His Own Words: 100 Years of Semiotics, Communication and Cognition*, Berlin: De Gruyter Mouton, 527–35.
Farias, P. and J. Queiroz, (2017), 'Visualizing Triadic Relations: Diagrams for Charles S. Peirce's Classification of Signs', *Information Design Journal*, 23 (2), 127–47.
Favareau, D., ed., (2009a), *Essential Readings in Biosemiotics*, Dordrecht: Springer Nature.

Favareau, D., (2009b), 'The Evolutionary History of Biosemiotics', in D. Favareau, ed., *Essential Readings in Biosemiotics*, Dordrecht: Springer Nature, 1–77.

Fisch, M., (1982), 'Introduction', in *The Writings of Charles S. Peirce, Volume 1: 1857–1866*, Bloomington: Indiana University Press, xv–xxxv.

Fisch, M., (1986), *Peirce, Semeiotic and Pragmatism: Essays by Max Fisch*, K. L. Ketner and Ch. Kloesel, eds, Bloomington: Indiana University Press.

Freadman, A., (2004), *The Machinery of Talk: Charles Peirce and the Sign Hypothesis*, Redwood City: Stanford University Press.

Gare, A., (2019), 'Biosemiotics and Causation: Defending Biosemiotics through Rosen's Theoretical Biology or Integrating Biosemiotics and Anticipatory Systems Theory', *Cosmos and History: The Journal of Natural and Social Philosophy*, 15 (1), 31–90.

Genette, G., (1976), *Mimologiques: Voyage en Cratylie*, Paris: Éditions du Seuil.

Guarda, R. F., M. P. Ohlson and A. V. Romanini, (2018), 'Disinformation, Dystopia and Post-Reality in Social Media: A Semiotic-Cognitive Perspective' *Education for Information*, 34 (3), 185–97.

Guerri, C., (2016), *Nonágono semiotico: un modelo operativo para la investigación cualitativa*, Buenos Aires: University of Buenos Aires Press.

Guerri, C., (2019), 'The Semiotic Nonagon: Peirce's Categories as Design Thinking', in T. Jappy (2019), ed., *The Bloomsbury Companion to Contemporary Peircean Semiotics*, London: Bloomsbury, 277–302.

Heidegger, M., (1982), *The Question Concerning Technology and Other Essays*, New York: Harper Torchbooks.

Hoffmeyer, J., (1996), *Signs of Meaning in the Universe*, Bloomington: Indiana University Press.

Houser, N., (1992a), 'On Peirce's Theory of Propositions: A Response to Hilpinen', *Transactions of Charles S. Peirce Society*, 28 (3), 489–504.

Houser, N., (1992b), 'Introduction', in *The Essential Peirce: Selected Philosophical Writings, Volume 1: 1867–1893*, N. Houser and C. J. Kloesel, eds, Bloomington: Indiana University Press, xix–xli.

Jakobson, R., (1957), 'Shifters, Verbal Categories, and the Russian Verb', reprinted in Jakobson, (1971), in *Selected Writings Vol. 2: Word and Language*, The Hague: Mouton, 130–47.

Jakobson, R., ([1959] 1985), 'Sign and System of Language: A Reassessment of Saussure's Doctrine', in K. Pomorska and S. Rudy, eds, *Verbal Art, Verbal Sign, Verbal Time*, Oxford: Blackwell, 28–33.

Jakobson, R., (1965), 'Quest for the Essence of Language', Reprinted in Jakobson, (1971) *Selected Writings Vol. 2: Word and Language*, The Hague: Mouton, 345–59.

Jakobson, R., (1971), *Selected Writings Vol. 2: Word and Language*, The Hague: Mouton.

Jappy, T., (1999), 'Iconicity and Inference: Peirce's Logic and Language Research', in M. Shapiro and M. Haley, eds, *Peirce Seminar Papers, Volume 4*, New York: Berghahn, 41–76.

Jappy, T., (2013), *Introduction to Peircean Visual Semiotics*. London: Bloomsbury Academic.

Jappy, T., (2016), *Peirce's Twenty-Eight Classes of Signs and the Philosophy of Representation*, London: Bloomsbury Academic.

Jappy, T., (2018), 'Speculative Rhetoric, Methodeutic, and Peirce's Hexadic Sign-Systems', *Semiotica*, 220, 249–68. DOI: https://doi.org/10.1515/sem-2016-0075.

Jappy, T., (2019a), 'Introduction', in T. Jappy, ed., *The Bloomsbury Companion to Contemporary Peircean Semiotics*, London: Bloomsbury Academic, 1–32.

Jappy, T., (2019b), 'Peirce's Conception of Semiosis', *The Bloomsbury Companion to Contemporary Peircean Semiotics*, London: Bloomsbury Academic, 101–132.

Jappy, T., (2019c), 'Hypoiconicity, Semiosis and Peirce's Immediate Object', *Language and Semiotic Studies*, 5 (2), 1–36.

Jappy, T., (2021), 'Peirce's Other Ten-Class Typology', *Language and Semiotic Studies*, 7 (1), 1–33.

Jappy, T., (2022), 'Three Problems for Peirce's Metaphor', *Revue Roumaine de Philosophie*, 66 (1), 11–28.

Jappy, T., (forthcoming), 'Diagrams, Semiosis and Peirce's Metaphor', in C. de Waal, ed., *Oxford Handbook of Charles S. Peirce*, Oxford and London: Oxford University Press.

Johansen, J. D., (1993), *Dialogic Semiosis: An Essay on Signs and Meaning*, Bloomington and Indianapolis: Indiana University Press.

Kent, B., (1987), *Charles S. Peirce: Logic and the Classification of the Sciences*, Kingston and Montreal: McGill-Queen's University Press.

Ketner, K. L., (2009), 'Charles Sanders Peirce: Interdisciplinary Scientist', in E. Bisanz, ed., *The Logic of Interdisciplinarity: The Monist-Series*, Berlin: Akademie Verlag GmbH, 35–57.

Kull, K., (2012), 'Advancements in Biosemiotics: Where We Are Now in Discovering the Basic Mechanisms of Meaning-making', in S. Rattasepp and T. Bennett, eds, *Gatherings in Biosemiotics*, Tartu: University of Tartu Press, 11–24.

Lakoff, G. and M. Johnson, (1980), *Metaphors We Live By*, Chicago: University of Chicago Press.

Legg, C., (2021), 'Discursive Habits: A Representationalist Re-reading of Teleosemiotics', *Synthese*, 199, 14751–68, Doi: https://doi.org/10.1007/s11229-021-03442-8, pagination according to the on-line version, https://www.researchgate.net/publication/355193693_Discursive_Habits_A_Representationalist_Re-Reading_of_Teleosemiotics (Accessed October 2022).

Liszka, J., (1996), *A General Introduction to the Semeiotic of Charles Sanders Peirce*, Bloomington and Indianapolis: Indiana University Press.

Liszka, J., (2000), 'Peirce's New Rhetoric', *Transactions of the Charles S. Peirce Society*, 36 (4), 439–76.

Liszka, J., (2018), 'Reductionism in Peirce's Sign Classifications and Its Remedy', *Semiotica*, 228, 153–72, Doi: https://doi.org/10.1515/sem-2018-0089.

Liszka, J. and G. Babb, (2019), 'Abduction as an Explanatory Strategy in Narrative', in T. Jappy, ed., *The Bloomsbury Companion to Contemporary Peircean Semiotics*, London: Bloomsbury, 205–34.

Locke, J., ([1690] 1964), *An Essay Concerning Human Understanding*, abridged and edited with an introduction by A. D. Woozley, London: Collins.

Marty, R., (1979), 'Trichotomies de l'icône, de l'indice et du symbole', *Semiosis*, 15, 5–18.

Marty, R. and A. Lang, (2012), '76 Definitions of The Sign by C. S. Peirce, with 12 Further Definitions or Equivalents', https://cspeirce.iupui.edu/rsources/76DEFS/76defs.HTM (Accessed September 2022).

Marty, R., (2020), 'The Simplest Model for the Ten Classes of Signs', https://www.academia.edu/44347570/The_simplest_model_for_the_ten_classes_of_signs. (Accessed January 2023).

Merrell, F., (2001), 'Charles Sanders Peirce's Concept of the Sign', in P. Cobley, ed., *The Routledge Companion to Semiotics and Linguistics*, London: Routledge, 28–39.

Mioni, A., (1983), 'Italiano tendenziale: osservazioni su alcuni aspetti della standardizzazione', in P. Benincà and G. B. Pellegrini, eds, *Scritti linguistici in onore di Giovan Battista Pellegrini*, Pisa: Pacini, 495–517.

Misak, C., ed., (2004), *The Cambridge Companion to Peirce*, Cambridge: Cambridge University Press.
Morand, B., (2004), *Logique de la conception: figures de sémiotique générale d'après Charles S. Peirce*, Paris: L'Harmattan.
Murphey, M., (1993), *The Development of Peirce's Philosophy*, Indianapolis: Hackett Publishing Company.
Noë, A., (2004), *Action in perception*, Cambridge, MA: MIT Press.
Noë, A, (2009), *Out of Our Heads: Why You Are Not Your Brain, and Other Lessons from the Biology of Consciousness*, New York: Hill and Wang.
Nöth, W., (1990), *Handbook of Semiotics*, Bloomington and Indianapolis: Indiana University Press.
Nöth, W. and I. Jungk, (2015), 'Peircean Visual Semiotics: Potentials to Be Explored', Review article, *Semiotica*, 207, 657–73, DOI: 10.1515/sem-2015-0058.
Ogden, C. K. and I. A. Richards, (1923), *The Meaning of Meaning: A Study of the Influence of Language upon Thought and the Science of Symbolism*, London: Routledge and Keegan Paul.
Parker, K. A., (1998), *The Continuity of Peirce's Thought*, Nashville: Vanderbilt University Press.
Peirce, C. S., (1931–1958), *Collected Papers of Charles Sanders Peirce*, 8 Volumes, C. Hartshorne, P. Weiss and A. W. Burks, eds, Cambridge, MA: Harvard University Press.
Peirce, C. S., (1982), *The Writings of Charles S. Peirce, Volume 1: 1857–1866*, M. Fisch, C. Kloesel, E. Moore and D. Roberts, eds, Bloomington: Indiana University Press.
Peirce, C. S., (1992), *The Essential Peirce: Selected Philosophical Writings, Volume 1: 1867–1893*, N. Houser and C. Kloesel, eds, Bloomington: Indiana University Press.
Peirce, C. S., (1998), *The Essential Peirce, Volume 2*, Peirce Edition Project,eds, Bloomington: Indiana University Press.
Peirce, C. S., (2009), *The Logic of Interdisciplinarity: The Monist-Series*, E. Bisanz, ed., Berlin: Akademie Verlag GmbH.
Peirce, C. S. and V. Welby-Gregory, (1977), *Semiotic and Significs: The Correspondence between C. S. Peirce and Victoria Lady Welby*, C. S. Hardwick, ed., Bloomington: Indiana University Press.
Pharies, D., (1985), *Charles S. Peirce and the Linguistic Sign*, Amsterdam: John Benjamins Publishing Company.
Rattasepp, S. and T. Bennett, eds, (2012), *Gatherings in Biosemiotics*, Tartu: University of Tartu Press.
Romanini, V. and E. Fernández, (2014), 'Semeiosis as a Living Process', in V. Romanini and E. Fernández eds, *Peirce and Biosemiotics: A Guess at the Riddle of Life*, Dordrecht: Springer, 215–39.
Russell, B., (1950), *An Inquiry into Meaning and Truth*, London: George Allen and Unwin.
Ryle, G., (1946), 'Knowing How and Knowing That', *Proceedings of the Aristotelian Society*,46, 1–16.
Ryle, G., (1949), *The Concept of Mind*, Chicago: University of Chicago Press.
Samuelson, B. L. and K. Wohlwend, (2015), 'Embodied signs: Expanding representations through and with bodies', in P. P. Trifonas, ed., *International Handbook of Semiotics*, Dordrecht: Springer, 565–72.
Sanders, G., (1970), 'Peirce's Sixty-Six Signs?', *Transactions of the Charles S. Peirce Society*, 6 (1), 3–16.

Saussure, F., ([1916] 1972), *Cours de linguistique générale*, Paris: Payot.
Savan, D., (1988), *An Introduction to C. S. Peirce's Full System of Semeiotic*, Toronto: Semiotic Circle.
Schapiro, M., (1994), *Theory and Philosophy of Art: Style, Artist and Society*, New York: George Braziller.
Sebeok, T. A., (2001), *Signs: An Introduction to Semiotics*, Toronto: University of Toronto Press.
Shapiro, M., (1983), *The Sense of Grammar: Language as Semiotic*, Bloomington: Indiana University Press.
Shapiro, M., (1998), 'Sound and Meaning in Shakespeare's Sonnets', *Lg.*, 74, 81–103.
Shapiro, M., ed., (2002a), *The Peirce Seminar Papers: Essays in Semiotic Analysis, Volume 5*, Oxford: Berghahn.
Shapiro, M., (2002b), 'Aspects of a Neo-Peircean Linguistics: Language History as Linguistic Theory', in M. Shapiro, ed., *The Peirce Seminar Papers: Essays in Semiotic Analysis, Volume 5*, Oxford: Berghahn, 108–25.
Shapiro, M. and M. Haley, eds, (1999), *The Peirce Seminar Papers, Volume 4*, New York: Berghahn.
Short, T. L., (2004), 'The Development of Peirce's Theory of Sign's', in C. Misak, ed., *The Cambridge Companion to Peirce*, Cambridge: Cambridge University Press, 214–40.
Short, T. L., (2007), *Peirce's Theory of Signs*, London and Cambridge: Cambridge University Press.
Sowa, J., (1984), *Conceptual Structures: Information Processing in Mind and Machine*, Reading, MA: Addison-Wesley.
Spinks, C. W., (1992), *Peirce and Triadomania: A Walk in the Semiotic Wilderness*, Berlin: Mouton de Gruyter.
Stjernfelt, F., (2011), *Diagrammatology: An Investigation on the Borderlines of Phenomenology, Ontology, and Semiotics*. Dordrecht: Springer Verlag.
Stjernfelt, F., (2014), *Natural Propositions: The Actuality of Peirce's Doctrine of Dicisigns*, Chestnut Hill, MA: Docent Press.
Tesnière, L., (1988), *Éléments de syntaxe structurale*, Paris: Klincksieck.
Thaler, R. H. and C. R. Sunstein, (2008), *Nudge: Improving Decisions about Health, Wealth, and Happiness*, New Haven: Yale University Press.
Thellefsen, T. L., (2001), 'C.S. Peirce's Evolutionary Sign: An Analysis of Depth and Complexity within Peircean Sign Types and Peircean Evolution Theory', *Semiotics, Evolution, Energy, and Development*, 1 (2), n.p, https://see.library.utoronto.ca/SEED/Vol1-2/Thellefsen.pdf (Accessed October 2022).
Trifonas, P. P., ed., (2015), *International Handbook of Semiotics*, Berlin: Springer.
Varela, F. J., E. Thompson and E. Rosch, (1993), *The Embodied Mind: Cognitive Science and Human Experience*, Cambridge: MIT Press.
Vasari, G., ([1568] 1991), *The Lives of the Artists*, J. C. Bondanella and P. Bondanella, trans., London: Oxford University Press.
Vehkavaara, T., (2003), 'Development of Peirce's Classification of Sciences: 1889, 1898, 1903', https://www.academia.edu/5148145/Development_of_Peirces_classification_of_sciences_1889_1898_1903 (Accessed July 2022).
Velmezova, E., K. Kull and S. J. Cowley, eds, (2015), *Biosemiotic Perspectives on Language and Linguistics*, Dordrecht: Springer.
Weiss, P. and A. Burks, (1945), 'Peirce's Sixty-Six Signs', *The Journal of Philosophy*, 42 (14), 383–8.

Wilson, J. J. and H. Price, (2018), 'Courtroom Data and Politeness Research: A Case for Neo-Peircean Semiotics in Interpersonal Pragmatics', *Journal of Politeness Research*, 14 (1), 63–95, https://doi.org/10.1515/pr-2017-0056 (Accessed December 2022).

Wohlwend, K. E and B. L. Samuelson, (2015), 'Embodied Signs: Expanding Representations through and with Bodies', in P. P. Trifonas, ed., *International Handbook of Semiotics*, Berlin: Springer, 565–72.

Zuboff, S., (2019), *The Age of Surveillance Capitalism*, London: Profile Books, Ltd.

Index

abduction 12, 16, 50, 88, 135, 136
action of the sign 34, 40, 44, 45, 56, 63, 69, 73–5, 87, 91, 108, 146, 148, 151, 170, 171, 178, 187. *See also* semiosis
analogue as diagram 68, 69, 71, 157, 163, 166, 168

Beatrice 163, 164
Bellucci, F. 21, 22, 87
Benedict, G. 40, 59, 73
Bentham, J. 9, 10, 13, 14, 16, 125, 173
biosemiotics 1, 4, 13, 14, 16, 19, 42, 50, 60, 114, 129–32, 140, 156
    and language 113, 125, 129, 131, 132, 134, 136–40, 148

Cameron, M. 163, 164
category 24, 27–9, 34–8, 46, 47, 51, 54, 55, 59, 62, 64, 66, 71, 74, 75, 81, 83, 88–92, 101, 105, 110, 111, 125, 126, 132, 133, 135, 146, 147, 157, 168, 177, 181
causation 83, 108, 184
cenoscopy 10–16, 19, 21, 30, 31, 49, 60, 113, 125, 128, 129, 135, 139, 173–5
classes of signs 12, 17, 19, 23, 30, 34, 35, 39, 45, 51–3, 56, 60–3, 65, 78, 80, 88, 94, 95, 106, 109, 115–23, 129, 152, 160, 184, 185
classification of signs. *See* typology
collateral acquaintance with object 82, 93
collateral experience 82, 93, 97
collateral observation 79, 81, 82, 93
correlate order in semiosis 50, 100, 101, 119, 153, 154
coupled system 126, 130, 137, 140, 185

Deely, J. 13, 14, 41, 42, 59, 108, 114, 135, 138, 170, 175, 176, 187
    Deely and cenoscopy 13–14

degeneracy, phenomenological principle of 46–8, 62, 64–7, 101, 102, 178, 184
determination, definitions of 102–4
determination flow 56, 109, 124, 135
determination process 44, 56, 95, 100–9, 113. *See also* action of the sign, semiosis
diagram 13, 16, 29, 48, 54–9, 68–71, 85, 105, 114–18, 124, 149, 157, 158, 163, 164, 167–9. *See also* analogue
diamesic variation 148, 149, 187
dynamic interpretant 64, 65, 78, 85, 95, 98–100, 121, 153–5, 185
dynamic object 49, 56, 64, 69, 72–7, 79, 80–2, 85, 93–8, 100, 103, 104, 107–11, 113, 142–5, 147–50, 153, 155, 156, 162, 164, 166–70, 185, 186

effectual interpretant 77, 98
embodiment 18, 19, 73, 74, 125–8, 134, 140, 147, 168, 174, 185
emotional interpretant 82, 83, 143
enaction, enactivism 4, 31, 113, 126–30, 135, 137, 140, 185
energetic interpretant 82, 83

final interpretant 56, 62–5, 76, 78, 85, 95, 96, 98–100, 103, 106–10, 113, 135, 142, 153–5
Firstness 35–38, 52–5, 58, 64, 68, 71, 72, 75, 111, 158, 160, 178, 181

Houser, N. 23, 25, 26
hypoicon 29, 34, 49, 54–6, 59, 68–71, 141, 156, 157, 160, 162, 167, 170, 178
hypoiconicity 30, 34, 57–9, 156–61, 164, 167, 168

icon 24, 28–30, 34, 40, 46–50, 52–8, 60, 64, 65, 67–74, 85, 87, 109, 129, 135, 142, 157, 158, 161, 162, 167, 171, 177
    redefinition of the three icons 68–72
iconicity 29, 34, 48, 55, 71, 145, 151, 169, 175
iconicity and language 28–30, 48–50
idioscopy 10, 12–21, 29–31, 54, 71, 108, 113, 125, 128–30, 173, 174
idioscopy and semiotics 11–16
image (hypoicon) 29, 48, 54, 55, 57, 58, 68–71, 157, 158, 162, 167, 177
immediate interpretant 60, 64, 65, 83, 94–100, 103, 110, 146, 153, 154, 179, 183
immediate object 5, 29, 60, 64, 73–6, 81–3, 90, 93, 95, 97–100, 103, 106, 107, 121, 146–53, 155, 156, 161–4, 166–71, 179, 181, 182. *See also* mediatization
implication principle 29, 37, 47
index 16, 17, 24, 28–30, 34, 40, 46–50, 54, 55, 60, 64–8, 80, 87, 109, 129, 142, 177
inference 12, 18, 133–140
    signs recognized solely by 134
intention 69, 80–82, 107, 108, 113, 144, 145, 150–3, 162, 163, 170
intentionality 69, 75, 81, 82, 98, 99, 108–10, 123, 146, 147, 149–53, 155, 156, 162, 164, 168–71
interpretant order controversy 95–9. *See also* Savan

Jakobson, R. 17, 28–30, 48, 54, 55, 129, 175

Kruger, B. 164, 165

Lakoff, G. and M. Johnson 31, 125–8
logical interpretant 83, 84, 85, 96, 180
    first, second and third logical interpretants 84
'looking' 4, 13, 15, 31, 37, 113, 124, 125, 129–140. *See also* observation

Marty, R. 117, 170, 178
mediatization 137, 141, 146–51, 155, 161, 162, 167–71

medium 57–77, 85, 109, 111, 123, 135, 141, 142, 146–70, 177, 178, 180, 187
    air as 57, 83, 144, 146, 149, 153, 159
    paper and ink as 74, 149, 167
    skin as 75, 148
metaphor 29, 48, 54, 55, 57–9, 68–72, 85, 125, 126, 135, 158–60, 164–71, 178
mind 113, 119, 124, 126, 127, 129, 131, 134, 137–40, 146
    Peirce's definition of 139
Mioni, A. 148, 149, 187
mode of representation of object 48, 49, 54, 56, 60, 144, 162
Mona Lisa 74, 156, 157, 161, 162, 170

Noë, A. 31, 127, 128, 135, 138

observation 4, 9, 10, 12–16, 31, 35, 37, 108, 113, 114, 124, 125, 128–31, 134–6, 139, 140, 150, 173, 176
observer and object 4, 15, 31, 113, 124, 126, 129–31, 134–6, 140, 154, 170
organism and environment 4, 31, 113, 124, 127–30, 134, 137, 139, 140, 185

perception 14, 41, 59, 67, 126–8, 130, 132–40, 171, 186
perceptual judgement 133, 136, 186
phaneroscopy 15, 28, 49, 69, 70–3, 81, 83, 85, 87, 88, 91, 102, 105, 108, 184
phenomenology 10, 11, 15, 19, 28, 33–9, 49, 51, 58, 64, 65, 72, 83, 85, 89, 91, 108, 111, 129, 133, 150, 181, 184, 193
post-scriptum table 114–117, 120–4, 139, 142, 145, 151, 152, 169
pragmaticism 8, 15, 65–70, 77–9, 85, 86, 99, 133
pragmatism 3, 8, 18, 23, 47, 53, 59, 65–7, 79, 84, 92, 93, 108, 133, 146, 179
prescission 36, 38, 39, 47, 51

quasi-mind 75, 76, 85, 108, 111, 171

relevance of Peirce's legacy 3, 4, 12, 17, 22, 30, 31, 124, 125, 129, 139, 140, 171
representamen 34, 38–43, 46–8, 50, 51, 54, 56, 60, 63, 69, 72, 104, 119, 160, 176, 178, 184

Savan, D. 26, 95, 96, 102, 106, 181, 182
Sebeok, T. 17, 31, 47, 114, 129–40, 174, 176, 186
Secondness 35–8, 48, 52, 55–8, 64, 72, 75, 85, 86, 111, 133, 157, 160, 181
semiosis 1, 3, 4, 5, 7, 14, 17, 20, 22, 23, 26, 27, 30, 34, 37, 41–9, 53, 56, 59–63, 66, 70, 76, 79–83, 86–8, 94–8, 103–11, 113–15, 117, 120–4, 129–31, 135–53, 156, 157, 161, 162, 164, 168–71, 174, 176, 178, 180
Short, T. 8, 15, 16, 20, 21, 22, 24–6, 55, 110, 175
sign 1, 2, 3, 6–9, 11, 12, 16–21, 24–30, 34, 38–66, 69–97, 100–11, 113–41, 142, 143, 144, 145, 146, 148, 150–71, 174, 176, 177, 178
sign defined 38, 42–5, 72–6, 89, 92
sign or representamen controversy 38–45
sign relation 40, 42, 114, 115, 147
sign=triadic relation fallacy, 60, 115, 178, 183
symbol 24, 29, 34, 40, 46–50, 54, 55, 58, 60, 63–8, 70, 85, 87, 109, 129, 132, 135, 142, 144, 146, 150, 155, 160, 164, 177, 178
symbolistic 46, 67, 68, 70, 79

Thirdness 36–8, 48, 52, 55, 59, 62, 64, 68, 72, 75, 85, 111, 181
triadic relation 38–44, 56, 60–2, 72, 74, 102, 104, 111, 114–19, 145, 176, 178
typology 4, 17, 23–6, 34, 45, 55, 56, 60–9, 76–8, 85, 87–97, 100–11, 113–24, 139, 141–6, 150–5, 179
four six-division typologies 1904 61–5; 1906, 72–7; 1907, 83–5; 1908, 92–5, 102–6, 151, 152

universe 28, 34, 48, 62, 88, 89, 90, 91, 92, 95, 99, 102, 103, 105, 106, 108, 109, 110, 111, 115, 122, 150, 152, 153, 155, 169, 181, 185, 186, 190
universe or category controversy 88–92
universe of discourse 92, 181
universe hierarchy 95, 102, 185

Varela, F., E. Thompson and E. Rosch 31, 126, 128–30, 185
volition 80–2, 107, 108, 110, 155

Your Body Is a Battleground 164, 165

www.ingramcontent.com/pod-product-compliance
Lightning Source LLC
Chambersburg PA
CBHW052116300426
44116CB00010B/1681